the electronic adventures

**Following**

*of the chestnut man - · →*

# FOO

the electronic adventures

# Follo

of the chestnut man

HarperEntertainment

*An Imprint of HarperCollins Publishers*

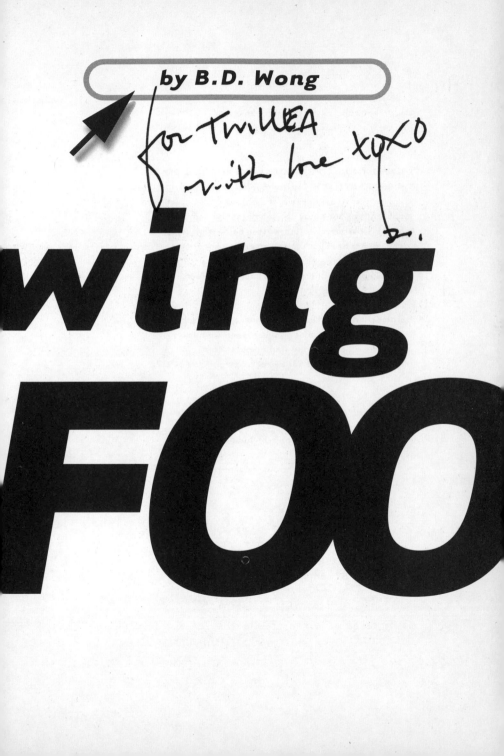

by B.D. Wong

*for Thillea with love xoxo*

# wing FOO

**FOLLOWING FOO: (THE ELECTRONIC ADVENTURES OF THE CHESTNUT MAN).** Copyright © 2003 by B.D. Wong. All rights reserved. Printed in the United States of America. No part of this book may be used or reproduced in any manner whatsoever without written permission except in the case of brief quotations embodied in critical articles and reviews. For information address HarperCollins Publishers Inc., 10 East 53rd Street, New York, NY 10022.

HarperCollins books may be purchased for educational, business, or sales promotional use. For information please write: Special Sales Department, HarperCollins Publishers Inc., 10 East 53rd Street, New York, NY 10022.

FIRST EDITION

*Designed by Judith Stagnitto Abbate / Abbate Design*

Library of Congress Cataloging-in-Publication Data
Wong, B.D.
    Following Foo (the electronic adventures of the chestnut man) / by B.D. Wong
        p.   cm.
    ISBN 0-06-052953-9
        1. Wong, B.D.—Family.   2. Actors—United States—Biography.   3. Gay parents—United States.   4. Wong family.   I. Title.
    PN2287.W66A3   2003
    792'.028'092—dc21
    [B]                                        2002038895

03  04  05  06  07  ❖/RRD  10  9  8  7  6  5  4  3  2  1

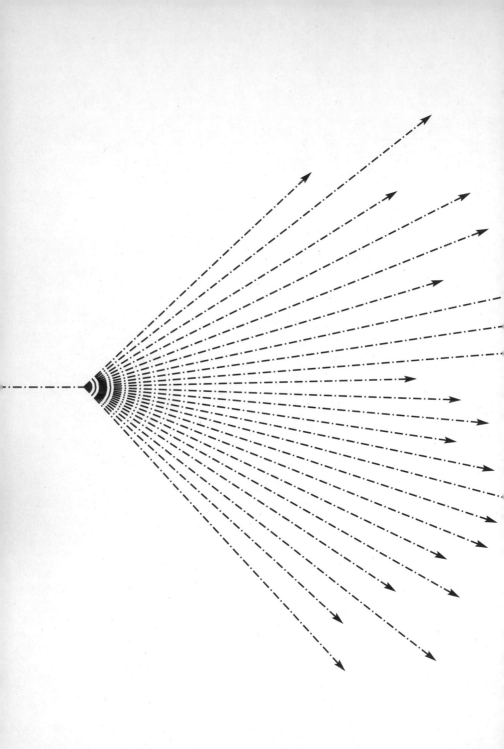

To

**Randy**

&

**Carol**

&

**Sue**

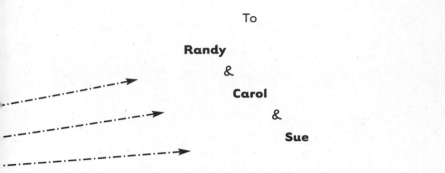

in the hopes that,

during the time in which these events took place,

I gave even a fraction

of the devotion and commitment

that I have since seen pour from them

and to

**My Parents**

for everything that those two words entail

Throw your heart over the fence
and the horse will follow.

—a saying in the horse world >>

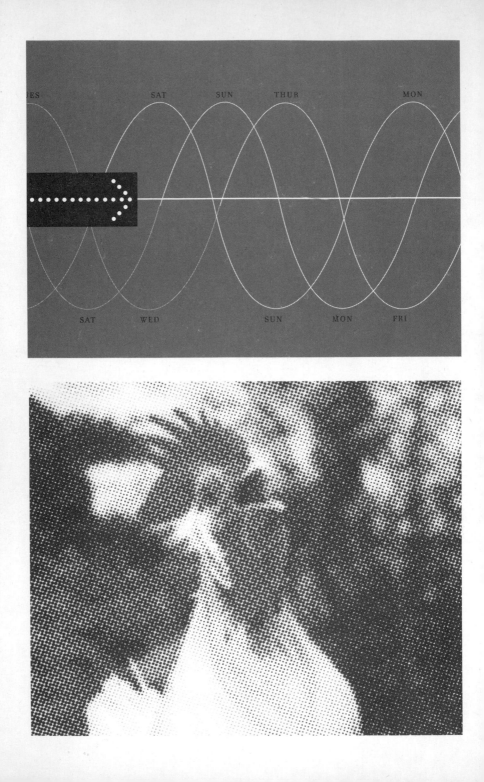

# PREFACE
## or "PRE-UP"

(WRITTEN AFTER THE FACT,
FROM THE BIG APPLE)

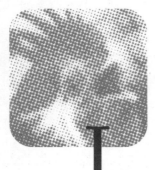

I t was a hot California Central Valley evening on the last Memorial Day weekend of the twentieth century when the sky opened up.

The Weather Channel had not predicted this. The Weather Channel or Al Roker *might* be able to tell you what color the sky will be tomorrow, but they can never tell you when the sky is going to open up. This is beyond their meteorological jurisdiction. Plus, there was no Chicken Little to run excitedly through the town to warn the other animals. Technically, I think this might be because the sky didn't really *fall*. It *opened up*. I can't really say it any other way.

I was standing right under it when this happened.

It was like the sky was the navy blue jumpsuit of a beautiful sky diver. As her graceful body somersaults to earth, she casually reaches into a zipper in her billowing, ripstop nylon uniform for a stick of Wrigley's spearmint gum, so that her landing might not only be triumphant, but accompanied by fresh breath, just in case there're members of the press waiting. What happened to the sky was just like that little zippered pocket, flashing open with the dexterous tug of an athlete's gloved, well-versed fingers.

However, along with the gum a lot of other unexpected things came tumbling out and clattered to earth, all around where I was standing, uncharacteristically minding my own business. As I squinted up into infinity and watched everything hurtling through the slash in the silky, deep blue fabric toward me, a pair of green-handled elementary school "lefty" scissors (the blunt, "safety" kind), went careening by my right eyebrow and stuck into the grass—*thwack!*—like the handiwork of a carnival knife thrower. I stared numbly up and wondered whether a person jumping out of airplanes should really carry so much stuff around in their pockets. Ballpoint pens, a Swiss Army knife, pennies from heaven . . .

You might ask, was this a *good* thing or a *bad* thing?

Tsk, tsk, tsk. What do you think this is, the Magic Eight Ball?

## ASK AGAIN LATER

I guess you just have to read on, and then you can give the ball another shake.

Still, with all the stuff tumbling down from above, I had no clue what to do. Would you? I wasn't alone, as you will soon learn. But I was far from home, wandering around in this boundless and exquisite grassy void dotted with whimsical topiary. I watched with my dry mouth hanging wide open by the sheer weight of my jaw, frozen as a weathervane rooster, and just as two-dimensional. I hadn't been forewarned (or, more accurately, *screeched at*) like all of those barnyard animals in Chicken Little's town, and like I said, I wasn't alone. See, in my experience, when things happen in this enchanted forest, animals flock from all points of the compass to help you, or bring you feed, or hug you. But I was far, far from home.

So I did something that Chicken Little could never do. I went to a computer and I wrote my friends and loved ones an electronic letter. You see, not only did the original Chicken Little live in a land where there were no computers, but in junior high he elected to take plastics shop, instead of signing up for typing like I did. Tough. Now Chicken Little flips burgers, and I got myself a literary agent and a publisher.

When I wrote my electronic letter to the other inhabitants of the jungle, I didn't really know what I was doing, or even why. Like Chicken Little, I was hysterical, and I just sat down at the computer, and all of this squawking came out of me,

**4**

# EE-I
## EE-I O.

I've never thought of the computer as a very serious way to communicate. I think of myself as one who would sooner use the telephone, or write a "real letter." But it's been years since I actually licked a postage stamp with my bifurcated tongue (which, contrary to popular belief, tells it like it is . . . ). Furthermore, I'd never seen the sky open up like that before, and it sure was something. There were so many subjects of the animal kingdom I wanted to tell about that, and of course I could reach a whole lot of barnyard folk by writing just one E-letter, so that's what I did.

I just wrote what happened.

I didn't try to be clever or funny or literate. I just told the story plainly. I wanted to get all the facts down straight because I thought this might help some of my fine feathered friends to not be so anxious or afraid or sad about the sky situation, and it would also start the grapevine (because, as I'm sure you know, in the animal kingdom word sure travels fast). Also, this would help me to not have to explain it all to every single creature I ran into. So I did it for only the most practical of reasons.

When I nervously pushed the "send now" button to mail that electronic letter with my paw, I realized I felt better about things right away. The computer helped me bridge thousands of miles. This was amazing, since Before This I had only thought of the computer as a way of *casually* communicating with someone. You know, I might say, "How are you?" or "Can I borrow your corn pone recipe?" but I would never say, "The sky is falling, the sky is falling!" I would never say anything *that* important or serious or personal. I just didn't think I could use an electronic machine to crow that the sky had opened up. But nowadays, people use the computer to say lots of things, don't they? They'll say, "Whatever you do, don't vote for Bushy-Tail," or they'll say, "Please sign this petition to save our furry friends," or they'll say, "Hey, I'm dumping you, you weasel, you." The stories the computer tells are getting more and more important these days. Why not? So I told mine, too.

Another neat thing about the ( **Electronic Letter** ) is how fast it gets delivered, even when you're across a whole continent from somebody. You can send a letter and get an answer back just minutes later sometimes! I was really surprised so many wrote back right away. They wrote the most beautiful things; they almost all said they'd go right outside and shout up at the sky,

## "*Please,* no more scissors!"

until it let up. Plus, they asked me to tell them what was falling through the zipper from then on. They were so worried that someone in my family was going to get hit by a blunt object. But thanks to the computer, it almost felt like they weren't far away at all.

After just a few days had passed, more happened, so I wrote again. I was running out of the house on my webbed feet to go and check what was falling that particular day and I wrote, "This is what I expect today . . ." and I sent it off. Again, I wasn't trying to be clever or funny or literate. Like I am now.

After that, even more wrote to say they were going outside to shout,

## "Hey, you up there,

# no more scissors!"

at the sky.

So I wrote back again, and again . . .

As time passed, some of the residents of *this* zoo told neighbors in *other* zoos about the updates, and the electronic mailing list began to grow and grow and grow. Pretty soon there were hundreds on the list, not even including *a lot* who passed the updates on to others even though I didn't even know about it. So many of the animals weren't even animals I had ever met before (even though I've met *an awful lot* of animals).

Four months later and I'd written ten updates in twelve installments. I guess all the shouting up at the clouds that everyone had been doing must have done some good. Knock wood (we jungle beasts can be pretty superstitious). The sky's still wide open, mind you, but now the stuff that's coming down to earth is mostly soft, nonlethal, pretty things, like . . . like bubbles. Bubbles are some of life's few perfect things. Sometimes, though, it seems like you have to jump out of the way of a lot of scissors to see even just a few bubbles blow your way.

Anyway, by the fifth or sixth update I gradually discovered something surprising: that I kind of *was* beginning to care about being clever or funny or literate, quietly at first, and then in a voice that sang out with more and more *vibrato*. As the objects swirled around me in that dizzying maelstrom, I fell deeper and deeper into that rabbit hole of a creative process through which I passed on the story. I began feeling a responsibility as the messenger of the saga, a responsibility which was as close to a reason for being alive as I'd ever had. Not only that, but sometime during all of this, I also met a nearly new part of myself, a writer, and he was another great reason to be alive. As it all continued over the misty months to spill out, good ol' Chicken Little became increasingly more invested in every new installment, and more and more diverted, and guess what? Soon he wasn't such a little chicken anymore.

You know, it isn't very often that we get to go through God's pockets. Most of the time, we just look up and *wonder* about God, and we rarely get to experience those events that God can orchestrate in a really big way. Most would say, "Thank goodness!" but I've learned that when God opens a pocket, you owe it to yourself to start rummaging. So, as the "poo hit the propeller," and I dodged the fallout (boy, some of that stuff really stains), I always tried to remember everything, if only so that I could write it all down and tell others. I just didn't want to waste the biggest opportunity I ever had to see the master sky diver, God, do her thing firsthand, by not reporting what was behind The Iron Zipper. You know what? I was amazed not only by all of the things that I saw, but how writing about them made me feel better, and how reading about them seemed to make the rest of my world feel better, too.

The point of all this is that now I'm inviting you, someone outside the original bestial congregation, to hear Our Story . . .

This feels funny because I've often wondered how our story would affect someone who doesn't know me. You know, whether anybody else would give a fig. Then I remembered that a lot of the nearly one thousand electronic-letter recipients on the original list didn't know me either, and that didn't matter to them. So you just might relate to what happened to me and my family as a Fellow Creature of the Universe.

The way I see it, when things fall down on us, we just have to tell other creatures, as many as we can reach, or we'll just keep going on and on in our own little pigpens or chicken coops or beehives or lions' dens or ant hills and some may never get the chance to experience certain things, unless we pass on what we've seen. Some of y'all might think you'd be just as well not seeing such stuff. It can be pretty dark inside the zipper. But it zips both ways. It's one of those two-way, industrial-type zippers. When you're on this side of it, it seems like you can't see anything good in there. But when you're in the darkness looking out, the light shines back at you through the cracks in the little teeth real nice, if you brace yourself and open your eyes. Keep reading, you'll see.

If someday you do get the chance to go through God's pockets, you might recognize some of the stuff you find there, having read what I wrote, and you won't feel so alone.

If you haven't yet had the chance, you'll at least be able to say you kind of know what it's like.

Or maybe reading this might just help you keep the faith that maybe there actually is a God, and that God actually has pockets, and there's something in them. That's cool, too.

Even though I definitely haven't seen the absolute worst of what God's got in there, some of the stuff I *did* see was kind of scary. But the other stuff, the bubbles, I've been lucky to see some of those, too. In fact, they were definitely worth ducking all those green lefty scissors for.

So I know from personal experience that if you are ever standing under the sky when it opens up, and all of this stuff just starts *falling* on you, and it soon seems like it's almost more than you can take . . .

. . . and you get hundreds and hundreds of glorious animals of various species, from neighboring wildlife preserves, to look up at the sky, shake their fists (and claws or hooves and paws or fins or wings) and shout,

## "HEY, YOU UP THERE,

# NO

# MORE

# SCISSORS,

# PLEASE!"

*FOLLOWING FOO*

. . . if you can do that

(and I suggest you do it ( **ELECTRONICALLY** ) );

before you know it,

just like magic,

there *will* be bubbles.

Trust me.

—C. LITTLE
NEW YORK CITY, OCTOBER 2002

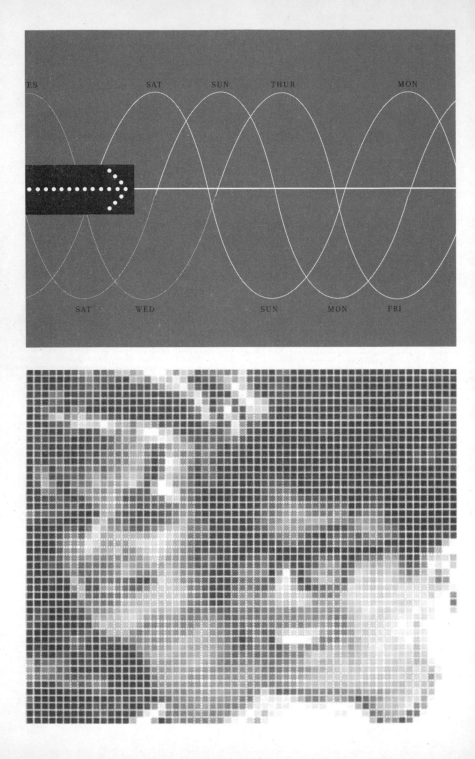

# UPDATE #1

JUNE 6, 2000
SAN FRANCISCO, CALIFORNIA
written at my mother's dining room table

## << Hi! B.D. Wong here! >>

I just want to tell you before you dive into this that it's VERY LONG.

I'd love you to sit down when you have the time and read it all . . .

Dear Ones:
Well, where do I begin? This is going to be difficult for some of you, because so many of you, in different relationships to me in my life, will have greatly varying levels of understanding of this situation. Many of you aren't aware of what Richie and I have been dreaming of and planning since August of 1998;

some of you aren't even aware that there is "a Richie" . . . !

I have experienced something which I need to share with all of you. It is very important to spread the dominant emotions of this situation, Joy and Hope (rather than

**B.D. WONG**

any of the many others), and I feel that contacting you all myself is real important, and will help this end.

The best way to begin is that on Sunday, May 28, 2000, at 9:42 P.M. . . .

## << I became a DAD! >> :-)

This miracle, as only some of you know, has been a couple of years in the making. I don't have time for all the fantastic details of this preparation, but I have a feeling it will eventually be known and maybe become legendary one day! While on the road with *You're a Good Man, Charlie Brown* prior to opening on Broadway, I told few that I was driving into Chicago to deposit my DNA in an Oak Park, Illinois, laboratory . . . one of the first steps in this whole journey . . .

Don't worry, I'll spare you all the gory details of *that* part of the saga . . .

**15**

Now I must fast-forward to the matter at hand. Richie and I have been the proud expectant parents of identical twins since last December, the blessed due date: August 16. Our dear, amazing surrogate mother, Shauna, became quickly quite enormous (pregnantly speaking), and we had a brief scare with (among many other things along the way) preterm labor, a mighty serious condition, when she began having some contractions on Friday, May 19, where she lives near Modesto, California. Richie and I were home in New York, so it was a torturous night . . . after a nervous call from one of Shauna's girlfriends on her behalf from the hospital, and about forty-eight hours of anxiety on both coasts, her contractions were stopped and under control. She was sent home for strict bed rest and medication, and the following week was a bit scary, but looked good.

At twenty-seven weeks, it was way too early for the babies to come into the world without complications. Like most twin births, we knew they'd probably come a bit early, but more than two and a half months early??? We hadn't even had a baby shower!

I was about to start work acting in an odd Castle Rock movie called *The Salton Sea* which was shooting in Los Angeles, and my first days were Wednesday and Thursday of the following week (May 24 & 25). I flew to L.A., and the shooting was uneventful. Periodic phone contact with Shauna was reassuring. I also had the all-important first rehearsal with the band for my cabaret show at Joe's Pub back in New York scheduled for Monday, May 29 (the gig was set for June 5 & 19). Then I was scheduled to work again on the movie back in L.A. on May 30 & 31. But since it was Memorial Day weekend, the movie producers wouldn't release me to fly all the way back to New York for the rehearsal.

I was furious, because the band would be playing on without me, which doesn't really make a lot of sense, when you think about it. Oh, well. So instead of going back to New York, I resourcefully decided to spend the weekend with my mom and dad up in San Francisco, and flew up to the Bay Area from Los Angeles (I guess as long as I was still in the state, the movie people were okay . . . ). Shauna lives about two hours away from San Francisco, so I spontaneously decided to drive down on Sunday afternoon (5/28) for a nice visit. (Our entire pregnancy was peppered with "quality time" visits . . . accompanying Shauna to doctor's appointments, or just being with her and her husband and two toddlers, or with her fellow surrogate girl-friends). I arrived in Shauna's town around noon, and we had fun watching television, chatting, and having "take 'n' bake" pizza (I had never had it and

Shauna was dying to introduce me to it). At around 5 P.M. we started watching the video of *American Beauty*. I warned Shauna I wasn't sure it was "her kind of movie," but I think she enjoyed it. At a little after 7, right between when Chris Cooper tongue-kisses Kevin Spacey and the latter gets shot, I turned to Shauna and routinely asked her how she was feeling. She said, "I've been having a lot of contractions, actually." After taking the very reliable medication, they did not subside.

In half an hour I was getting directions to take Shauna to the hospital (about a half hour away) from her best girlfriend *who takes her everywhere and did not have the car that night*. We decided to play it "better safe than sorry" at this point . . .

The drive to the hospital, though much more physically uncomfortable for her, was really scary for us both. Her contractions timed to about four to six minutes apart (way too often for my taste), and they were obviously very intense. She also, while writhing in the car seat next to me, was saying things like "No no no, stay in this lane" through gritted teeth . . . having a severely irritated uterus and navigating your own way to the hospital should never have to go together, poor thing. I realize now we were both awfully afraid, but not a word was spoken about our fears. By the time we pulled into the parking lot, I was convinced that another shot of magnesium sulfate would once again stop this preterm "scare."

Well, something happened in that walk across the parking lot to the maternity registration, we think. I had asked Shauna if I should run and get a wheelchair. She had never been one to take me up on things like that before. Trouper and proudly independent woman that she is, she walked herself. You know how they always make the overdue pregnant lady and her bleary-eyed husband walk up and down the halls of the maternity ward? I think I finally get why.

By this time Shauna had the drill down. We checked in at registration and they still had her on file from her preterm false alarm the week prior. As she answered their dumb and dumber questions, she was clearly uncomfortable; uncomfortable physically, and uncomfortable with the check-in nurse, who appeared to us to be moving and speaking as if she were suspended in a jar of molasses. Shauna was put in a kind of Labor and Delivery examination room to be hooked up to all the monitors and evaluated. I quickly called Richie with my cell phone, and woke him up: it was after 11:30 P.M. in New York, and I had already said good night to him. I told him as gently as I could that Shauna and I came to the hospital "just in case," and that she was being hooked up. I told him not to worry (not an easy task for him, believe me) and that I would call him again as soon as things were under control—i.e., Shauna got some medication or something. Shauna and I were happy to be there, but the sweet older nurse, Ginger, soon checked Shauna's cervix since her contractions weren't letting up and she was dilated to four centimeters (all week she had been steady at less than two) . . .

Shauna waited until Ginger left the room and then sadly turned to me, between contractions, and defeatedly admitted, "If I'm at four, I don't think they can stop it . . ." I will never forget the sobering, sweet sadness of her face. But inside I'm thinking

*you've gotta be kidding me...*

as my heart began throbbing simultaneously with adrenaline and terror.

I could barely comprehend what was happening. My denial was magnified exponentially by my inexperience in this particular situation. Ginger handed the case over to a fantastic and confident and compassionate nurse, Kari Carper. Kari had just walked in from assisting in the delivery of a twenty-six-weeker, and her head was spinning. It spun faster when she heard that Shauna was only at twenty-eight weeks.

"I'm **NOT** letting you deliver those babies tonight," she commanded emphatically. I didn't feel a whole lot better, but Kari was very experienced, and clearly determined to stop Shauna's labor.

Shauna's contraction's were very, very intense, though, and it seemed soon that Kari could not keep up with their frequency. Kari kept asking, "You don't feel like pushing, do you, hon?" and Shauna kept saying, "No." However, she couldn't express more resolutely how fierce they were getting, and she was quickly turning into that writhing, desperate, perspiring woman I had only seen in bad movies. I was trying not to ask too many stupid questions, but I didn't have a clue how to read the monitors, what to expect, how to act, or how to help my friend.

The next part happened very, very, VERY fast.

Shauna asked if four centimeters was too small to have an epidural. Kari said, "Honey, I'm setting up your IV right now!" This really pleased Shauna. She almost smiled! She'd never had any pain management for her own two kids, and always maintained that this time she

19

would. Then, as Kari tied the rubber tourniquet thingie around Shauna's bicep, Shauna had another soul-splitting series of contractions.

They were, even from my civilian's viewpoint, intolerable, and Shauna was clearly more tortured than previously. Kari made Shauna "present herself," and felt beneath Shauna's gown, between her legs.

Then, all she said, and I'll never forget it, was the word "Crap."

I am not exaggerating when I say that in seconds, at the military summoning of Kari, a phalanx of nurses was in the room, releasing the brakes to Shauna's bed. We were in the exam room, *not* the delivery room, and though Shauna's OB had been paged, he had not responded, nor had any other physician in the hospital made their presence known. It was just a bunch of well-meaning nurses, a terrified twenty-two-year-old pregnant woman, and a somewhat moderately talented actor.

But the latter was feeling very alone. If only Richie wasn't three thousand miles away.

There was a frantic conversation between all the nurses about whether or not Shauna would even *make it* if they tried to wheel her down the hall to the delivery room, just yards. Apparently, there was a baby's head *right there,* so the nurses turned to Shauna:

"Shauna, honey, if we move you down the hall, do you think you can make it? Can you hold on till we set you up in the delivery room? It's not too far, but we'll have to disconnect you and push you down the hall, and hook you up again. Can you do it?"

In the tiniest little girl's voice, Shauna said, "I think so."

Then this mighty army of women in psychedelic scrubs was racing down the hall pushing the bed and all the equipment, and I was chasing them, like Noah Wyle from *ER* when he hasn't read the script. I was finally convinced at this point that

**<< this was really happening. >>**

They threw me this silly-looking jumpsuit and shower cap thing and left me outside the door.

One of the last things I remember seeing as Shauna disappeared behind the big swinging door is the blue rubber tourniquet, lamely half tied around her arm. She had weakly asked, "Does this mean I don't get my epidural?" and Kari said with effortless irony, "No, Shauna, no epidural for you." Outside the door I could hear Shauna screaming every minute or so, and the ladies warning her not to push. There was no doctor in sight. I broke the hospital rules and called our New York number on the cell phone over and over frantically, but I could not get a sufficient signal. A few minutes later they let me in so I could be by Shauna's side. A doctor had arrived, so any second they would let Shauna go for it, but the doctor seemed unsure, and I thought I heard her say, "What do I do?"

The nurses said, "You'll be fine, just deliver like a normal birth." Later I heard, though I'm not certain, that this was a first-year resident at the hospital (perhaps the only doctor available right after supper on Memorial Day Sunday?!). Regardless of her experience, she soon put on her game face and told Shauna to open her legs. When Shauna said, "I don't know what you mean," the seriousness of the premature nature of this situation

21

soon became clear to me. Shauna had had the experience of delivering her own two babies almost effortlessly before . . . why wouldn't she open her legs? I tried to put myself in Shauna's place. So young and so early in this pregnancy, carrying twins, feeling so responsible. The answer came easily.

"She's afraid," I told the resident.

I imagine now, that Shauna, knowing all too well the implications of their prematurity, was probably trying doggedly to keep the babies from being born by the sheer force of her will, once it became clear that was all she had. I imagine that she fiercely held her legs together from the time we left her house till this moment, an exercise in futility. I imagine that she might not have even been aware she was doing this. If determination and will were the only factors, I'm positive Shauna Barringer could've carried our precious cargo all the way to the finish line.

Perhaps something about what I said galvanized the "resident." She really stepped up to the plate, steadied our Shauna; Shauna grunted, and with one swift, smooth effort, at 9:42 P.M., there was a tiny baby in the "resident"'s waiting hands that wasn't there before. It was indescribable. The child was very pale, and hardly moving, but moving. Thank Gosh for the nurse's soapbox derby, for the delivery room was directly adjacent to Neonatal Intensive Care through a tiny pass-through window, and so in seconds after the "resident" cut the cord, the baby swiftly disappeared.

Everyone congratulated Shauna for doing so well, and I realized that I was so intent on looking for the slightest signs of life that I hadn't even noticed the gender of our child. Shauna had known for months, and was real good about not slipping, so she finally got to say, sweetly, and with not a small portion of defeat that this had all come about this way, "Do you want me to tell you what they are?

They're *boys* . . ."

Then we quickly hugged and kissed and battened down the hatches for round two.

They were all waiting to make sure the second twin's orientation would not further complicate things before they let Shauna push. By then another, more experienced doctor who had been paged had entered the picture. He was still suiting up and scrubbing as he rushed through the doors, and got right to it. Then he announced that Shauna's water hadn't actually broken yet! So he told her to push, and I couldn't help but notice him holding his rubber-gloved hands *in front of his face* as she bore down. I soon saw why. When Shauna's water went, it was as if this entire roomful of medical personnel (about a dozen people) were a big Memorial Day barbecue, and Shauna had taken two buckets of water and completely **PUT EVERYONE OUT.** This was truly surreal. Everyone was amazed, startled, and a bit amused. Shauna felt immense relief from the pressure. It actually wasn't that surprising, because she had grown so large in the last couple of months!

**23**

Soon after, Shauna's real OB finally walked in! This was a relief. He had rushed over from a delivery at another hospital in Modesto. Again, in one swift, obviously excruciating but seemingly effortless push, at 9:58 P.M., there was another baby on this wonderful planet. Again, with an unwinding and cutting of the cord, the baby disappeared through the pass-through window. This little guy was bright red, and yelped out and writhed, clearly a bit stronger and more vibrant than his older brother. I had very strong feelings of hope that the unseen team of people on the other side of the window would stabilize them both, soon enough.

So after all the placenta and afterbirth things, and Shauna had been cleaned up and all, we went back to that same little exam room and waited. Then I finally got a call through to Richie, and told him the unbelievable news. I told him I would call him as soon as the boys were stabilized, and there was something more to tell.

So Shauna, and I, and her girlfriends Debbie and Anita (may you all have friends like these women are to Shauna) just waited. We waited, and waited, and waited and waited. Then, two and a half hours after the second baby was born, at around 12:30 A.M., a doctor and a social worker came to find me.

They had "that look" on their faces.

Again, my only frame of reference for "that look" was bad television. I wished they would just *talk* already; it seemed like it took them **so long** to get it out. It was a million times worse than the nurse who checked Shauna in, what seemed like ages ago. Finally time froze, and the doctor spoke:

They were unsuccessful in stabilizing the firstborn. We had lost him. His younger brother only looked "okay."

24

As you can imagine, all of my hopes and dreams and expectations of the last couple of years (particularly the last six and a half months, when I was wholly embracing the magical notion of raising twins with such staggering thrill), ground to a very quick halt in this one, breath-catching, I-can't-believe-I'm-standing-here fraction of time. The adjustment was such a curious one. One moment I was rolling my eyes at the naive excess of it all: surrogacy, modern medical science, identical twins, baby showers, parenthood. An embarrassment of riches. The next, I was being given the Great Pop Quiz: life's inevitable test of acceptance.

"Today???

**There's a test _TODAY???_**

**You didn't tell us you were giving us a test**

# _TODAY!!!_"

I suppose it's just as well. There isn't a lifetime of cramming that can get you ready for this one.

So it was then that I decided firmly (without much effort, actually, but a bit numbly, and tentatively at first, but soon enough with increasing conviction) to put all of that hope and energy I had been storing up in such overflowing abundance until this night into the survivor. To honor the son we'd lost by turning our grief for him into light, and laser-beaming that light into his brother's heart, so that he just might make it.

*FOLLOWING FOO*

But before I could do that wholeheartedly, I had to tell Shauna and Richie what had happened.

This was a task that even I, who arrogantly proclaims that I am up for just about any assignment you might throw me, was stumped by. I hesitated outside of Shauna's door for a stymied moment, reminding myself to breathe, and summoned Kari, Shauna's hero nurse.

"How do I do this? What do I say?"

There I am, asking a total stranger (one who had proven herself so valiantly, but a stranger nonetheless) if she carried the key to this particular door in one of life's more perplexing halls.

The nursing veteran answered almost immediately. "You just say it," she gently said, sweetly shrugging.

26

She also said that she would stay with me, by me, and so we both went into Shauna's room, pulled aside the noisy curtain, and I shared with Shauna and Debbie and Anita what had happened as simply as I could. I am so grateful Shauna and I had these experiences together, that Shauna was not alone (which she probably would've been if I didn't happen to be visiting). The drama and trauma of the delivery, I'm sure, must've made it nearly unbearable for her. But we held each other, and as I spoke I heard myself urging us all to turn the hope we'd been storing into a kind of light, and using the energy from our grief to shine it into the surviving twin's heart. I don't know. Was I just saying the "right sounding" things? It was, at least it seemed, something we could *do*.

Then I called Richie again, who I would say must've felt the loneliest and most anguished of any of us. There he was, three thousand miles away, all alone in our apartment in New York, in the middle of the night wondering for two hours what was going on. I promised him it would be all right, because I really felt it would, and he immediately made arrangements to fly out. We would all be together soon enough.

During this memorable phone conversation, Richie and I named the Angel, whose visit to what we all know as Earth only lasted a bit more than an hour and a half, Boaz Dov Wong, and his younger brother, who was by this time stabilized in the Neonatal Intensive Care nursery, thanks Jackson Foo Wong.

That night, the doctor and the social worker said I could visit them both, and I got to not only say everything I needed and wanted to Boaz, and bawl, but I got to bring him to say "good night" to Shauna, take a few pictures with a camera provided by the hospital, hold him tight, thank him for everything he did for his brother, and celebrate him. They dressed him in an adorable little dressing gown and knit hat, and swaddled him gently in a blue blanket. He truly looked like an angel. Even in death, he carried a dignity that would make any father proud. He actually looked like he knew what he had done for his brother, and seemed almost pleased with himself.

You see, Boaz and Jackson had what is known as Twin-to-Twin Transfusion Syndrome (TTTS), a condition that is not uncommon in identical-twin pregnancies. Because they share one vascular network, one of the twins with this condition (the "donor" twin) passes much of his blood to his sibling (the "recipient"), and the result can be fatal for both. The donor twin almost always suffers from anemia, and the recipient may have heart failure

because of the overabundance of blood in his circula-
tory system, as well as many other complications.

It is very clear, and actually inspiring, to Richie and me
what happened between our two beautiful and excep-
tional boys, and I hope it will be to you.

Some time around Friday, May 19, when Shauna had her
first preterm labor scare, the boys were already transfusing, unbeknownst to any of us. Though we had been
aware of a size difference (often a sign of TTTS), it was
not an abnormal one, or so we were told. I guess only
they, still in Shauna's womb, knew how much trouble
they were actually in. They tried to be born at this time,
but the doctors stopped it with a good dose of magnesium sulfate. However, responding to the wake-up call
the boys were sounding, the doctors also gave Shauna
two steroid shots, to aid in their lung development in
the event that they were to be born prematurely. If they
were to be born more than forty-eight hours after these
shots, they had a much better chance of having the
appropriate lung development to survive. Shauna didn't
actually deliver for another nine days, so by the time
they were born, Jackson's lungs were in much better
shape than they would have been without the steroids.

When Boaz was born, he was about two pounds, five or
six ounces, pale and anemic. He had given his brother
nearly all of his blood, and at this point they, as one
doctor put it, "demanded to be born," because they
must have sensed their own distress. I am told Boaz's
hematocrit level was 4, Jackson's was 80. (I have no idea
what the heck "hematocrit" is, but it has something to
do with the amount of blood in your system. Even with
my lack of medical knowledge, "4 vs. 80" kind of tells
the story.) Jackson couldn't tolerate much more of

Boaz's blood than he'd already been given at the time of their birth. If they had stayed much longer in utero, they would surely both have perished.

I figure they must have known all of this. So they made a break for it, and Boaz gave everything he had in the effort, including, of course, his life. (Like the last few minutes of *Titanic,* when Leo DiCaprio saves Kate Winslet, and then goes down . . . ) The little guy gave his blood and everything he had to his brother so his brother would have the best chance possible.

Richie and Jackson and I will always be grateful to Boaz for that gift. We are sure that he will always continue to look out for Jackson, in that extraordinary *heavenly* way, and that is a birthday present no money can buy. So when we think of this we are inspired and uplifted, and count our many, many blessings. This experience has caused Richie and me to be so ultimately thankful. For everything. For each other. I guess I'm taking the time to write all this to you, my friends, so it might do the same for you.

I am writing to you **A WEEK AND A DAY** after Boaz and Jackson were born. Jackson is doing relatively well. It certainly has been interesting. During this past week, the doctors noticed that Jackson had a distended stomach and diagnosed some sort of intestinal perforation which might eventually require him to undergo surgery, which they do not perform at the Modesto hospital, so they suggested he be moved to the Neonatal Intensive Care Nursery at the University of California at San Francisco. Nifty, because it's just a stone's throw from where my parents live. Life continues to be full of apparent coincidences.

So quite dramatically, last Friday, Jackson and I rode in two ambulances and a tiny fixed-wing plane (again, me as Noah Wyle), leaving Richie's fearful feet firmly fixed on the ground: he met us at the hospital. Our little family is now all in the same city and Richie and I are staying with my folks, while Jackson is getting state-of-the-art care at UCSF.

We are happier, and much less lonely and disoriented (as well as getting fatter, thanks to my mom) and less worried about Jackson, and going one day at a time. I am writing this all to you on Monday, June 5 (the original, now canceled Joe's Pub date!), and we had a well-deserved good day. The doctors decided not to operate on Jackson's tummy for the time being; perhaps whatever's going on in there will either heal itself, or he will eventually have some kind of procedure later on . . . but if he does, the longer they wait to perform it, the stronger and more tolerant he will hopefully be of it. Secondly, the results of his brain-hemorrhage ultrasound, which came back today, were good: he had a grade 1 bleed on a scale of 1 to 4, which they say is virtually the same as no hemorrhage at all. That was a real scary one. Thirdly, there is a rumbling that sometime this week they will take him off air support . . . no more ventilator! This is amazing, and of course probably in large part due to those magic steroid shots the Brothers Wong conspired to make us give them! As a parent will I always be so easily manipulated? I hope so.

I know this is the **l o n g e s t** E-mail you've ever gotten, but I'm sure you can understand that it has helped me in so many ways to write this all to you. Richie and I are doing better and better every day. We are grateful for each other, and the magic Jackson, and the legendary Boaz, and thankful for your calls and love and energy. Please call us, if you like, on our cell phones: 917-555-3599 (me) or 917-555-1671 (RJ). We just love to hear from any/all of you.

Friends, I think I can see it. I think it's peeking around the corner. This will turn out to be a glorious thing. Let's not worry. Let's keep praying (or like Richie's brother Mark says, "I don't really pray. I *ROOT*. I'm *rooting* for you").

I hope that you are all well, and happy, and not too sad over what I've just told you, but rather transcendent and full of the same strange joy as I am.

As I am thankful for my everyday blessings, I hope you will be, too.

I love you all, B.D.

P.S. check out his Web site!

http://www.geocities.com/jacksonfoowong

I wasn't really thinking about the replies that we would receive when I ardently sent out that first E-mail.

I wasn't really thinking about all the different things that people might write.

I certainly wasn't thinking about where it would lead.

Electronically, the world rushed to our front porch with open arms and covered dishes, and Richie and I just weren't prepared. I guess I was so used to unceremoniously deleting corny forwarded E-mails about some child I didn't even know who had fallen into a city sewer and lived with the rats for a fortnight, or another who overcame adversity after being born with the usual two arms, but only one arm*pit* (and you know how cruel the kids at school can be), that I just expected half of the people on the list to skip over it. Okay, so I'm a boob. Between my friends and family and Richie's, plus some of Richie's colleagues from both the West and East Coast offices of his company, the list was about one hundred E-mailers strong, and I don't believe there was a single person who didn't reply immediately.

I can't print them all. But if I had to choose one that represented the spirit of them all, it might be this one:

**hey bd and richie . . . and jackson:**

**if you guys could know about how new york city is brimming over with prayers for you, you would think you were watching it's a wonderful life. we are all trying not to cry, but that is hard since you are so far away. we are just sending it up to clarence in the sky who I know is taking good care of**

boaz, and just so determined to get jackson set up right and off of the bridge. and I can already hear the bells ringing that give everyone their wings, and if you check, any minute you will find zuzu's petals in your pockets. you are the richest men alive, if all of the love and care and worry and prayers are any indication. New York, Broadway, the wardrobe union, the basement of the palace, we all Love you, and we just can't wait till we meet the amazing jackson. i am one of those old-fashioned people who pray, and boy howdy have i been going at it. you are all with me, in my heart, every day, and I am going to keep you there until, well, forever. Love you guys . . . . . . Love and rainbows, terri

> · **TERRI PURCELL** *is a Broadway wardrobe supervisor, and now, a mom. It's fitting that the only words she capitalized were New York, Broadway, and Love.*

Some people could not help but share how Jackson made them think of their own origins . . .

**33**

. . . I too was born premature at 3 pounds and dropped to a pound and a half. You can survive and thrive as I am sure that Jackson will . . .

> · **CARLTON SEDGELY** *is the owner of Royce Carlton, Inc. (my speaker's bureau), and a father.*

. . . or think of their own children and loved ones . . .

Dear B.D.

I just finished reading about your amazing earth-spinning crazed glorious journey. I was weeping with such a mix of emotions, most of which I would have never known a year ago. But since Isabelle Moon came into this world . . . I have a deeper sense of, well, everything. I can't even imagine what it was like for you, but I am awed by the simple enormous majesty of creation. You were witness to an Angel of the highest degree, and now stand by a living god, your son.

Isabelle and I thank you for your insight and knowledge of life's power, and send our blessings to two new souls—one of this earth, and one of the clouds.

May your constant love shine Jackson's way on. Love is the key. Unconditional. Forever.

Gratefully—Jace

- **JACE ALEXANDER** *is a television and film director, and a father.*

. . . while reading your note I was interrupted by my little guy Brandon pouring fish flakes all over (his brother) Nathan. I was angry and at the same time thankful—what a range of emotions! . . .

- **STEPHANIE LOUIE** *is my cousin, and now a mother of three.*

. . . The birth of a baby is such an awesome gift from above, and as you know, something to never take for granted. We thank our lucky stars every day for our little Max. We know he is truly a blessing.

Bruce and I just experienced a loss of our own. I had a miscarriage a couple of weeks ago. It was a huge disappointment, and it really hit me how fragile life is.

Our prayers are with you guys. Please take care of yourselves. Jackson needs you to be strong too!

- **BRENDA LOUIE** *is my cousin, Stephanie's sister, and now a mother of two.*

. . . i too lost my first little guy . . . jeremy . . . at 5 days . . . so your story was so evocative . . . . . . jennifer was born a year or so later, and order (what is order, anyway?) was restored . . . we adopted james 4 yrs later and the family was defined . . . looking forward to standing in line to welcome and hold JACKSON . . . jg

> · **JOEL GREY** *is an Oscar- and Tony Award—winning actor, and a father.*

. . . We were so lucky with Sam, all the complications ended when he was born. God was with you and Jackson! . . . Babies *are* Angels sent with so much hope for the world, and Boaz was obviously sent to help Jackson have a safe landing. And now he's back with God! (Don't worry I haven't been born again. But since Sam came—well you know) . . .

> · **DAVID SPAGNOLO** *is a photographer, farmer, and father.*

Kindred spirits . . .

My dear friends . . . . . more than anything, I just wish I could be there to look at the blessed new Jackson and hold your hands . . . so, for now, I send my love and energy and blessings and will ask my David to keep a look out for Boaz in case he needs a hand to hold . . . . . my love, Bob

> · **BOB HARBIN** *is the former head of casting for the Fox Broadcasting Network.*

There were dear friends, with their distinctive personalities . . .

well! I'm a mess!

I just read "it" and I'm bawling like there's no tomorrow. But not because I'm sad. Because I'm happy that you can see through a tragedy such as this and see the precious gift of Jackson. !!! Praise God! Boaz IS a hero in my eyes . . . I have been praying every day, and even rooting! haha Mom has too . . . if you can, keep me updated . . . Kristin

· **KRISTIN CHENOWETH** *is a Tony Award—winning actor.*

You know, I've been so depressed, down, low, just plain 'ole poopy lately . . . AND then I get an email from a dear dear dear friend about the birth of his babies, the loss of one & the survival of the other . . . and am reminded I ain't got it so bad . . . yes I know everything is relative . . . my thang seems huge . . . but dwindling little by little . . . While reading your email I cried but I laughed . . . laughed hard . . . 'cuz dammit . . . thank goodness for our sense of humor . . . it has gotten us through the most frustrating & ridiculous moments in our lives, yeah? . . . I send nothing but love to you & Richie & now . . . your family . . . what a nice word . . . family . . . is what I feel with you . . . If there is anything at all I can do . . . please do not hesitate to ask . . . I'll be in touch . . . I have to . . . —Deb

· **DEBORAH NISHIMURA** *is an actor.*

**Dear Moderately Talented Actor & Richie,**

B.D., I loved your overture . . . How stressful. How wonderful. I will find some perfect books for him. (Can a parent be called "Richie"?)

**Love, Neufeld**

· **PETER NEUFELD** *is a semiretired Broadway producer.*

Some of our newest friends said the nicest things . . .

. . . you have enabled everyone who is out there with you (even though in the physical sense, we are here) to understand in a more complete way the relationship that the twins shared, and the miracle of the bond that they will always have . . . I thank you for allowing us all into that room with you, where you stood, experiencing it step by step.

I am honored to share in the blessing that is your son.

    · **MARC AYRIS** *is a writer who also works for an advertising agency.*

. . . One of the hardest parts of being a nurse where we work is that once "our" little ones leave us, we often don't hear from their parents or get updates for months, or even years, if ever! Often we have taken care of these babies day and night for 3—4 months and do get a little attached, so your being willing to let us know what is happening in your lives is really special. Thank you so much for including us.

    · **SUZANNE ERWIN** *was one of Jackson's first nurses at the hospital in Modesto where he and Boaz were born.*

. . . We have a saying in the horse world that goes "Throw your heart over the fence and the horse will follow," which essentially comes down to the fact that if you refuse to accept defeat in the face of anything you really want, you will succeed. You and your story are proof of that. I am so proud of you and your fatherhood and proud to know you . . .

    · **KARYN WAGNER** *is a cinematic costume designer. She designed the film* The Salton Sea, *which I was working on when the sky opened up.*

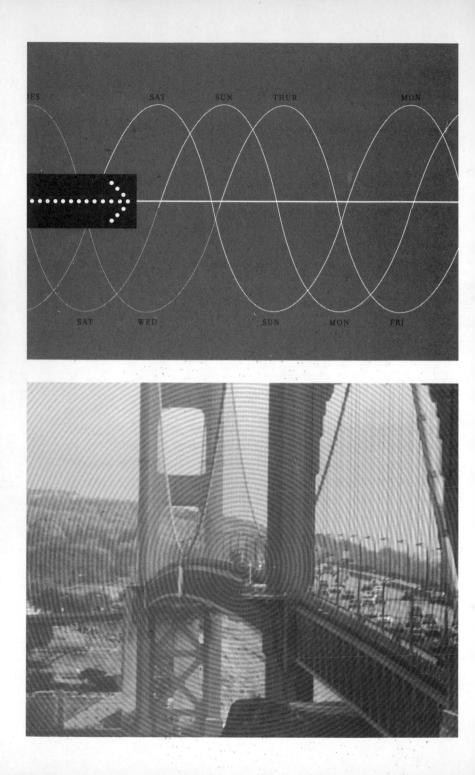

# The SKY OPENED, The EARTH MOVED

## THE BRIDGE B.D. BUILT:
## "POST-UP, PRE-OP"*

*It wasn't until after Update #4 that I began most thoroughly reporting nearly everything that happened between updates. Here's my after-the-fact "Golden Gate" spanning Update #1 and Updates #2–#3.

A s I had been doing ever since Richie and I decided to start a family, at random times when I thought one interesting thing or other was happening in the lengthy process of "preconceived notions," conception, pregnancy, and preterm labor shenanigans, I had a tape recorder rolling when Shauna went into labor. As we left Shauna's house that night to drive to the hospital, I had the little machine with me, and as soon as we got into the labor exam room, I pushed "record." Hours later, I looked down, and I was still clutching the machine; it had preserved a good part of this unearthly experience. Richie and I can't really bring ourselves to listen to the entire recording of that night and the following day quite yet, but when we do, the tape itself will be easily identifiable from its label. Ever the recycler, I had been recording over a lot of discarded cassettes, and this particular tape was one of Jackson's one-day-to-be-godfather Stephen Spadaro's old, relentlessly pounding seventies disco compilations. It was already in the tape recorder when Shauna started having contractions.

Stephen had curiously labeled it

## << EPICENTER >>

It seemed like Shauna and I (and Anita and Debbie, with Richie in New York) waited forever for news about what was happening with the boys, who had been whisked away before we'd even held them or taken their finger- or footprints. Besides giving birth so early in the first place, here was one of the main issues of defeat for Shauna on this night (not having Richie there was probably primary, and not getting an epidural maybe secondary . . . ), because Shauna had always tried to prepare Richie and me for that magical moment when the babies were to enter the world. "Don't worry about me," she urged firmly. "The babies will bond to the sound of the first voices they hear. You have to go with them and talk to them while the nurses wash them and take their fingerprints and footprints. Just leave me alone, I'll be fine." That just about sums Shauna up, I'd say.

People sometimes asked, how can you trust this young woman? How can you be sure that she won't change her mind at the last minute and want to keep the babies? Why is she doing this? You just don't understand, we would say. She's doing this so that two people who can't have a baby themselves can start a family. There's really not much more to it than that. Aside from an amount of money that she could much more easily earn working at McDonald's, what she will receive in return is a feeling of unparalleled distinction that very few mortals can claim. Her behavior for the duration of our relationship with her has pretty much been commensurate with all of the above.

41

But instead of Shauna's selfless plan, the boys were instantly popped through that pass-through window, like the one in Mary Tyler Moore's TV kitchen, into Intensive Care, just like the *two* servings of "Veal Prince Orloff" that Mr. Grant accidentally helped himself to in that classic episode. There was no triumphant, ceremonious cutting of cords, no traditionally jubilant "It's a boy!," no first cries marking the Grand Opening of the Parenthood Superstore, not to mention no pre-coached moment of abandoning Shauna for that sacred ritual of babies bonding to our reassuring, welcoming exclamations.

There was just barely five pounds of baby, divided between their *two* miniscule bodies (#1 weighed about two pounds five ounces, #2 about two pounds thirteen ounces), spirited off to a place I fervently hoped was as well equipped and full of life as Santa's workshop. Then, equally as suddenly, there Shauna and I were. Alone in a delivery room once bustling with people, left stunned, with a single nurse attending Shauna's after-delivery ablutions as the other personnel shuffled off to do other things. The two of us wearily looked at each other, saying, "What happened? Where did everybody go? Remember us? The ones with the emergency?"

Shauna had called her sisters-in-surrogacy, Anita and Debbie, when we first got to the hospital, and there they were, having seemingly arrived in nanoseconds to hold Shauna's hand during her preterm labor agony (part two), only to discover that both the Kit and the Kaboodle had already arrived.

The wait was pervaded by a sense of quiet, fearful defeat. We spoke softly, and our words were positive and hopeful, but I know that deep down we were all afraid of something we dared not articulate. We were all such nice darn people! That unspoken thing couldn't really happen to us, could it? I tried to be as upbeat as possible as we recounted the story of the delivery to the girlfriends.

Aside from the gloomy feeling in the air, I'll always remember how beautiful Shauna looked—a tiny sign from God that though everything appears to have gone horribly wrong, something great indeed has taken place. I, on the other hand, was another section of the newspaper altogether. I was still wearing the preposterous jumpsuit and shower cap made of that disposably sanitary yet unfashionably synthetic, eternally nonbiodegradable, institutional-blue material, and the whole outfit was still lightly splattered with some of Shauna's blood, as was my grindingly clenched face. I was managing, as I recall, to be pretty held together emotionally, *clear* even, but the few photographs that were taken during this long wait depict a man who appears to have slightly snapped. Like a stop sign in a hurricane.

While we waited, I left the room to call my mother on the phone, who had fully expected me to drive the couple of hours back to San Francisco that night in time for dinner!

Guess what?
Shauna started having contractions again.

Guess what?
I drove her to the hospital.

Guess what?
You've got two more grandkids!

Yeah, Ma, I *know* they were due in the middle of August.
I *know* it's the end of May.

Guess what, Grandma, they're *here*.

*FOLLOWING FOO*

The celebration of my fatherhood was dampened at the hospital that night by our numbness, by disappointment, by not having Richie there, by our fear, and of course, by not knowing what was going on down the hall in the Intensive Care Nursery. We replayed the drama of the scene, and subtly (but kind of desperately) tried to find relief in the parts of the story that were remotely diverting: Shauna's water breaking like a tidal wave, the almost absurdly youthful demeanor of the "resident." We called Shauna's husband, Kenny. As I said, I called my mom.

But before any of that, of course, I called Richie.

I literally closed my eyes and tried to imagine what all of this was like for him. After all, I was there, digesting every moment of the drama, and in one jarring phone call, he would have to be completely apprised. How do you tell a New York Jew who never steps off the curb until the light turns green something so fraught with peril and uncertainty? I knew he was literally waiting by the phone, wondering whether or not Shauna's labor had been stopped. I had to remind myself to rewind the video and replay it to him, frame by frame. Alas, I feared that no amount of retraced steps could ever be a satisfactory journey for him at all, no matter how carefully trod.

"You're not going to believe this, but you're a dad," I said.

That's always a good way to start, I think. Unless, of course, the person to whom you are speaking is not a dad.

Trying to tell Richie everything that happened, without robbing him completely of that joyful revelation which usually blesses a man when he crosses the threshold from Son to Father, was like walking an electrified high wire in a monsoon. So was trying to couch everything so that he wouldn't fret himself silly. *Further* fret himself silly . . .

But I soon realized that witholding information would be dishonest. So I told him everything, reaching through the tiny holes in the receiver and trying to hold his hand with my voice. Yet I barely had any information myself, when it came down to it. I could only promise him that I would call him again as soon as somebody told me something. We just had to wait.

He listened quietly, the silence roaring with his fear.

All he could do, while I had the company of Shauna, Anita, and Debbie, was stare at the TV, all alone. It was about 3:30 A.M. by now in New York, and a VH1 *Behind the Music* marathon was on. Richie still says he now knows more about Stevie Nicks than anyone in their right mind would want to know.

Kari Carper, Shauna's solid-as-a-rock Labor and Delivery nurse, was also around during this time. Kari had been expert in preparing Shauna for delivery, and came very close to delivering the babies herself, but at this point she was at least two degrees separated from knowing any better what was going on than we did. She had prepared Shauna brilliantly for the three (!) people who delivered the babies, who in turn, literally passed the babies to Intensive Care. But she did offer her professional, no-nonsense opinion.

"The second one looked okay, but I have to tell you, and I've been a nurse a long time, the first one didn't look too good," she said.

I realized later that Kari was saying this to explain why it was taking so long, not because she specifically thought the baby wouldn't live. She was warning us to expect it to be a long night, and though my heart sank when she said he didn't look good, I wasn't that worried about losing him. Maybe I was just naive. Or in denial.

It was after midnight when the doctor and Karen Farwell, the social worker on duty, came to me, like the police on the front porch in a scene from a cautionary driver's ed movie.

I thought, this is what it feels like when a "big thing" happens. This is that event you wonder whether you would survive if it occurs. Hysteria seemed completely inappropriate and counterproductive; crude, indulgent. I felt such sympathy for this soft-spoken, sweet man who not only was unable to save the baby using the skills he had committed a large part of his life to learning, but was further forced by the tradition of his function to actually report to me of his unsuccessful attempt. What a punishment that must feel like, I thought. How *mean* to make a man have to do that. I remember monitoring my response, using that weird inner third eye that probably exists only in performers.

If I overreact, will I seem ungrateful for his efforts, like I'm blaming him?

Will they be worried that I'm going to lose it, tackle me, sedate me, *institutionalize* me if I cry, like Randle McMurphy or Frances Farmer? Would they put me in the "Cuckoo's Nest"?

Shouldn't I say something *intelligent* soon, so that he will know that I have comprehended what he has told me; that I still have "got it together"?

So I said nothing, and stared at them/him, trying to maintain eye contact but intentionally nodding my head, to illustrate (in actorspeak, to *indicate*) that I indeed comprehended what he was saying.

When he was all done, I said something like "I see," and I intentionally thanked him, for I felt from the sadness I saw in his eyes that it surely must have been as bad a night for him as it was for me, and hey, I hadn't even tried to save anybody's life.

It was after they told me that I could go visit the boys in the nursery that I asked the doctor and social worker to wait for me outside Shauna's room. Then I told Kari. When Kari reacted with shock and immediate compassion, I realized that she hadn't intended to make it seem like she thought Boaz was going to die back when she said he didn't look good.

That's when I told Shauna, and then called Richie.

Richie tells people that if you ever have to get bad news, you should have me tell you. I'm not so sure about that, but I did try to imagine him at home watching Stevie Nicks and late-night replays of Oprah—remembering her darn spirit—like a zombie, just waiting for me to call when our phone finally rang. It was pretty rough, but perhaps he was expecting the worst, and I made that effort to put our energy into moving forward.

I would go visit the boys, one to say good-bye to and one to say hello to, and while I did, Richie would call the airline to find out when the next flight was. It was at this time that Richie and I decided what to name the boys. Richie and I had settled on names not long before. We agreed from the beginning that the first name of one baby, boy or girl, would be Jackson, Richie's family name. We put my dad's original Chinese name, Foo, in the middle if he were a boy, because we both liked the way it tripped off the tongue. Jackson Foo Wong. "Foo" is hard to translate from Chinese. It loosely means "rich," but I believe it's a rich that transcends monetary wealth, though I'm not absolutely sure. It matters not to me. It's my dad's name.

The other name we had chosen, if the babies were boys, was Boaz Dov Wong. Richie and I were immediately both drawn to the name Boaz, a name from the Old Testament; "Dov" is the Hebrew word for "peace." My father's "American initials" and my brothers' initials are all "BDW," and we wanted to continue that tradition.

On that night, coast-to-coast long distance, the question became whose name was whose? Richie and I both wanted a child named Jackson (to keep both our surnames alive in the family).

But living, or in memoriam? After some thought, the name Boaz Dov seemed like the only choice for the mighty sacrificer. A biblical name and the Hebrew word for peace. It was easy to "give up" my BDW monogram for a name that sounds like the name of a fleet-footed heavenly messenger. What's a monogram when someone has given their whole life?

When I rejoined the doctor and the social worker (Karen), the latter gave me a disposable camera, compliments of the hospital. She explained that a local one-hour photo lab would develop the film free of charge for any family who had lost a child like we had, and gave me a coupon. She warned me that though I surely would not feel at all like taking pictures of Boaz, I would most certainly regret not having the pictures later if I didn't take some. I marveled at the forethought of this gesture. She really had it down. It made me even sadder to realize that Karen must have given out a camera like this one on more occasions than she'd have liked. It was also curious that this jolly device, most definitely invented to document life's most joyous moments, was tonight being "pressed into memorial service."

In the Intensive Care Nursery, there were about a dozen or so babies in different kinds of beds being attended by various nurses.

They led me to Boaz's bed, which was one of those small clear plastic trays, padded with foam, open on top. Our hero was laid ever so carefully on it, dressed crisply in a soft flannel dressing gown tied with a ribbon, little blue booties, and the smallest blue knit cap. Perhaps a tiny wreath of laurel might also have been fitting. My little dove was so true to his name, so peaceful, his triangular mouth slightly open, his large eyes quietly closed, no sign of the trauma he no doubt experienced. I felt the kind presence of several nurses surrounding me peripherally, reminding me of the serene handmaidens in a Rembrandt, which normally might have inhibited my behavior, but I just had to speak to him right away. I had turned the tape recorder on at some point during this, though I still haven't the spine to listen to the recording to this day.

I just started talking. I suspect I went on a bit: about what a fine boy he was, how proud I was, how thankful I was for him, and how I hoped he'd look after Jackson. It was not hard at all for me to imbue him with all of the human qualities that I had already given him prebirth; Shauna and I had long since decided "Twin A" (Boaz) was most definitely the selfless one from looking at the ultrasound images. It was almost always impossible to capture Boaz's face, in sharp contrast to the full-on, dramatic pictures that we always got of the hammy "Twin B"—Jackson—from every angle. We always thought of Boaz as the camera shy one, the one who most certainly would eschew the limelight so the other could bask in it. How spectacular that this indeed turned out to be so.

I had not wept at all the entire evening, not in talking to the doctor or Kari, not in all of the phone calls to Richie and my mom, not in telling Shauna. But as soon as I started talking to Boaz, in this bizarre, publicly intimate, "act now, don't delay" moment, Niagara finally fell—and when she lost her balance, one could understand why she was one of the Seven Wonders. My legs never went out from under me or anything like that, but a pert, bespectacled woman in a kind of Amish-looking nurse's cap named Connie wordlessly and sweetly kept pressing dry tissues into my hand, as if she had done it a million times. Knowing this was an opportunity that would pass even quicker than Boaz himself did, I talked until I had not a single thing left to say. I don't remember specifically what I said. Yet these moments are tattooed on the cortex of my brain.

I thought that I should not botch this moment for Boaz and me. Not gloss over, trivialize, be embarrassed by, or avoid the intense feelings of it, but that I should try to get to the closure point as quickly as possible, for us both, for all three of us, for all four of us. I wanted to memorize Boaz's face (no wonder they give you a camera), I wanted to always remember being there, and I wanted to *feel* as much as possible, so that I could sooner rinse away the sadness and begin chasing felicity. This is the Jewishness that has rubbed off Richie's family onto me over the fourteen years I've known them, perhaps. *Never forget.* We have decided that the celebrations for Jackson cannot begin without a celebratory remembrance of Boaz.

I had a mortifyingly embarrassing moment at my grandmother's funeral years ago. I stood by her open casket and just stared at her for a protracted moment, completely unaware that a long line of people also wishing to pay their respects had formed beside me, and that I was holding up the entire proceedings with my indulgence. My uncle had to gently grasp my elbow and pull me away from the coffin until I understood what had happened, and it felt awful. I promised myself to avoid experiences like that in the future by never again letting my emotions freeze either me or time, as they had that day.

But the night the boys were born and the sky opened up, I felt no compunction to move things along. For a rare moment in my life, I was unconcerned with the possibility of embarrassing myself. I spoke my piece, without self-censoring or hurrying, I wrung my heart out like a wet sponge until I was completely parched, I halfheartedly took a few pictures, and then I finally nodded to Karen the social worker that I was content with my visit.

She nodded back and gestured toward a corner of the room. Then, as if I was a movie (sometimes I still don't know that I'm not; just kick me when that happens), the camera slowly panned to reveal what all the other nurses were looking at. Each of them glanced furtively at me, hoping that what I would see might be something that could brighten my world.

In all of their combined years of professional wisdom, they were never more right.

A few steps away, in a little glass house, was the living, breathing, struggling Jackson Foo Wong.

Nowadays, there isn't a night that passes without a thought about Boaz in it somewhere, some kind of wondering.

Even so, at that moment in my life an incredible new journey commenced.

One minute, you're overcome by the drowning sense that life just isn't fair. How unfair to beg for the responsibility of parenthood, for what you think are all the right reasons, and to have the responsibility revoked, without warning or sense, before the license is even activated. There's no chapter about grief, or what if your baby dies or something goes horribly wrong, in *What to Expect When You're Expecting* (although that book does manage to put the fear of God in you when it comes to just about everything else under the sun, and Richie and I weren't even carrying!).

It's not fair, it's not fair. Why is life so unfair? Where's the raft, the preserver, the plank of wood randomly floating by to grab on to?

Then, with a turn of your body and a few paces, your head breaks the surface of the water, and the oxygen nourishes your brain, and suddenly, you're swimming circles around *unfair*. You passed *fair* way back in the first lap. With a stop, a step, and a start, you're quickly approaching *grateful* and gaining on **lucky.**

If I might be so "more experienced than thou" to say so, I do think the emotional confusion experienced when a parent loses one of two twins close to the time of their birth must be among the most unrivaled insanities. I don't wish to be misunderstood. Other tragedies must be unquestionably more difficult to bear, more, well, tragic. But I don't think that in any other equation is the phenomenon of elation and grief served in more equal portions. There just aren't many travel agencies in life that can book you a trip to visit the North Pole and the South Pole at the very same time.

We are taught, particularly as Americans perhaps, to feel things fully. To live life with gusto, to have a point of view, to attack from a definitive position, to make up our minds; black or white.

As an Asian-American, boy have I ever learned that there's a hell of a lot more to life than just black and white.

So when that arguably definitive moment in a person's life, the birth of their first offspring, occurs, and splatters random brilliant color passionately onto the walls in an unbridled mural of exultation, how can we lead the world over the poppy-scattered knoll of celebration, when simultaneously the giant ogre has trampled the wildflowers into the earth with one fiercely cruel, thundering step? When it's a sunny day, we say God is smiling, and when it's icky out, we say God must be in a bad mood. It's all so neat and tidy, because we know that for every giddy day there's a somber one to keep life deliciously balanced.

Then the sun is beating down on the roof *at the same time* a storm is raging, and it's so rare and so impossible to fathom that it almost certainly will cause a fuse to blow somewhere in the house.

My, those extraordinary moments in our oh so short earthly tenancy: these earthquakes and twisters! Their unexpectedness— the fact that we're never offered options or choices, in some ways actually makes things easier. Whether in anticipation of the tornado or in the aftermath of the earthquake, you just have to *feel*. There isn't time to decide *how* to react or *how* to feel; all of a sudden you're just feeling these things, and the feelings pull you down the white water at their own speed, in their own fashion. I guess that's what happened in this freaky moment in the Intensive Care Nursery in Modesto. I never got the chance to say, "First I think I'll feel this, and then I'm sure I'll feel that." I just felt a Whitman's sampler of humanity's top ten emotions every step of the way, and the baby, living or dead, who happened to be directly in front of me dictated whether I would feel the potent emotions of bereavement or the potent emotions of jubilation.

Lying there in that little glass house, Jackson didn't exactly look strong enough to throw stones. Don't worry. If he had started the windup to pitch a pebble, I would have said something discouraging. I am his dad, after all. Besides, it was Plexiglas.

Jackson and Boaz were bigger than those impossibly tiny preemies that fit in the palm of your hand, but much, much smaller than your garden variety newborn. To give you a frame of reference, the nurses had placed inside the isolette with him a flannel doll, which they called a "preemie pal." The preemie pal has long arms and legs, and because a preemie can be handled and cuddled so infrequently, this featherweight friend can be placed on top of the baby, with its fabric limbs wrapped around him, to give the baby a sense of comfort. Jackson was the same size as the preemie pal. The preemie pal was a wee bit bigger than a Beanie Baby.

Afraid I'd miss something, my eyes were practically bugging out of my head, refusing to blink. I tried to soak up everything I saw and heard, for later, for Richie, forever. I didn't really look at the people around me. I just focused on the babies intently, shutting out everything else.

I listened to the doctor as he calmly told me the prognosis; Jackson was considered "stable," and was in no imminent danger.

"But," the doctor cautiously added, "looking after a premature infant is a bit like riding a roller coaster. No two preemies are alike, or become well in the same way. Be prepared for a lot of unexpected things to come up on a daily basis. There's no way to predict how quickly he'll get strong enough to grow on his own, or what problems that we don't see now which might develop."

I'm not sure if the doctor was particularly convincing, or if I was listening more intently than usual. Maybe Boaz's death had prepared me for the absolute worst. But from that moment, I was surprisingly easily resigned to Jackson being in the hospital for a long, long time, and I was officially braced for any number of crazy outcomes. Maybe I was just grateful he was alive. But eventually, many of those crazy outcomes actually occurred, and when they did I was sometimes more ready for them than not. This was the first of Boaz's many gifts to us. The gift of accepting whatever adventures were in store for Jackson, and not being particularly surprised or resistant to them. The gift of strength.

As the short paragraph of Boaz Dov Wong's life came to a close, there opened an entire bookful of material on the humble journey of Jackson Foo Wong. Literally, I suppose. An *Encyclopaedia Britannica* of thrills and chills.

Richie and I have a little Wong family trivia that makes us smile. Whenever my family watches my brother Barry's wedding video, there's a moment during the ceremony when I'm singing (well, not exactly singing, it was more like sniveling, but anyway; it was one of those all-time great weddings). While I'm singing, the camera zooms in on my macho brother's emotional face, and you can hear my voice in the background, swelling to a wobbly climax.

Whenever we get to this part of the video, my dad always points his finger, arm fully extended, at my brother's face in one specific instant, and he exclaims, in his wisely sentimental, impish voice, "There! That's when he grew up! Right there!"

I wish I had a videotape of the night the sky opened up.

The moment I turned from Boaz to Jackson would be the moment that my dad would be pointing at.

## << ATTENDING THE WOUNDED >>

By the time I visited our boys that first (and last) time, it was past one in the morning.

I stayed with young Jackson for a long time. It felt as though anything could happen to him in the trice I might have stepped away from him to make a phone call or use the bathroom. So I didn't.

When I touched his hand with my finger, he immediately grasped it tightly (his entire hand could barely wrap around it), and the pang of surprise and relief it made me feel was a Kodak moment. It was as if, even with his eyes tightly shielded from the light and his lungs hooked up to a machine, when I thought it was me who was comforting *him*, he was ironically applying that mighty mite of pressure to comfort *me*. To say, "Whew, Dad. That was something, huh?" You know what? He knew his stuff. I felt a little better. He squeezed my fingertip reflexively like he was grabbing a relay baton.

55

## Run, boy, run.

I was a little less alarmed by his unnatural purple hue because I had been warned of it, I guess, and because I knew that he could never be as dark as the grief I felt for his brother. At any rate, the extra blood in his body was being drawn from him, in a kind of antitransfusion, and they said his color would become more normal in the days to come; more like the *inside* of a radish than the *outside*. He was being given a roster of drugs for various things—a surfactant to help open his lungs, morphine, and others—and there was a large, invasive respirator tube down his throat and taped to his face with thick white tape. His apparent lack of resistance to this obviously comfortless state was reassuring.

I unabashedly sang songs to him through the little hole in the isolette, and said the kind of overoptimistic things that you say to someone who is in a coma.

When I realized, having talked to the doctor and the nurses, that the most traumatic portion of the evening had indeed passed, I prepared to say good night to him. I could have stayed singing more show tunes to him all night through the open Plexiglas porthole like an old drunk ex-hoofer in a Greenwich Village piano bar, mind you, but I knew that Shauna would want a full report, and that I should call the sleepless Richie once more to prepare for him to arrive in that whirlwind of heartache and uncertainty. I was relieved that Jackson's breathing was controlled by the ventilator, that the nursery staff was calm, and that there seemed to be no other immediate complications, but I still said good night to him as if it was ...

good-bye

... just in case.

Shauna was ensconced in the postpartum ward, and they had thoughtfully assigned her a private room, anticipating that I might need to crash on the floor. I told her everything, and then suggested we try to sleep. It had taken an awful long time to stop Shauna's post-delivery bleeding, and by now she was rather weak and dopey, two words that one would never normally use to describe her. I tucked her in, and reminded her that I was indeed happy, and profoundly thankful for her presence in our lives.

Alas, her sadness was palpable, and yet her (and my) emotional wounds were too freshly inflicted for us to discuss them.

A salty but warm older nurse had set me up on the floor with as many blankets and pillows as she could round up, and I lay on the cold linoleum feeling bony and restless, though I was bleary-eyed with weariness.

Shauna and I said "good night" from our respective areas of the clinical room, like *The Waltons*. It was after three in the morning.

Richie had called the airline immediately, and got on the first flight out Monday morning, arriving in San Francisco around 10:30 A.M. or so, just about twelve hours after the birth. My parents were going to pick him up at SFO and drive him directly to the hospital in Modesto. I could tell when I bid him "safe flight" on the telephone that he was anxious, confused, and rather beside himself, and I attributed this state not to his famous cautiousness and nervousness, but to the cruel prank of his unnatural detachment from the nucleus of the drama. When I spoke to him immediately after I left the nursery, I promised him that he would feel much better when he finally saw Jackson. Jackson was real, and witnessing that miracle was grounding and focusing—even if he, too, was to be soon taken away from us. Watching his tiny concave chest rapidly rising and falling was at once terrifying and reassuring. "When you see him," I told Richie, "you'll feel like it's going to be okay, I promise."

I really believed this. Looking down into his tidy plastic Habitrail, as scary and barely on earth as he was, one couldn't help but feel hope in something so cliché as "the miracle of life," even after so much had gone awry. From then on he would be, among a million other things, a reminder to us that dreams do come true, and that sometimes there is a dear, dear price to pay for such a pure, splendid truth.

As soon as I knew that the time Richie's plane landed had come and gone, I began looking out for him at every turn. I was afraid that he would get lost and roam the halls of the surreal institution, wandering into strangers' inhospitable hospital rooms, perhaps stumbling into a surgery or two, disoriented, his nerves eventually fraying completely, alone. For two hours, while I knew Mom and Dad were driving down, I overanxiously awaited their arrival.

While I waited, I made a handful of crucial phone calls between multiple visits to the nursery.

"Uh, guess what . . ." I always began.

Maybe the most important call was to Gary Gersh, a colleague of Richie's, and eventually one of Jackson's three godfathers, who not only is one of our closest friends, but who immediately became the hinge-leaf of the J. Foo grapevine, at least until the creation of my Electronic Updates #2 and #3. I started from the very beginning, and told him everything that I have told you, predicting accurately he would meticulously and lovingly assume such a role. He is a true-blue friend.

When somebody asked me, "Well, what does Jackson look like?" I didn't know where to begin. I thought about what people say, that you don't look like you did when you were a baby again until you are very old, and I just blurted out, "Um . . . he looks like . . . he looks like . . . a little **CHESTNUT MAN.**" I think this was mostly because his face reminded me of the wise old man selling chestnuts to the Christmas shoppers on a winter New York street corner, warming his hands over the coals, making his living, never giving up—not because he actually physically *resembled* a chestnut at all. I think. I'm not absolutely sure why I said it, actually. It just felt right. His head *did* look a little scrunchy and morsely, come to think of it.

When I finally stepped outside of Shauna's room to see Richie walking tentatively down the long, cold hallway toward me with my parents, our inevitable embrace was like the clenched vise grip of people who have been reunited after some sort of Great War, though it had been just less than a week since we'd last seen each other. I remember catching my parents out of the corner of my eye over Richie's shoulder, both of them having nowhere else to look while the dads stiffly rocked one another, doing the Frankenstein slow dance. I recall noticing them witnessing this rare and necessary moment of distraught intimacy, while they dealt with their own emotions of the situation overlapping with their shyness.

That morning, while we waited for Richie's arrival, Shauna thought of something that could make her feel a little better while she recovered. She asked to rent a breast pump, and began pumping breast milk to nourish Jackson. This was never part of our arrangement with her, and we never would have asked this of her, particularly since we live in New York and Shauna lives in California. But it was Shauna's idea to draw the life potion from her body to eventually help strengthen the baby, since it was clear we would now be in California indefinitely. She started that first day with an orientation from a lactation specialist, and drew a modest amount of the precious colostrum, which is the crucial mother's milk from the first few days after birth, chock-full of all this crazy stuff that's good for the baby. It's so concentrated that it's a salubrious golden color. So we showed the fruits of Shauna's first efforts to Richie and my folks, and then I took the newcomers all down to the Intensive Care Nursery to view the prince in the plastic castle.

Those of you couples who have children will understand what I mean when I say how fun it is to step back a couple of paces and observe how your baby transforms the person you live with. You don't yet even need to know that Richie is a very paternal soul to begin with, who soars through the air gripping the banner of fatherhood with a breathtaking rapture. There must be something to the notion that a baby enhances and deepens a relationship. One of the reasons I think this may be so is that a baby is one of the very few things in the universe which can coax out of each of us the godliest and most shining parts of ourselves, and when those parts come into focus on the face of a person who you set out to bring a child into the world with, that's mighty tasty gravy.

So I just backed up and watched Richie peering into the see-through dollhouse devotedly, getting his finger squeezed, politely introducing himself to the mini-man. I had tried to prepare him for Jackson's red-as-a-raw-ribeye-steak complexion, how small a less-than-three-pound baby actually is, and about the baby's subway map of tubes and wires, so I think it wasn't as bad as he'd feared. I watched that permanent bond form before my eyes, and I thought about the time to come, God willing, in sickness and in health.

A baby in the Intensive Care Nursery at the hospital in Modesto can only have two visitors at a time, and after Richie met Jackson, it was Grandma and Grandpa Wong's turn to scrub up. If I ever had any silly, self-deprecating worry that my mother and father didn't quite know what to make of me becoming a parent, it was soon enough rinsed away by the bright, clear stream of love freely flowing from them as I led them to Jackson's station in the nursery, one at a time, peeking ever so cautiously. I often think that they must have thought they weren't getting any more than the five grandchildren they already had. Yet there I was, at Christmastime just six months earlier, announcing that "we" were "pregnant"! As Mom and Dad first laid eyes upon him, the fragile state of the "bonus boy" somehow made Jackson even more special to them than his status as merely the grandchild they never expected.

He was a boy whose place on earth, and in our family, would in no way be earned easily, from the effort and thought it took to bring him to fruition, through his difficult birth, through his uncertain hospital stay to come. On this day, my parents, who would celebrate their fiftieth wedding anniversary later that year, would commit themselves to being Jackson Foo Wong's principal cheerleaders, mascots for the underdog. For every moment of the summer that was to follow, they would be there for him in more ways than you can imagine.

For better or for worse.

That reminds me . . .

When the appropriate nurses, learned that Richie had arrived, they prepared the part of Boaz that was still earthbound so that the two of us could have a visit with him. They laid him in a little basket, and put him in one of their tiny "hospitality rooms," and escorted us there when we said we were ready. Sadly, they apologized to us and warned us that because of where he had spent the night, he would be very cold.

This was dizzying. As I led Richie into each new room of God's fun house—Shauna's room, Jackson's nursery, Boaz's hospitality room—I somehow reexperienced everything again for myself. The two of us wandered gamely around the building, staring at ourselves in the wacky mirrors, feeling together such a kaleidoscope of new emotions and sensations. Even the day after what I thought was the *worst* of everything, I still felt like I was under water. Introducing Richie to each new thing, and preparing him, required so much thinking ahead. Even though I had all of the drills down pat (who to talk to, how to scrub your hands, what the rules were, etc.), I was barely much more up for each obstacle in the labyrinthine course than Richie was.

We went into the hospitality room and tried to take pictures, though through our watery eyes not one of the pictures we took with our own camera came out in focus. It's just as well. If you look at them, you could practically see it all pretty much as we did. Blurry, as if through tears. Richie bravely holding the steadfast tin soldier up, so tiny and lifeless, the fluorescent light so unforgiving. I was relieved to feel that his skin was still soft, and his body was pliable, though he was indeed very cool to the touch. Cool as the clouds in the sky.

I left Richie alone in the room for a few moments, as I had been with Boaz the night before (though I had had that "audience"), and I gave him the tape recorder and asked him to try to say something "meaningful." What a stupid thing to suggest. How could any true expression, no matter how emotional or incoherent, be anything less than meaningful?

When I returned, Richie looked so, so spent, and confirmed that he was as content as a person could be under the circumstances. Indeed, I didn't think he could bear more. Then, though we were resigned to accepting the little one's passing as best we could, simultaneously we had that moment when we both realized "this was it"; that we would not be able to see him anymore, ever. He might as well have died all over again right then, because the thought of permanently passing him from our arms into the intangible corridor of our memory of him was excruciating (no matter how heroically grand or sweetly fragrant we thought we'd dressed that corridor). Sure, the nurses had all whispered gently that anytime in the next couple of days, if I wished to see him again, I could, and I had eagerly told them I most certainly would, but it was far more emotionally draining to see him the second time than I had anticipated. I decided that I should wail now, and save my valuable energy for the little brother who needed it so. I knew that every time I asked for another visit with Boaz, it would never be any less wrenching. It would never be "a nice little visit." It would always be this huge thing. There are no small operas.

I have this thing about going home at the end of big parties. A half hour before Richie wants to go home (and trust me, he always wants to go home at least a half hour before I do), he'll politely (and wearily) say, "Can you start saying your good-byes now?"

Then I painstakingly go through the whole house and say my farewells to each person I know in each room, with their full attention. I'll wait for a conversation to end before I duck in to say so long. Once I've said parting words to a person the way I see fit, if I happen to cross through the same room again, I can just smile at anyone I've already covered, or wave, as long as I feel I have already given their particular adieu the proper weight. Then, when I feel like I've said "see you" to everybody well enough to allow me to rest if a safe falls on me (or them) outside, I say, "Let's go."

Sure, you think this is crazy. It takes a lot of energy to do it. Yeah, yeah, it's very anal. But once you've said good-bye thoroughly, you don't have to say it again and again and again. In fact, you shouldn't.

You just have to have faith that it will last as long as you need it to.

That if a long, long time passes before you see a certain someone again, when you finally do, they will remember you.

63

## << SURVEYING THE WRECKAGE >>

Well, Richie flying into San Francisco and my parents rushing him down to Modesto served a dual purpose. It wasn't just so we could be all together, and so Richie could be with the boys as soon as possible.

I was scheduled to shoot again on that movie, *The Salton Sea*, in Los Angeles the next day (Tuesday) at dawn, so my parents were going to leave Richie in my place, and drive *me* back up to San Francisco to the airport for *my* flight, on *their* way home to nearly collapse of emotional and physical exhaustion. There's that relay motif again.

More about the filming later. For now it will suffice to say that Tuesday and Wednesday were naturally unbearable (well, let's get some perspective: *being decapitated* is unbearable; this was really really hard). I really do like being a part of making movies, but I will have to admit that there are aspects of the process, and the entire world revolving around it, that as time goes on seem less and less the things I want to have anything to do with. When something so humbling and real as everything that happened Sunday night and Monday happens, it makes taking moviemaking seriously seem so embarrassing.

After the first day of work, I spent the night in the little green cottage that we had been renting in Los Angeles for me to use when I'm working there, and it was arguably the loneliest place on earth; not the usual rustic, artsy refuge from Hollywood that I always looked forward to.

Blessedly, Jackson's condition had not worsened. Richie gushingly reported on every new thing he discovered about the baby, as well as his rapport with the nurses, who were always cheery and upbeat. They would shake their heads and roll their eyes behind a doctor's back whenever they felt like the doctor was saying things to Richie that were too worrisome or unnecessarily complicated. If Jackson could keep going along, he might just make it, though the doctors and the nurses warned us that it was impossible to predict the many things that would invariably happen to a preemie like Jackson at a moment's notice. It would almost always be *something*; an infection, or a reaction to a drug, or an up-to-that-moment-completely-functioning-but-now-failing organ, anything. Sometimes it might be a huge fallen Sequoia in the road, sometimes an anthill. They said we should fasten our seat belts for a long and bumpy ride. We most certainly shouldn't think of bringing him home until at least his birth due date (August 16). I always took the doctors' and nurses' warnings seriously, and constantly told myself to be ready for anything.

In the meantime, Richie had homework.

One of the mind-blowing modern things that Richie, Shauna, and I had legally arranged in preparation for the boys' birth was a judgment from a California family court judge, who would put *only* Richie's and my names on the babies' birth certificates as their parents, as opposed to *one* of our names and Shauna's. This judgment hearing was scheduled for Thursday, June 2, in plenty of time for Shauna's *August 16* due date.

Richie called the lawyer we were working with.

"Uh, guess what . . . ?" he began.

Richie always handles these types of things. Me, I just type the E-mails feebly explaining them afterward. He does all of the calling and finagling and yes, negotiating, and then he drops a sheaf of papers down on the table with a thud and says, "Sign here . . . and here . . . and here . . ." like I was Judy Holliday in *Born Yesterday*, you know, sitting around eating bonbons out of a big heart-shaped box in my silk PJs and not assuming my intellectual potential.

Anyway, after a lot of fancy footwork, the judgment was secured. Richie's really quite a dancer.

Two days after our boys were born, we were officially parents, and so acknowledged by the State of California on paper.

After a split second of hesitation early Wednesday morning, while I was still off being in a movie (of all of the mature, down-to-earth, parental things to be doing at a time like this), Richie called his mom (Grandma Carol) and asked her if she would fly out from her home in Long Island, New York, to be with her youngest son (and *his* youngest son).

Immediately, on that afternoon, Grandma Carol hopped on a plane. Just say the word. I know she was anxious to see her lilliputian grandson anyway, but I have to hand it to the Jackson clan: they're always there for one another.

That's one of the reasons why, I reckon and hope, *Jackson* is such a good name for *Jackson*.

## << REVISITING THE SITE >>

When I returned on Thursday night Grandma and Richie let me know what the doctors were saying, including that they thought Jackson's lungs were in pretty good shape, thanks to the steroids Shauna had been given the week before the boys arrived.

When I saw Jackson at the hospital, he was markedly less burgundy colored, and that was terrifically reassuring. He had lost some after-birth weight as predicted, but everything else seemed "okay" for the time being. It had been about four nights since he'd been born, and he still hadn't pooped. They didn't seem too worried, but he was under careful and constant watch. He lay there under the bili-lights (to keep jaundice at bay), with a hilarious eye shade covering his eyes, like the kind of sleeping mask an old rich lady wears on an overnight flight to Paris, except that some wise guy at the eye shade factory had the ridiculous idea to silkscreen a pair of Ray-Bans on the outside, giving the baby an incongruous, sunbathing-beatnik kind of look.

That night, I stayed up late with him (my new favorite pastime), crooning still more corny, baby-friendly show tunes while Richie snoozed.

Before I went down to L.A., the hospital had referred me to a nearby motel because it was clear that we were going to be in Modesto indefinitely (August 16 was almost three months away!).

66

We had made an inquiry about moving Jackson to a hospital in San Francisco because that's where my parents live, but they told us that it would be a tremendous expense, and that our insurance wouldn't cover such an elective move, and besides, Jackson was in much too fragile and delicate and sick a state to transport. (They kept using that word "sick," which always made *me* sick). He was in Intensive Care, after all. Richie and I felt so dumb after we asked. *Of course* he can't be moved to make *our* life a little easier!

Richie had checked us into the Motel Tropicana while I was in L.A. They gave a discount there to parents who had kids staying in the Intensive Care Nursery. It was just a quick walk across the parking lot (though, take it from Shauna, a lot can happen during a quick walk across that parking lot), and the staff was very sympathetic and mindful there. The Motel Tropicana was exactly the kind of place that you think would be called the "Motel Tropicana." It reminded me so much of summer vacation trips with my family to Disneyland; we couldn't really afford the "official Disney hotels," so we always ended up at a place with AstroTurf, a big sign that says THERE IS NO LIFEGUARD ON DUTY, and free shuttles. There were no free shuttles at the Motel Tropicana, mostly because there was absolutely nothing to take a free shuttle *to*, but it was loads better than sleeping on a cold linoleum hospital room floor, or commuting to Mom and Dad's. So that's where we settled in to spend One Day at a Time.

One day at a time. One minute. One second. If you can just go day by day, eventually you can get anywhere, if nothing gets in your way. Yeah, that's always so easy to say. That's always easy for people to say when you're trying to scrape your way out of prison with a toothbrush, or you're waiting in an air pocket under an avalanche for a helicopter to find you. One day at a time. Let's face it, One Day at a Time didn't really work for Mackenzie Phillips, at first. I mean, look what happened to *her*. She ended up on an *E True Hollywood Story*. Still, I reminded myself that that's all it was. Jackson would just have to go one day at a time, even with all the unforeseen challenges to come that everybody was talking about, but soon enough, before we knew it, it would be the middle of August, and we would be able to go home, God willing. I went back to the Motel Tropicana that night more tired than the whole week, with all the traveling and worrying. Not to mention that singing the entire Rodgers and Hammerstein songbook into an incubator for a sleeping audience of one can sure take a lot out of an old ham.

I pulled aside the floral synthetic bedspread and got into the unfamiliar Motel Tropicana bed, with the grounding sound of some very familiar snoring beside me.

As soon as I gave my weight to the mattress, the snoring stopped. Which was very unusual.

Alien surroundings. 911-phobia. Fatherhood.
A faint whisper. Even more unusual.

**"Is he okay?"**

Of course, one could guess that I wouldn't be slipping into bed so quietly if he *wasn't* okay. But there's a time for everything, and I figured I could allow Richie his trademark nervousness tonight, these days, even until Jackson was home in New York with us. All right, all right, dammit, forever.

I might even try not to drive so close to the car in front of us for a while. Might.

"Yes, I think everything's okay. Try to go back to sleep. I love you."

"I love you."

Then I closed my eyes, and for lack of any fancy way of putting it, I wondered what was going to happen next. Here we were, finally a family. It took a lot for us to become a family, I'll tell ya, and here we were, wondering if it would all be cut off. Would he live? If he did, what problems might he have later on? Would he be a "normal" little boy, and be able to have a "normal" life? Was he intending to stay with us on earth, like Richie and I intended to stay at the Motel Tropicana when we checked in? Or would he find the accommodations inadequate and join Boaz in heaven, where there *are* lifeguards on duty?

Was I being honest every time I made a concerted effort to be thankful? Or was I just a really pissed-off person *pretending* to be thankful because that's what you're supposed to do? One day at a time. Sigh. I guess it doesn't have to be all that bad, I thought.

After all, Mackenzie Phillips eventually *did* get her act together, didn't she? It just took a while.

*69*

## << TRANSPORTING THE INJURED >>

I didn't really sleep well until it was dawn, and then I was out cold for about two hours. So when I woke up, I was completely disoriented, misplaced, and not rested. I'll say one thing for the Motel Tropicana. They got their money's worth from those plastic room-darkening curtains. It was pitch black. I had that physical feeling that all my organs had slowed down during my hibernation, which was rudely interrupted by the jarring ring of the telephone that started me out of bed, jumping, fishing around the room blindly for the apparatus as it repeatedly nagged, stumbling on the rust-colored indoor-outdoor carpeting, seizing and reeling in the cord to try and locate the source of the alarm. I think it was my brother Barry on the line, to let me know that he and my sister-in-law Doris were going to drive down today to see the new heir. Sure, sure, I told them; great.

When I hung up, I had fully intended to go back to sleep, but once I was awake, my mind began wandering around the rambling discount warehouse of our situation, *browsing* all over again, and I will confess, there is never any stopping me once I've started shopping.

It was about 9:30 A.M.

I realized then that Richie was not in the bed or even in the room. I knew that he would have risen early (as always), and that he and Grandma Carol would go get coffee and visit the baby, but I worried that I was missing something. I was too alone to sleep, which I must admit is so unlike me, because taking over the bed, for me, is always kind of a Christopher Columbus–esque experience. Move over, Mr. Native American. This is MY land. Plus, the dark silence of the room really created an atmosphere of paranoia—I began to be convinced that Richie and his mom weren't there because they were at the hospital dealing with some new emergency, and it was an ominous feeling, so I hastily brushed my teeth, pulled on some clothes, and stumbled out onto the blinding motel landing on my way to the hospital.

70

Outside the nursery I performed the elaborate, three-minute, up-to-the-elbows scrub ritual. The scrubbing would almost become a kind of daily superstitious rite: can't expect "good things" to happen if you haven't performed the sacred purification that earns you passage into the sanctuary. After weeks of this, I would get bloody scabs on my arms from scrubbing so hard and so frequently . . .

The washing neither woke me up nor calmed me down any. I groggily peeked through the window in the nursery door before I entered, to locate our main characters.

From the moment I looked in through the window, everything went into a kind of bizarre combination of slow motion and hyperspeed.

For the next seven hours, time raced by like mud, and after it was over, I was spent, and in a place I never expected to be, meeting people who would change my life that I never expected to meet, learning things about, well, everything that I never expected to know.

## << FRIDAY: THE FIRST HOUR >>

*We were moved. He was moved.*

After I pinpointed Richie and his mom through the nursery window, as I was moving to open the door, I saw that they were speaking intently with a person who was obscured by a row of babies. Even through my grogginess, and the wire-reinforced glass, I could immediately see Richie's serious, set countenance.

I felt a sinking feeling as I quickened my pace toward them.                    **71**

"Good morning," Richie said, not wanting to cut to the chase.

"What's happening?" I said, wanting to cut to the chase.

Richie introduced me to the doctor, and then added, "He thinks we might have to move Jackson to another hospital."

By now it was Friday, and my five-day-old Jackson still showed no sign of pooping. Thursday his belly began to distend a little, which they watched carefully. This morning his tummy was even more bloated, growing larger and larger like a balloon. I had noticed it on Thursday, but the nurse didn't seem particularly alarmed. This morning his belly was even bigger, and the doctor was afraid there was some kind of perforation in his intestines. This happens to a lot of premature infants (one of the first things the doctor had told me on Jackson's first night on earth was that his digestive system was woefully underdeveloped), and Jackson was a prime candidate for having gotten some kind of perforation because of his prematurity and high blood count from transfusing in utero with Boaz.

In my stupor I was still having trouble processing all of this information.

"Oh . . . uh, so that's bad, isn't it, and, uh, what do we do?"

I was just mumbling for no good reason. Luckily Richie and Grandma Carol had been there a good half hour digesting all of this properly, probably with some good strong coffee in their systems as an appropriate cerebral foundation.

So I let Richie and Grandma Carol do the interpreting.

"The doctor thinks we should move Jackson to another hospital where they can give him more specialized care."

My mind felt like a sponge. Not a particularly absorbent sponge, either. A dried-up, useless mass of hardened sea-cells. I started asking meaningless questions, like whether or not he was suggesting Jackson be moved because the care would be better, that that would just be . . . er, better, or because he was starting to look like he was in trouble right this minute.

Carefully, I sorted through the doctor's diplomatic jargon, looking for raspberries in a thorny thistle patch. He said that another hospital would be better equipped to deal with an advanced state of Jackson's condition, should it worsen, and that it was precautionary, because at this point Jackson was not in immediate danger. However, he also said that Jackson should be somewhere else if he *were* to become in immediate danger, and he could enter the danger zone at any time, without warning. Even in my semiconscious state I could tell he was waffling. Noncommital. It was, after all, a big decision.

"So, we're moving him? Or you're *suggesting* we move him?"

"Well, I have a call in to the doctors at Stanford in Palo Alto, and I'm going to go over the baby's situation with them and ask them for a recommendation. It's ultimately the parents' decision, though."

Grandma Carol had heard enough. "That's ridiculous. We're moving him! We definitely have to move him! Why should we wait to ask them? Obviously, we should move him, right?"

Richie and his mom had wanted to move Jackson for days, and this did seem like the obvious opportunity to do so. I did not want to move him only for the sake of moving him, just because staying at the Motel Tropicana kind of sucked, or because we were far away from our support system. But I was also naively assuming the medical care in Modesto was as advanced as it could be. The doctor's namby-pamby recommendation was hardly a vote of confidence for staying.

"Is that where we would go, Stanford?"

"I would suggest Stanford, in Palo Alto, yes. The two hospitals equipped to deal with this kind of condition are Stanford and UCSF. But we have worked with the doctors at Stanford on numerous occasions, so for that reason I would recommend them, only because I'm familiar with them. Both Stanford and UCSF are world-class neonatal facilities."

Then, once we told the doctor that my parents were in San Francisco, he agreed that that would be the logical place to move Jackson. His relationship with Stanford was merely a way to tip the balance on the scale weighing our options.

I kept turning to Richie, trying to sort it all out:

73

## "Okay, so we should go, right?
## He's not saying we have to, but we should,

Richie was (relatively) very calm. He clearly was relieved to have the opportunity to leave Modesto, but I could also see that he was reacting with clarity.

"I think we have to. If he has a perforation, they can't treat it here. They don't have an anesthesiologist. They don't have a surgeon. If he starts bleeding or his stomach keeps blowing up or he needs an operation, they can't do anything about it, they could only just try and make him comfortable."

I turned to the doctor. "How do we move him?"

"Probably by private airplane. We would check with the hospital you choose, say UCSF, and find out what their transport situation is for the day."

"When should we move him?"

"As soon as possible."

First they say, "Hey, here are your options, it might be better for him over there instead of here, think about it," and then in the next breath they say, "As soon as possible." When I got to the end of the conversation I realized that most of it was spent trying not to alarm me. Words like "choose" and "if" and "perhaps." It was the emergency that was never couched as one.

My day had officially begun with all of the fun and frenzy of *Apollo 13.* "Modesto, we have a problem . . ." We officially nodded to the doctor that we would like Jackson to be moved to UCSF in

San Francisco. He went to find out if they would accept him, and what time they had a transport team available to come pick him up. The insurance lady (with our tireless business manager and friend Dean Michaels via phone in New York) got right on the case to see if my insurance would cover Jackson being moved to UCSF under these particular circumstances.

Tracy Kempf, the regular ICN social worker on duty, went over the transition with Richie, and told him that she had had a conversation with the social worker at UCSF and put in a good word for us.

"You'll like her," said this friendly lady from a small California Central Valley town . . .

". . . she's a New York Jew."

# GOING ONCE, GOING TWICE . . . SOLD . . . TO THE JEWISH-AMERICAN TALENT AGENT IN THE GLASSES WITH THE SERIOUSLY ILL NEW-BORN. 75

The nurses hurriedly began preparing for the transition. Richie and I had a lot of loose ends to tie up if we were going to move. People were working on the case all over the place.

Soon they returned with the verdict that UCSF had a space for us, and could have a transport team come pick Jackson up at around 2:00 P.M. It was about 10:30 A.M. then. I called Barry's cell phone and caught Doris and Barry en route, and told them that when they got here for their visit, guess what, we'd be turning right and all going back to San Francisco. The whirlwind of activity that had begun when I saw Richie's intensely set face through the window in the nursery door picked up tremendous speed, and soon we were all running around doing various tasks to prepare for this big event. We had a lot of things to work out, a motel to check out of, lots of paperwork, and a plane to catch. There was not a minute to lose.

I felt like we were on an America's Cup team, pre–starting gun, where everyone has their own specific function. Whenever I looked into Jackson's show-and-tell box, I could swear his little stomach was getting larger and larger, the skin around his belly button drawing tighter and tighter, practically ready to burst any minute. When I was little we had this party game which was a hand pump that you fastened a balloon to. You would pass the apparatus around in a circle, and roll a die or spin a wheel, and it would tell you how many times you had to prime the pump. The person who popped the balloon was "out."

I think it was called **KABOOM.**

I knew there was nothing that I could do to make our 2:00 P.M. departure any earlier, which could have considerably less-ened Jackson's chances of being the "KABOOM loser," so I just prayed that his condition wouldn't worsen too severely before we got him somewhere that they could take care of whatever it was he had, this mythical UCSF place. Richie's, Grandma Carol's, and my relief that we would be able to go to San Francisco after all was qualified. The one thing that we had thought would make life a little easier for us, to have Jackson stay at a hospital in a city where we had a support system, was plopped right into our lap. But of course the emergency nature of the situation was the gold we gave for that magic bean. For the "convenience" we would have, we had to endure the first of the bumps in the ride that all the doctors and nurses had warned us to fasten our safety belts for.

The nurses were, as always, supportive and loving, and whispered quietly how good the care was up there. One of them even nodded knowingly, saying, "I'm glad he's going there," her emotions obviously mixed. We could tell they were all as worried about him as we were, and that sure felt good. In just a few days they had bonded to him like mother kangaroos with warm, comfortable pouches. One of them tried to explain the whole transport to me in as much detail as possible (probably sensing what an "info-holic" I am), showing me the cumbersome isolette that was especially for the airplanes, with oxygen tanks and whatnot to make it completely self-sufficient.

"Or, they might bring their own portable setup," she said.

## << FRIDAY: THE SECOND HOUR >>

*The delegation . . .*

After all responsibilities were assigned, there was one thing looming on our checklist that we hadn't thought of when we were talking to the doctor.

**Boaz**.

I believe it was Wednesday when little Boaz's remains were sent away for cremation. We were unable to have any kind of ceremony or have anybody in attendance, partly because the hospital was way down in Modesto, partly because I was in Los Angeles, and partly because we weren't even sure what we wanted to do. Richie and I didn't have a clear picture what our most desired scenario was, so we just went ahead with the cremation and did not plan a ceremony. We hoped that we would have some kind of memorial gesture when we celebrated Jackson's coming home with us, whenever that would be. When I look back now, I am kind of sorry about this. I wish I could have been there for him, even alone, to say a prayer at the cremation, to acknowledge his tiny/tremendous presence in my life in some small way. But everything happened so fast . . .

Anyway, Richie and I realized that we didn't yet have Boaz's ashes in our possession, nor did we have a death certificate for Boaz, nor a birth certificate for either of the boys. We couldn't just leave Modesto without having signed all the proper papers and filed all the appropriate documents. A lot of things that we would normally coordinate over days or even weeks needed to be done in less than an hour. It was a lucky thing that we had gotten the judgment naming us both Jackson and Boaz's parents, so we did have everything we needed for the right person to put the proper information on the certificates.

Richie and I have always had extremely distinctive roles in almost everything that we have ever done. When we had our apartment gutted and remodeled four years ago, he turned in his keys and said, "Go for it, I don't want to hear a word about it," and didn't come back in for eight months while I picked out all the faucets and the doorknobs and grout colors (we lived in sublets in the meantime). Whenever I got into a fight with the contractor (and there were many), I would sic Richie on him, for hell hath no fury like a talent agent crossed. Richie dealt with all of the negotiating, as well as all of the administrative and financial aspects of this huge war, with august panache, like Eisenhower organizing the troops, and I dealt with all of the creative fun with reckless artistic abandon, like Mamie wielding a brush and a bucket of pink paint attacking the Oval Office. When it comes to getting most things done, we make a great team. (Why am I always the *woman* in these analogies??? Basically, it's a left brain/right brain thing.)

So we huddled and strategized, and when the huddle broke, Richie went to deal with insurance, birth and death certificates, parental rights, and funeral parlors, and I stayed in the nursery with the baby to be with the nurses as they began preparing him for transport to his new home away from home. There would be a lot of things to remember, medications and various things, and even though there would obviously be a lot of phone communication between the doctors here and there, and charts and all, I didn't want to be asked elementary questions about my own baby's treatment on the other end, and not know at least a few of the answers. Some of the questions might be crucial. Alas, Richie is the type of person who might say to our new doctor,

## "Yes, I know EXACTLY what medicine he's been taking.

**"**

**Um, I think it starts with an 's' . . .**

At the end of this second hour Barry and Doris arrived, and boy, that was a relief. My brother was a paramedic before he became a fireman, and I knew that he would help keep me *grounded* in the midst of all this crazy air-transport talk. I introduced Doris and Barry to Jackson for the first time, and was able to briefly enjoy their amazed, though fearful, responses to him. Barry grabbed our camera and started taking pictures right away, because he knew that Richie and I were not in a photographer's frame of mind. He's an emergency-mode-type guy, so you can always count on him to do exactly the right thing, coolly, during a crisis, and then some, *con machismo mucho*. The many pictures he took during our last hours in Modesto really tell the whole story. He eventually put a lot of them on Jackson's Web site, which became the home base for many people who found out how things were going by logging on to it periodically.

79

Like the lucky fortune of my being in Modesto on the very evening that Shauna (who was by now back at home getting over everything) went into "official" labor less than a week before, Barry and Doris were on their way to visit Jackson, Richie, and me right when they were most acutely needed. Sure, my mom and dad were there the day after the birth, and then Richie sent for his mom, Grandma Carol; we'd asked them to come. But Barry and Doris were fortuitously on their way down while the decision to move Jackson was being made, and they arrived in the eye of a tumult of activity, rolling their sleeves up and absorbing the workload like the quicker-picker-uppers they are.

Richie called the funeral director to coordinate the arrangements we had made for Boaz. He asked both of us to come to the home to officially sign for Boaz's cremated remains, which we would have to return to Modesto to pick up on a later date.

Our plan was to quickly drive over to the funeral home to sign the papers, and then return to finish getting ready to leave. Mom and Dad's Toyota Camry was out in the parking lot.

But the car wouldn't start.

There were any number of reasons why the car wouldn't start, and let's face it, they're all completely moot at this point.

It was yet another unbelievable example of the "noncoincidence" of Barry and Doris having driven down. Richie and I and Grandma Carol all hopped into Barry and Doris's car and found our way to the funeral home for a bit of a field trip, which, like all good field trips, was quite an education.

## << FRIDAY: THE THIRD HOUR >>

*Permission slips (and other things) signed . . .*

Please note: the names have been changed to protect the scary.

In the middle of a typical sweltering California Central Valley landscape of Modesto minimalls and fast-food restaurants outlined by countless farms, was an anachronistic Victorian structure and the rather formal signage in front of it identifying it as

STIMSON & SOAMES.

Why does the name *Stimson & Soames* sound unmistakably like a funeral home? Why is that? It doesn't sound like a law firm. It doesn't sound like a comedy team. It doesn't even sound like a one-hour television drama about two cops from opposite sides of the tracks, or a boy and his imaginary friend. It just sounds exactly like a funeral home, don't it? You would think that Mr. Stimson and Mr. Soames had lunch one day and said, "Hey, I like you. Let's go into business together. We'll call it 'Stimson & Soames.' Why, that sounds like a funeral home, doesn't it? Sounds good!"

That's what it was, all righty.

We all walked up to the front porch of the large, worn house, fully expecting it to start raining as we stepped onto the property while it stayed sunny and blue skied outside it, and pulled open the imposing white doors. I felt like a child tiptoeing into the Museum of Natural History with a chain of other kids, holding sweaty hands, one step at a time, footfalls echoing through the corridors, just waiting for one of us to flinch beneath the gargantuan reassembled Tyrannosaurus Rex. Then the whole pack of us would scramble screeching from the premises, cascading down the front steps into the blinding sunlight, only to reconvene at the tree house later to pass, like a hot potato, the blame about who ditched first.

I remember as we drove up and I first saw the home, and I thought, Oh, man, that's creepy. Is this a joke? I can't believe we gotta go in *there* to do *this* . . . Richie even said something like, "There it is. Oh. Isn't that comforting." I mean, it wasn't the hardest task there ever was. We just had to stop in and sign a few papers. But I wasn't in the mood to have my emotions tested, and I felt like Indiana Jones, going into the Temple of Doom to rescue the Holy Grail, wondering if I would ever come out.

The inside of Stimson & Soames was even more like the set from *Dark Shadows* than the outside. Well, I'm so sorry, but it was.

We gathered inside the foyer and closed the tall front door behind us carefully, as if we were entering the gallery with the stretching walls at the beginning of the Haunted Mansion at Disneyland. There was drab wallpaper, large stone urns with dusty artificial flowers in them, and a heavy ornate wooden balustrade that led up a musty carpeted staircase to a second floor.

What the heck do you suppose was up there???

I felt even more like a Disneyland tourist in the shorts and T-shirt that I had pulled on that morning when I left the Motel Tropicana and walked across the asphalt, past that good old, painfully applicable, NO LIFEGUARD ON DUTY sign. It was all like the home movies of my family's summer vacations, as directed by Roger Corman.

A dour, elderly woman came out of a room off the foyer and asked if she could help us. She did not offer us any poison apples, and we did not conspire to push her into any ovens. We just explained that we had an appointment with a Mr. Stoddard to sign some papers. Well, all five of us didn't, but she understood, and ushered us into a parlor to wait for him.

When I say that it was a "parlor," I think you can get the picture. It was a room furnished with antique furniture that was probably not antique when the furniture guys delivered it. The wallpaper was just as depressing, and there were fake flowers and tchotchkes all over, you know, on doilies and stuff, like somebody's grandmother, or Miss Havisham. It was a room for having a piano lesson, or waiting nervously for your new sweetheart's father to come down to grill you before your first date to the ice cream social.

All five of us were a little uneasy, because we were so worried about getting everything ready to move Jackson in time, plus whether Jackson would even be okay to boot. I personally was so stressed out by having to face the fact that I was going to sign my little Boaz's release papers that the atmosphere actually served to break the ice a little. Stimson & Soames was so absurdly spooky that I couldn't take it seriously at all. I just kept making jokes about everything I could see that was remotely macabre, and believe me, it was Chock Full o' Macabre. I guess I was kind of afraid that the signing of the papers would be an emotional thing for me, and I didn't want to get messy again. I was also worried that our surroundings would make Richie sad, too, so I kept looking over to him, but he seemed okay. We just waited, maybe ten minutes. My hopes that we could be in and out and on to the next, non-death-related errand were dashed.

When Mr. Stoddard finally came in and introduced himself, I was relieved. This is because I had always wondered what ever happened to the actor who played Barnabas Collins. Seriously, he was a tall, thin, older man dressed in what looked like an even older suit, whose demeanor was not out of step with the decor. He regarded us cryptically, and sat down at a desk. The five of us quickly shifted seating arrangements so that Richie and I sat in the chairs opposite the man, like we were applying for some Transylvanian home loan or something. Actually, I think Barry just got up out of the chair because he was uncomfortable sitting so close to "Lurch." I didn't feel like sitting at first, but I eventually did.

Mr. Stoddard opened Boaz's file and studied it scrupulously. He confirmed Boaz's name, to make sure he had the right family. Richie handed Mr. Stoddard the judgment credentials we'd just gotten the night before, and all the birth and death certificate information naming Richie and me both as Boaz's parents.

Whenever Mr. Stoddard was busy, I would look over to Doris and roll my eyes, or over-enunciating-ly mouth the words,

## OH MY GOD or I AM SO FREAKED OUT.

I did this because Doris is usually really easy to get a laugh out of, and I knew if I could see her smile I would feel better about this whole thing. She obliged, à la Mona Lisa.

Mr. Stoddard (who, to elaborate further, also reminded me of the monologist Spaulding Gray in a one-man show about the life of Vincent Price) studied the papers calmly, and then confirmed that Richie, whom he had talked to on the phone, was indeed the "Richard Alan Jackson" of the paperwork.

Suddenly, I became nervous about what he was going to say next. You know, about *My Two Dads*. Living the big-city life, you forget what a fish out of water you can be in a place like Modesto, until there you are, washed up on the blistering sidewalk, gills working overtime, hoping that someone who hates fish won't kick you or step on you with their logger boots till your guts squeeze out onto the pavement unappetizingly. We call this "bass bashing."

**84**    Mr. Stoddard looked up again, and around the parlor, and at all of the *five* people in it. He looked at Doris, who was sitting with Barry. He looked at Grandma Carol, who was, well, after all, a grandmother. He looked at me.

"B.D. Wong."

"That's me." I guessed he doesn't get cable.

"That's you."

"Yes."

He laggardly looked back down at the paperwork, for a moment that seemed like a minute.

". . . Who're the parents?"

"*We* are."

Then, after another creepy pause, without looking up or batting an eyelash, he flatly said, "Hmm. You're *both* the parents."

"Yes."

(A beat.)

". . . I see," he acknowledged.

When I finally exhaled, I tried not to blow all the paperwork off the desk.

Richie and I both had to sign these documents because we had no idea who would be the one to come back down to pick up Boaz's ashes once they had been prepared, sometime in the next few weeks. We both signed, so that either of us would be allowed to take him back to San Francisco.

When I eventually signed my name I was okay, but it *was* imbued with a finality which tugged at the apron strings of my heart just enough to get my attention. Finding myself in this indescribable town, in this indescribable building, in this indescribable parlor, with this indescribable Mr. Stoddard, made me realize what an indescribable situation we were in. Who would ever believe *any* of this?

When our business was done, we said good-bye to the Munsters, and left the House of Wax to complete our other tasks. Once we were out in the heat again I thought that it wasn't so bad in there after all. Sure, it was creepy, kooky, mysterious, spooky, and altogether oogie in there, but Mr. Stoddard, in his outdated old suit (who was probably the first person outside of our support system, or the hospital, that Richie and I exposed ourselves to *as a family*) actually seemed almost—how can I put this?—

well, *hip.*

That most common, everyday, conventional role, the role of the parent, which Richie and I were in some ways oddly helping to redefine, seemed even less *normal* in comparison to that bizarrely eccentric, sad old parlor from the past in which we were seated. But Mr. Stoddard acted as a bridge between those two polarities. He reached out of the old world, and gently touched the sleeve of the new world, all without saying boo. It's a good thing. "Boo" woulda scared me.

But was he merely being tolerant? Did he affect an air of non-chalance for our benefit, to avoid getting into it at all, or worse, to avoid some kind of altercation? Was he just afraid that we outnumbered him? Did he have the hots for my brother?

Who knows?

A few days later, Richie's cell phone rang. It was Mr. Stoddard, calling on behalf of everyone at Stimson & Soames.

"Hello, Mr. Jackson. I was just calling because we were wondering how the other twin was, the surviving brother. Is he doing all right?"

He had no further business to discuss with us that day. He was just calling.

As much as I'm tempted to make a joke at Stimson & Soames's expense, I assure you: Mr. Stoddard was not calling to try to "scare up some more business," hoping young Jackson might be his "next victim." No, when Richie reported that Jackson was "still with us," the gentle man was genuinely relieved . . .

. . . and no, when he answered the phone, Richie did NOT say,

**"You *raaaaa n g ?"***

## << FRIDAY: THE FOURTH HOUR >>

*". . . anyone traveling with small children, or who needs special assistance . . ."*

By the time we got back to the vicinity of the hospital, we had determined who would do what. Richie and I would go into the nursery, to greet the transport team from San Francisco, and learn whatever there was to learn about what was happening, and of course, to see how the baby was. Doris and Carol went to the room at the Motel Tropicana to pack up what little we had with us, so we would be all ready to check out. Barry was assigned not only to jump-start my mom and dad's car, but to help pack up all of Shauna's perishable frozen breast milk, which had to be transported very carefully. Barry ran out and bought a portable cooler and a sack of ice, for this was his big chance to pretend that he had to rush someone a new kidney or something.

Richie and I got back to the nursery in time to see that the transport team had just arrived. It consisted of one transport nurse (Andrew), a nurse practitioner (Beverly), and two pilots. Gentle Andrew was particularly mindful of our emotional state. He told us some news which relieved me, and terrified Richie:

                    ANDREW
          There's room for one of you
          to go on the plane with the
          baby. Which—

        B.D.                      RICHIE
   (simultaneously)         (simultaneously)
    *I* will.                *HE* will.

Andrew, Beverly, and the pilots asked me how much I weighed and told me to bring a sweater or jacket and put on long pants because it would be very cold. An ICN nurse sweetly lent me a sweatshirt with some nursing organization logo on it.

Beverly dealt mostly with Jackson's nurses, learning as much about the baby that was not on the chart as she could. Andrew dealt with preparing Jackson to be moved from his isolette to the transport isolette, no small feat with the infinite array of instruments that he was hooked up to. I just kept looking at the little Chestnut with the protruding stomach. The isolette was made of acrylic and, like Future, the linoleum floor wax, "transparent as glass, but a lot tougher." But was the baby inside it?

They had wheeled into the nursery a high-tech apparatus that included both the isolette that the baby would be put into and an ingenious, bright yellow rolling device that looked like a small cherry picker, which could support the isolette at any height.

Months later, I remembered this day, and how the well-meaning Modesto nurse had explained to me how the transport might work, showing me the equipment they used to transport sick babies. "Of course, UCSF might bring their own . . ." she had added.

Compared to the modernist sculpture that the San Francisco crew wheeled in, the Modesto setup might as well have been made of adobe and straw. How lucky we were that we had access to the luxury of advanced technology. When I contemplated the difference much later, it was scary.

The team needed about an hour to completely prepare before we headed out, suggesting I go and come back in time for departure. I made them promise they wouldn't leave without me, and they in turn urged me to be back in about half an hour, to be safe.

Everyone was just about done with their various jobs, and I had changed into my only long pants for the flight, when we realized that we hadn't eaten anything yet. We decided to have a hasty prelaunch lunch, and the five of us dashed over to the Denny's adjacent to the hospital. This Denny's had the distinction of having been a landmark for Richie and his mom earlier in the week when they were trying to find their Modesto bearings. They would tell one another, "You just take a left at the Denny's," but did not understand why they kept getting lost, until they discovered to their dismay that there were *five* Denny's on the same thoroughfare. It was a little like saying "Meet me at Starbucks" to somebody in Seattle.

So here we are at Denny's, where there isn't really a table to be had, because (1) it's the lunch rush and (2) as I've already mentioned, Denny's is *hot* in Modesto. A surly waitress indicated that we would just have to wait, until Grandma Carol frankly explained that we were medevac-ing a premature infant to San Francisco in exactly twenty-eight minutes and counting and that we needed to eat immediately. We got a table, and service with a warm smile to boot.

I guess when you're the guy with the emergency, your window for special treatment isn't huge, so you're actually kind of a jerk if you don't make the most of it. Pretty soon, before you know it, you'll only be a normal Joe again, and all of a sudden it's back to,

## "Hey mister, there's a LINE here, do you mind?"

We ate like entrants in a county fair pie-eating contest. Well, I did. Then, Richie and Barry and I ran back to the nursery, and Doris and Grandma Carol caught up with us a few steps behind.

Jackson was now inside the superfancy isolette, and everything seemed okay.

When Barry resumed snapping pictures, I was initially glad that he was documenting this once-in-a-lifetime experience, for us to look back upon way, way into the future. But then, there was also the unsaid: someday, would snapshots be all we had left to remember Jackson Foo Wong by? I was a little surprised that there were no more complications when he was moved from iso-lette to isolette. Everyone had their best faces on. Richie and I had too little experience with nurses, medical professionals, and this kind of situation to know what was real. Were they confident that he would make it to San Francisco and worried about what would happen after that, or was his making it through the trip at all an issue as well?

Richie and I took turns getting our finger squeezed by the All-Time Champion Finger Squeezer, and Barry kept grabbing photos. The one picture he took of Richie and me standing in front of the isolette, just minutes before we left, pretty much says it all. It's just a picture of a coupla guys who haven't the energy necessary to convincingly cover up how they are feeling at all.

We said our hasty so-longs to the nurses who cared for him so tenderly for such a brief time, his entire life. It felt more and more like an emergency as we cantered toward the door. Outside was the ambulance, with its open double doors beckoning like the entrance to a Coney Island "House of Horrors" ride. People walk-ing their dogs stopped to watch. Richie and I resignedly parted, and Richie said the six words that he has never failed to say before every single plane trip I've ever gone on since we've been two-gether:

"Tell the pilot to drive safely."

This time, it meant even more than usual.

As the ambulance doors closed with us on opposite sides of them, Richie and I wondered if we would ever get our fingers squeezed again by the Chestnut Man.

# << FRIDAY: THE FIFTH HOUR >>

*Final boarding call . . .*

The drive to the airport went as well as could be expected. There wasn't room for me to really move. After every turn, stop, start, or acceleration, I would look for Andrew's face, since I couldn't see the baby. Andrew would say, "He's doing fine." It wasn't a long ride, and the whole crew was obliging and friendly. The driver apologized whenever he drove over a bump, even the speed bumps in the hospital parking lot. I was positive that every jolt would disconnect some crucial connection or make all the needles and numbers go wacky, so I accepted his apologies gratefully (and infrequently, thank goodness).

We swiftly drove through a secured gate right onto the tarmac to the aircraft, *Casablanca* style, which was even smaller than I expected, apparently still parked right where the gang had left it on its way in. The two pilots jumped out and immediately began working to prepare the portable ramp. To my satisfaction they wasted no time, for anything more than pulling the isolette out of the ambulance, popping it into the plane, and immediately taking off was more than I had patience for. But I just sat cooperatively in the ambulance with my arms wrapped around my tucked-in legs, perfectly still. I was also overconcerned with staying out of the way. At first I had tried to get out and watch, but it was so windy that I could barely stand. I was terrified of unwittingly wandering into some high-speed propeller and pureeing myself, which would have unquestionably stolen Jackson's 911 thunder.

May it never be said that I competed with my own son for the limelight.

So I went back inside the ambulance and curled up in my spot. I could just imagine all the distraught parents who micromanage a transport crew with ridiculous, paranoid comments and needling questions, suggestions even, while the team is tripping all over itself trying to work. I was determined *not* to be the reason my son didn't get to San Francisco in one piece, and in time.

When they were ready, I ducked into the cab of the airplane, and I actually thought that this was all something I might find really cool under other circumstances. Maybe if they had just put out some giant chocolate-dipped strawberries and a free phone and shown a movie I wouldn't have been so uptight.

The plane was a four-seater, with all of the seats taken out. There was only space big enough for the isolette, which was probably two seats' worth, and Beverly, Andrew, and I were squeezed rather tightly around it. Beverly and Andrew were next to the isolette, so they could observe it, and I was at the head of it.

They fired up the sucker and the copilot turned to give me the standard orientation before we took off. This only added to my state of perturbation. Any speech that has to begin with the phrase, "In the unlikely event of . . ." was an oration my nerves had no tolerance for at this particular time. Please don't talk to me about "unlikely events." In the world of people having babies (thank goodness for the relative infrequency of a situation such as this), this whole week, this whole day, was one big unlikely event made up of a series of smaller unlikely events. It might have been better for the pilot to just say, "If or when we spiral downward in a fiery crash over the ocean, try to remember to do this . . ." I was ready for just about anything, and I'm not even the nervous one in the family.

I was constantly astonished whenever something reminded me that I was indeed experiencing all of this. That for once in my life, *I* was the haggard guy that the person walking their dog on the sidewalk sees, and stops and watches as a kid gets loaded up in an ambulance, making him shake his head and say,

**"Boy, I'm glad I'm not THAT dad."**

I kept stepping outside of my body to try and watch this movie, this thriller, because, hey, it seemed like such absorbing drama. At least three stars. Cliff-hanger. I pictured myself at the TV store where they have all of the TVs turned on to the same thing. I am frozen, in the middle of the sales floor, hypnotized and dwarfed by the images flickering from the endless wall of tiled, tiered television monitors. The TV department has trained the latest digital camcorder (on sale that weekend) on the very spot that I am standing, piping it into every TV of the display. As I raise my hand to scratch my befuddled head, I see a person wearing a Ben Folds Five T-shirt just like mine on all the screens. I freeze.

**93**

Wait, that looks like my shirt.

Hey, is that guy wearing my baseball cap?

I blink. He blinks.

## Oh, my gosh . . .

*that's me.*

I wave, self-consciously.

*Me* is waving back, mocking my self-consciousness.

"Hi, Me."

Then *Me* winks at *me*, like in the opening credits of *That Girl*.

I, of course, am only playing a supporting role in this particular film. Yeah, so what else is new? The main character, the
movie star getting all of the attention, is quietly resting in the
plastic mini–tanning booth next to me, while everyone fusses.
The studio has sent the private jet, and there he is, being waited
on hand and foot while the ancillary characters, like me, do all of
the histrionic emoting.

The takeoff was nothing I wasn't expecting, given the size of
the plane. There is, of course, a direct correlation between the
size of a plane and the quality of its takeoff and landing, though
I'm still not sure about the size of the wave in relation to the
motion of the ocean, or that the sweeter juice *always* comes out
of the darker berry, but that's all another book. My knuckles
whitened, but soon we were airborne, and Andrew again quietly
said, "He's doing fine."

We flew for about half an hour, after the half-hour ambulance
ride, and after that, we would take another ambulance another
forty-five minutes into San Francisco. As we were flying, Doris
was driving Richie and Grandma Carol in Barry and Doris's car,
while Mr. Fixit Barry was driving my mom and dad's car (which
he had resurrected) in case it pooped out again.

Once we had reached our (relatively low) cruising altitude,
Andrew began making conversation to pass the time. Andrew was
a large, sweetly soft fellow with an open, round face and a high,
nonabrasive speaking voice. He asked me about Jackson, and I
told him about Boaz, and the birth, and a few things here and
there. I am not accustomed to being very forthcoming about my
personal life, not even with people I know, so telling strangers
about all of the various nuances of Jackson and Boaz's creation
made me a little uneasy. (I guess writing all of this down is the
end of *that*).

Without the practice, this most personal story was a little
hard for me to tell freely, but I figured that Andrew and Beverly

had joined the Jackson Foo Wong family, so I tried to share more than I usually might. I found Andrew in particular to be a most open and easy listener. He constantly referred to Richie as my "husband," which amused me, since I don't even refer to Richie in such a manner. Not seriously. I assumed that Andrew must have a husband of his own. Maybe that was my mind's stereotype of the "male nurse," but it was also Andrew's soothing manner, as well as his unblinking usage of that twenty-first-century verbiage and the fact that he was from the San Francisco Bay Area. I mean, that's at least four telltale punches on the "is he or isn't he?" card, isn't it? We're not talking chads or dimples here, either.

I was much more interested in asking Andrew and Beverly questions about Jackson's condition and what I might expect. They'd only just met the Chestnut Man, but perhaps they were familiar with his symptoms, and maybe they could familiarize me with the hospital that we were speeding him to.

But I would have preferred that we all just sit and stare at the baby without uttering a word, which I certainly would have done if I could just see him. This way, no time would be lost discovering that some level or pressure in his body had risen or fallen to an alarming new high or low. But our quarters were so close that I suppose such behavior would have seemed socially awkward, even for a distraught father. So I tried to chat a little, and between the brief discussions, Andrew and Beverly fiddled with the knobs and dials.

By the way, Andrew later mentioned his "wife." I became very confused. Was he talking about his "wife-wife" or his "husband-wife"? Was his wife a wife to him like Richie was a husband to me? How much wood does a woodchuck chuck? I still get a headache thinking about this. I suppose, in the modern vernacular, that if Richie was my husband, Andrew's wife could be a cocker spaniel.

Or, to be fair, she could actually be a *wife*.

Then the pilot warned us of the very thing that I was dreading from the get-go. There seemed to be what you might call a "turbulence situation" ahead. I wasn't in the mood (*Gol-lee, surprise surprise, Sergeant Carter!*), though I was clearly the only one on the entire flight manifesto who was alarmed. The plane began to pitch, and the isolette began to slide back and forth within the space in which it was secured. Suddenly, it reminded me a little too much of a coffin in the back of a runaway hearse for my optimistic taste. When I impulsively threw my upper body over as much of it as I could to hold it still, I felt like Cornelia Wallace might have when George Wallace was shot. I didn't think about it. I just didn't want it to move. I didn't care that I looked like an idiot. Well, not till after.

My mind started babbling. What was it the pilot said to do "in the *unlikely* event of . . ."?

## Does an isolette float?

### Can it act as a *life preserver*?

What am I talking about?

# There's no water!

**B.D. WONG**

The state of mind that many people flip into during in-flight turbulence fascinates me. Have I done everything I needed to do? If I get one more chance could I make You a deal? Can't You at least wait until the end of the classic *Third Rock from the Sun* episode to bring us down? It's just split seconds really, but it never fails to be the gentlest little reminder that it can all be taken away, as easily as pulling Aladdin's magic carpet out from under him, completely spoiling the fantasy of immortality most of us entertain so naturally.

The turbulence continued as we descended to earth, no, not like a feather; I felt more like an autumn pine-cone diving toward the suburban asphalt, soon to be drafted into a makeshift neighborhood stickball game. Of course, the landing was as skillful as the pilot undoubtedly, proudly felt it was, but it was for me more like speeding toward the bottom of Victoria Falls in a barrel. Which was kind of what Jackson was doing, wasn't he? Packed all cozy in his high-tech wine keg as well as human beings could anticipate was necessary. As the plane touched down, we plunged beneath the dark surface of the foam for the briefest of moments, until we mercifully bobbed to the surface, the roar of the deafening elements which surrounded our heads shocking us as much as the impact of landing did. I peered into the "cask." Was all that bubble wrap and Styrofoam popcorn they had surrounded him with enough? Or would I find him in a million pieces?

No, he was in one piece, with the usual look on his face of peace, to boot.

## << FRIDAY: THE SIXTH HOUR >>

*Touch down, Forty-niners . . .*

Another great thing about flying in toy planes: there isn't all that taxing taxiing. There isn't that endless driving around in what seems like circles with you wondering how you're going to beat the old German lady in front of you to the overhead compartment the precise moment that the seat belt light goes off, while the urge to urinate increases with every lackadaisical announcement from the pilot saying that you're "in line for the gate," "being towed in," or just plain "stopped."

No, on Tonka Airlines, you just drive the plane right to your parking spot, like you're going to Costco. Wow, this is swell, I thought. Especially when you gotta medical emergency. Not that an increasing urge to urinate ain't.

"He's doing fine," Andrew said simply.

The crew repeated their Modesto transition performances, in reverse. An ambulance was waiting like part of a well-oiled machine. It went as smoothly as an Indy 500 pit stop.

During some moment of these preparations that neither of us were involved in, I had chatted with Bob Becker, the copilot, who told me that he was a part-time aviator when he survived a tough battle with eye cancer years ago. Because of his positive experience with medical professionals who had saved his life, he made a career change and became an air ambulance pilot soon after. As I shook his hand and thanked him and said good-bye to him and the pilot, I felt a sadness that such a remarkable man could only play such a brief, albeit major role in my family's life. Like so many of the people Richie and Jackson and I have met, we won't forget him, or the remarkable path he has chosen for his life—a path that *life* chose for *him*.

We hit the road. Andrew was glad the ambulance had its own oxygen tanks on board, and we could save Jackson's tanks for an emergency. I resisted the creative impulse to imagine such an emergency. I called Richie in Doris's car and told them we had landed safely and were on our way to the hospital, about a forty-five-minute drive. They told us where they were, and Andrew confirmed that they were making good time and that he wasn't sure which one of us would get there first.

Andrew and Beverly continued to monitor Jackson's levels and pressures; Jackson had been solid for two out of the three legs of this journey within a journey. But now, so close to our destination and yet so far, Andrew knit his eyebrows into a heretofore un-knit pretzel.

"Hmmm. *That's* not good," he mumbled, studying the gauges.

## Gulp.

I asked the obvious question. Andrew didn't meet my gaze as he responded, continuing to read the equipment.

"His blood pressure's dropping."

## Gulp. Gulp.

You know, I never have understood blood pressure. I don't understand what it is, how to read it, or how to tell if a reading is good or bad. It's one of those many essential things in life that I still just can't yet get over the grown-up hump of comprehension. Blood pressure. Driving a stick shift. Porn stars with breasts bigger than their head. Buying something at the manufacturer's suggested retail price. The Olympic sport of curling.

So my nervousness was not at all inflamed by understanding the medical ramifications of low blood pressure. It was from watching the silent movie of Andrew's face.

"It's okay," Andrew said, rather compromisingly, "we'll just keep watching it, make sure it doesn't get any lower or that nothing else changes . . ."

Well, at least I was off the hook from talking about my personal life for the time being.

Jackson's blood pressure stayed low for the next twenty minutes. I decided against mentioning it to Richie on my periodic calls. Andrew and Beverly proceeded much more cautiously from this point on. They called ahead to the hospital to report the change, to notify those involved that we would be arriving soon, and to be prepared to take Jackson right in. They were concerned that Jackson's stomach was in more distress, and that the hospital should be ready for some kind of immediate action, even surgery.

At this time I would much rather have been telling Andrew and Beverly about every intimate detail of my sordid past, present, and future. Funny.

Then, as we got closer to the city, traffic began getting tighter. It was Friday rush hour, and pretty soon we were inching forward in a way that was unsatisfactory to everybody in the ambulance, not only tightly wound, little old me.

I was just about to call Richie and say we were almost there (but still not mention anything else) when Andrew flatly said, "We're just going to do this, it doesn't really mean anything. Nothing's really changed. The baby's okay. The traffic is really bad, that's all."

"What? Do what?" I had been unable to decipher the cryptic mumbling between Andrew and Beverly. What are we going to do, Andrew? LOSE IT, as a group?

"We're just going to turn the siren on so we can get to the hospital as soon as possible."

Oy, vey.

Remember when you were a little kid, and your dad took you to the fire station, and the fireman let you sit in the fire truck and push the foot pedal to turn on the siren? Remember how shocked and thrilled you were at how loud it was? How you squealed with delight?

Remember your childhood fantasies about high-tailing through the suburbs in a cop car—"one Adam twelve, one Adam twelve, see the man, see the man"—with the cherry on top blazing and the only thing louder than the siren the screeching of the burning rubber? *Whee!*

Ever play a virtual video game where you're the space vigilante, eradicating the universe of galactic pirates and star bandits, breathlessly rubbing out the evil element, turning, banking, super stereo siren cranked to full blast in your own private, personal pod? *Get him! Yesss!!!*

**Remember the thrill**

**and the exhilaration,**

**the *high* of all that?**

**Take it from me . . .**

# THIS WASN'T LIKE THAT,

**okay?**

There was definitely an adrenaline rush. I will give you that there was definitely an adrenaline rush.

The driver went full "code three," and pulled out from behind the car in front of us into the skinny space between cars. I was literally dialing the phone to check in with Richie, but I flipped the phone shut *immediately*, like the jaws of a gator in the Florida everglades.

"This would not be the time to call Richie," I said, never more certain of anything in my life.

Our little "Mr. Toad's Wild Ride" had exactly the effect on me that I feared it would. The sound of the siren and the sight of the flashing lights intensified my anxiety one thousand fold. It didn't matter what Andrew had said. It felt like a full-out, bona fide emergency. Is the siren really on to make people get out of the way, or is it just screaming for you, so you won't lose your voice?

One neat thing happened. I hope I never have to experience it ever again, but it *was* neat.

In as Hollywood-biblical a way as you can imagine, the infinite sea of jammed cars before us parted, like Richard Burton and Elizabeth Taylor after their first marriage was over. Then the ambulance passed through, and the cars folded in once again behind us, just like Dick and Liz when they got back together again. This really surprised me. I don't always give mankind credit for coming through like that, cynical old me, but gosh darn it, it got right out of the way for Jackson Foo Wong.

Then, before I knew it, we were on top of the hill where UCSF is perched, like the Emerald City, where I hoped the wizard would have something in his black bag for little ol' me. It was the same hill where my older brother, Brian, went to medical school, minutes from the house I grew up in.

"We made it, Chestnut. If you keep breathing, I promise I will."

## << FRIDAY: THE SEVENTH HOUR >>

*Home stretch. Home. Stretch.*

At the emergency entrance, a bunch of people immediately came out of the building to help slide the fancy cookie pan with our little undercooked cookie on it out of the mobile Easy-Bake Oven.

Andrew and Beverly never left Jackson's side, and true to my MO of not wanting to get in the way, I followed close, but behind: another version of the memories I have of accompanying Shauna's rolling bed down the hall into the unknown, without having read the script.

After a few turns, a huge elevator took us to the fifteenth floor: Neonatal Intensive Care.

Jackson's entourage wheeled through a large door into one of the four wings of the Intensive Care Nursery. Andrew and Beverly went inside with the baby, I stayed out in the hall. They mysteriously told me that someone would come out and let me know what was up ASAP. The same feeling as waiting for Shauna outside the delivery room, or watching Boaz disappear through the little window into the ICN. Just wait.

Almost immediately after Andrew and Beverly disappeared, that whale of an elevator belched my Jonah (Richie) and his mother out onto that beach of a hallway. Washed ashore after the shipwreck, looking for other castaway members of the family; Doris had dropped them off. I told Richie and Grandma Carol that I didn't know much, and we could see flashes of Andrew and

*103*

Beverly and others vaguely surrounding Jackson's isolette through a window in the door, slightly around a corner. We might as well have been trying to lip-read a Fellini film with the sound off.

After a few minutes the fancy gurney, the extra personnel from downstairs, and Andrew and Beverly emerged, pushing the equipment back toward the big elevator. Even though intellectually I was not surprised, I gasped a little when I saw that the isolette was empty, and then had to remind myself that they had transferred the baby to a new home.

Andrew smiled very slightly, and said, "He looks okay. Good luck."

Then he and Beverly and the crew pushed past us.

I thought, Hey, *wait!*

Where are you going?

# You forgot the baby!

*How can you abandon him now*

*after all you've been through together?*

Don't you wanna hear
more intimate details about my life?

I could tell you about my cross-dressing phase.

*Come back! . . .*

**B.D. WONG**

But see, this is what these amazing people do, these people who have this remarkable job that most of us have never heard of before, or had the good fortune to ever witness firsthand. Or the bad fortune, depending on how you look at it. They go from hospital to hospital with scores of sick babies beneath their watchful eyes; their protective, fixed wings. They give everything they have and know to them for the brief time that the little souls are in their charge, and then they hand them over to the doctors and nurses who care for them in the longer term, the ones who get remembered. Some of them even calm the parents, too, for no extra credit. Then, when their unsung task is complete, there really isn't time to chat, or follow the baby they have gotten to know so intensely for such a short amount of time. The relationships they form become like the bonds that gypsies, or actors, or circus folk enjoy, roaming the countryside, touching folks here and there, diverting, witnessing loss, falling in love even, and then plaintively following the piper's rhythmic tattoo to another town. They are dedicated, tireless, and almost always *anonymous*.

So, for the record,

it was Transport Nurse **Andrew Garrick,**

Nurse Practitioner **Beverly Shoemaker,**

Transport Pilot **Assad Razaq,**

and Transport Copilot **Bob Becker**

who faithfully followed Foo, flying to Frisco.

Grandma Carol, Richie, and I caught up on our separate experiences of the last two hours while we waited. I fessed up to Richie about the siren, and about the blood pressure. Richie and Carol admitted they were terribly glad to be coming to San Francisco, and that on the way, Richie's brother Mark, who lives in

Tokyo, called Richie's cell phone "just to see how everything was." Boy, did he get a transpacific earful.

Eventually two women came out of the nursery toward us: pediatric surgery resident Dr. Jenny Ogilvy and neonatologist Dr. Susan Sniderman.

They were warm. They were extremely open, and honest, and crucially mindful of our emotional stress. They were funny, even at this rather serious time. To say they knew what they were talking about would be like saying, "Gee, that Great Wall of China sure is long," or ending your visit to Versailles by grunting, "Nice house, Lou."

We were so glad to be there.

Susan Sniderman explained that Jackson was indeed "very sick." His stomach was pretty severely distended, and this could be for any number of reasons. Jackson was so premature, and young, that operating on him immediately was extremely risky, and they all felt that at least a few days of observation were necessary to make a proper determination about what was best for him, as long as nothing worsened.

Jenny hastened to add that Jackson looked much better than they had expected him to look, given the manner in which he was whisked in. I was thankful for Andrew and Beverly's conservative approach. What the SF docs had decided, with our consent, was to insert a drain into Jackson's stomach. They hoped this deceptively simple apparatus would relieve the pressure by allowing excess air to pass out of his belly through it, as well as any nasty bilious substances, since it was clear that something was keeping Jackson from being able to pass anything all the way through his lower digestive system. Jenny said that this was a minor surgical procedure (gasp) but then quickly added (without taking a breath or adding extra punctuation) that it would be done right at the bedside, and would only take about twenty minutes. They wanted to do the installation immediately. Jenny always confirmed everything that Dr. Sniderman said, and infused it with even more optimism (very different from false hope) and positive energy, and I felt for the first time, awful as it sounds, that if Jackson was going to die, I wouldn't think that it was because he wasn't given his best shot. We gave our consent, after all three of us asked a few carefully pondered, but in retrospect probably unnecessary questions. It was fantastic to have Grandma Carol there. She thinks of everything.

Jenny said, "Try not to worry. It's a relatively minor procedure, and I'm sure he'll feel much better if we can give him a little relief."

Then, once more with feeling, the two experts disappeared behind the mysterious door, and we waited.

As soon as the door closed, Richie sighed and said, looking after Dr. Sniderman, "Thank God. Finally a Jewish doctor."

He was only half kidding. The lack of Jewish doctors in Modesto really disconcerted Richie. It was quite an adjustment. He had every faith in all of Jackson's Gentile doctors and nurses, it's not that he didn't. He'd just practically never even *heard* of a non-Jewish doctor before. Like Spencer Tracy in *Guess Who's Coming to Dinner?* he had to get used to the idea. We New Yorkers don't get out much.

Exactly twenty minutes later, the ladies reemerged. Jenny's radiant smile reached us as soon as they stepped through the door, down the length of the long hall.

"It went perfectly. You can come in now."

I got to learn a whole new scrub routine, and soon Richie and I and Jackson were reunited as a family once again, accompanied by Grandma Carol.

"Lower GI Jack" was lying in an open bed (a sort of shallow Plexiglas tray which is for babies that are handled frequently or might be going into surgery at a moment's notice) and, thanks to the candy man (or woman, as it were) resting sublimely. We met Jackson's first UCSF nurse, a very confident and sweet-spirited young woman named Abbie Hofstede, who had already fallen in love at first sight with *El Hombre Castaña*.

At first it looked like Jackson had a piece of ziti sticking out of the lower right-hand corner of his tummy, almost as if the wayward piece of pasta, swallowed whole, had wiggled its way out of his belly button instead of going out the proper channel. This was the infamous "drain." A one-inch piece of rubber noodle neatly stitched in place with little crosshatches. Just minutes later, Jenny and Susan seemed to think that the swelling had gone down already, relieving Jackson of that "I can't believe I ate the whole thing" look. As it turns out, this drain is a fairly experimental procedure, one of many that this pioneering teaching hospital was having great success with. From the word "go," the reasons why Jackson was forced to become one of the younger members of the "jet set" were becoming alarmingly clear.

After a relieved round of "finger squeeze therapy," we felt he was in terrific hands with Abbie, so we left to settle in at my parents', and came back later.

Where was my foil poncho?

Don't you get a T-shirt when you cross the finish line?

Wait a minute . . .

. . . that WAS the finish line,

wasn't it?

## << FRIDAY: THE EIGHTH HOUR >>

*A summery summary.*

   As we left the hospital, I was truly shocked to see what time it was. More than seven hours had smeared by since that phantom ringing telephone roused me from my labored slumber at La Maison Tropicana, like the alarms on a military submarine.

# MAN ALL BATTLE STATIONS.
# MAN ALL BATTLE STATIONS.

We all breathed a collective sigh of relief, like the one you might remember heaving as the end credits of *Jaws* started rolling.

I learned a lot about *time* on this day.

It only takes seven hours to sign away your firstborn and flee to safety with your second.

(Sophie's choice was made in a mere moment of her life.)

In the eighth hour, you can be *home* again.

In the eleventh hour, you can be tucked in your boyhood bedroom, fast asleep.

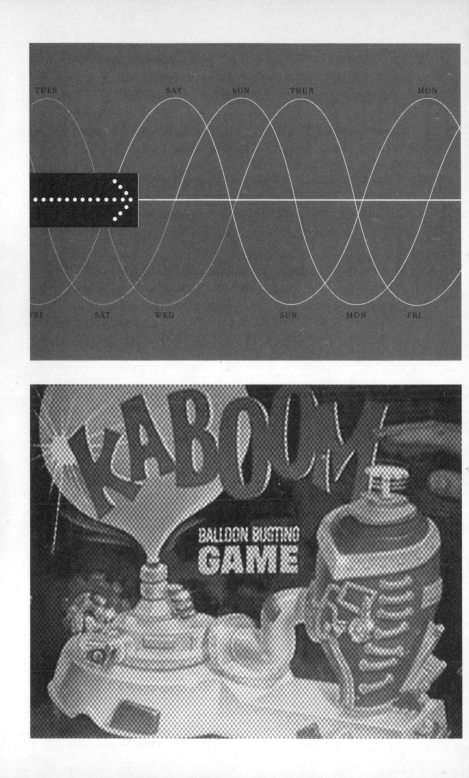

# PRƐ-OP

I am having understandable nightmares about Jackson needing surgery, and that is making me have more understandable nightmares about Jackson needing surgery.

Re: Jackson, here are my top ten most frightening references for "going under the knife":

10. That horrifying frog in Biology class.
9. My dad getting to know Hamilton Beach at Thanksgiving.
8. M*A*S*H.
7. The nasal difference between Cher Bono and *CHER*.
6. Carny Wilson.
5. Renee Richards.
4. The dental operation scene in the film *Marathon Man*.
3. The Face Formerly Known as Michael Jackson's.
2. *Frankenstein*, or even worse, *Young Frankenstein*.
1. Marie Antoinette.

—C. LITTLE

F or the next ten days, we settled into life in SF, at UCSF.

Early every morning, Richie and I would go to the hospital for our first visit of the day. We'd park the car and walk up the steep hill toward the sweeping, circular driveway at the main entrance. Ritualistically, we steeled ourselves for whatever we might find that day once we went inside. The doctors told us that you never know what to expect with preemies. Richie and I had witnessed this ourselves. Thursday his tummy was fine. Friday it was Jiffy Pop. So we tried to take this to heart each morning, wondering what might have happened while we slept.

"Okay, anothe:

"Let's make it a good one."

"Come on, J. Foo."

"No surprises today, please."

day."

"Anything can happen, *right*?"

"Right. Anything can happen."

*FOLLOWING FOO*

We met a lengthening roster of nurses who began rotating into the "round-the-clock rounds" taking care of Jackson in the most intensive unit of the nursery. One by one, the ladies fell for Prince Charming. Original nurse Abbie began a list of nurses who would each volunteer to be one of Jackson's "primary nurses." I am proud to say, as the dad, that in addition to Jackson's complete primary list there was soon practically a waiting list. He was very popular. Full dance card. Lady killer. Richie and I delighted in the attention lavished over him as nurse after nurse claimed him as "hers." It was so cool. It wasn't just that we were a "showbiz family." It wasn't just that we were an "alternative family." It was him. He was the love magnet of Intensive Care.

The residents and fellows and doctors we met were equally enamored of him, and made Richie and I feel that we were home there as well. Soon Richie and I had a routine down and spent a lot of time in the nursery, learning all of the brain-boggling things there were to learn. Dr. Susan Sniderman was at the end of a rotation when we met her, but she assured us that the doctor rotating on, Dr. Francis Poulain, was someone we would love, and that he had an equally lovable French accent. She was right on both counts.

Jackson's lungs did pretty well the first week he was in San Francisco. They dialed his respiratory settings lower and lower, and anticipated that they might actually extubate him (take him off the machine) sometime soon. Dr. Poulain felt that if Jackson needed to have surgery, it would be great if he could be breathing on his own for it.

Boy oh boy, they watched that little noodle sticking out of his tummy like the groundhog was going to come out of it or something. They watched his "other end" a lot, too.

By the time that Jackson was exactly two weeks old, June 12, there was still no sign of the groundhog, or to be more graphic, of *poo*. To be clear, by "poo" we're not talking about the silly old bear with his head in the honey pot. We're talking about what that bear does in the woods.

On Sunday, June 4, 2000, I decided to deal with the thing that had been gnawing at me since Shauna gave birth exactly a week earlier:

Telling our world what was happening.

"I think I have to tell people what happened, *from me*," I told Richie.

On Sunday night, I sat down at my trusty Blueberry iMac on Mom's dining room table to let people know that we were hanging in there. I thought I would tell them a little bit of what happened, and try to tell them not to worry.

Five hours later, ( **Update #1** ) was born. (There was a lotta birthin' going on back then.) It wasn't quite the thumbnail sketch I thought it would be. It was hard, and cathartic.

**115**

On Monday, June 5, 2000, at 2:32 P.M., after having Richie make sure it was all right, I sent the first electronic smoke signal to about a hundred members of our virtual tribe.

So here we are.

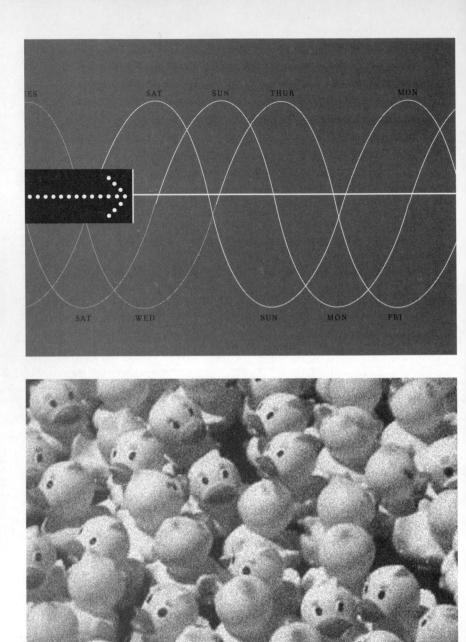

# *OP*

As I am writing the word-fragment above, I am reminded (good Chinese son that I am) that "op" in Cantonese means "duck." You know, as in "Peking duck." Or "sitting duck."

But when I type it in such oversized letters, it's like shouting.

## "DUCK!"

Hearing that word in my head and remembering the part of the story that follows both make me want to dive under my desk, facing away from the windows, like in a San Francisco elementary school quake drill.

"Children, stay down on the floor till the violent motion of the earth's crust stops. You could be seriously hurt . . ."

—C. LITTLE

A day or so after I sent (**Update #1**), while I jettisoned myself down to L.A. again to work another day or two on the movie, Dr. Poulain and surgeons Dr. Diana Farmer and Dr. Mike Harrison all agreed that it was probably finally time to go in and see what was going on in Jackson's little gut. Jackson was not in distress anymore, rather steady in fact, but between the X rays, the no poop, and a test or two that they gave him to confirm that indeed his gut had perforated somewhere and strictured (blocked itself), all the jagged signs in the scary forest pointed to the mad doctor's operating room perched on that foreboding, gothic San Francisco cliff.

They scheduled surgery for Tuesday, June 13, as an "add-on." This meant that it would be scheduled sometime spontaneously during the day, and after getting as much info as I could about it from Richie, he suggested I call Dr. Poulain myself so that I could get a more detailed assessment of the seriousness of this and the possible outcomes, giving me a nice fix to satisfy my jones for information (and therefore a false sense of control and comfort). Richie had already been given the whole, delightful, "here are all of the things that could go wrong" warm-up, and stuff like that does not sit well with him, especially when he has to pass it all on to me. Like I said before, he just turned in his keys when we remodeled, and hoped for the best.

When I spoke to Dr. Poulain, I had pretty much decided to fly home for the surgery, but I asked him to confirm how serious a procedure this was. It involved removing all four feet or so of Jackson's intestines, finding the "bad part," removing it, re-attaching, stuffing it all back in, and sewing him back up. There was no way to tell from the X rays how much of the bowel was bad. It could be a complete disaster when they opened him up, though Jackson showed no exterior distress signals to indicate that it might be. Furthermore, the bowel could be so immature and delicate that it practically disintegrates in the surgeon's hand, which is also very, very bad. Colostomy time. Surprises should never be ruled out. Enough surprises already. How about just a normal birthday party, we all have some ice cream, and call it a day?

One more thing, to give you a little frame of reference: at this time in his life (about to have such critical surgery), the Chestnut Man was just about the size of the book you are now reading. Closed. *Then folded in half lengthwise.*

I asked Dr. Poulain if he agreed that I should fly back home to be with Jackson for the surgery; what were the possibilities we could lose him, etc. Dr. Poulain had spent a day or two with the other father of my child, who was worrying enough for both of us in my stead. Dr. Poulain replied,

"Yes. I think it would be better if you were here . . .

*. . . for Richie."*

Richie and I are still laughing over that one.

**I am cautiously optimistic the baby will make it.**

It's *your partner*
**I'm worried about.**

On Tuesday, June 13, I was still a little concerned that I might have overstayed my electronic welcome when I wrote those volumes about what had happened two Sundays before in Update #1, and that people were down.

So, as brightly as I could, what immediately follows is all I wrote. When I read it today, it makes my face hurt from forcing myself to smile:

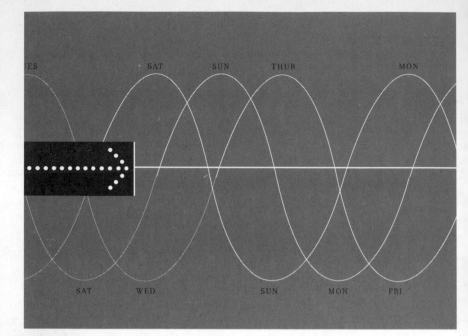

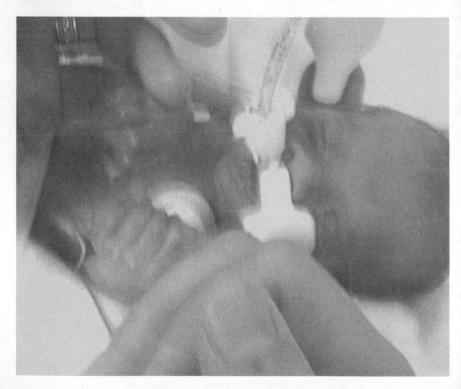

# UPDATE #2

SUBJECT:
"A SHORT UPDATE
FROM B.D. WONG"

JUNE 13, 2000
(ONE WEEK AFTER UPDATE #1)

at the dining room table

### << hi everybody! >>

you all have been so overwhelmingly supportive and
wonderful to us. thank you so much for *EVERYTHING*.
more formal thanks and replies to come, but i wanted to
give you an update . . .

today is a big day for jackson foo wong! sometime
this afternoon, he's going to have that surgery on his
tiny little intestines to fix that pesky perforation. the
doctors don't think it'll be too complicated; we're all
just hoping for no surprises in there!

so, this afternoon, Pacific Standard Time, keep thinkin
whatever you've been thinkin out there . . . so far,
it's been working like gangbusters! **root root root**

### << *GO TEAM JACKSON!* >>

we all love you and miss you more than words can
express.

Jackson, Richie, and B.D.

**B.D. WONG**

**B**etween the time I wrote #1 and #2, another fifty people had been added to the list. I started wanting to tell everyone, and began gathering more and more E-mail addresses and filing them into my address book. I continued to send out #1, as I got more addresses, and kept catching people up depending on where I was in the update process when they started tagging along.

This time, there was a goal, so a lot of the replies included some individual method of prayer; colorful and individual expressions of faith . . .

**WWWWHHHHOOOOOOOOOSSSSSHHHH!!!!!!! Could you feel that force of positive energy coming the TEAM JACKSON way? I will be thinking about you all!**

> • **ADENA FELDMAN CHAWKE** *is a talent agent who works with Richie, and a mother of two.*

Others added something that became a recurring theme; that they felt part of a community . . .

**I'll be thinking of the both of you and Jackson all day today, as I have been for the past couple of weeks. I think all of New York City is pulling for you guys these days—it's very impressive.**

**Love, Kisses, Congratulations and Powerful Thoughts of Surgical Success, Daniel**

> • **DANIEL SWEE** *is the director of casting for Lincoln Center Theater.*

There were predictions . . .

**. . . I believe that little souls who come into this world and have to overcome difficulties will grow to be the spunkiest and most compassionate and loving people, and will have the most to give the world. My thoughts will be with you . . .**

> • **DEB COFFEY** *worked in the contracts department of Richie's company.*

It was moving whenever people confirmed, without having been told, how anxious we were to become parents . . .

**. . . I know that every minute you are experiencing now will become the stuff of Jackson's legend and inspire his family forever and ever. I predict that you will be the greatest parents because you know what a miracle it is to be alive and healthy, what a great gift it is, what an honor to have this great and incredible responsibility you must have pursued with all your hearts . . .**

> • **NANCY NIGROSH** *is a literary agent at Richie's company.*

People continued to offer support from the experience of their own (or their loved ones') origins . . .

**. . . Fred was also a twin. His twin brother also died at childbirth and look at Fred today. He's 200 lbs. Our hearts and thoughts are with you today as your son undergoes surgery . . .**

> • **BARBARA KONG BROWN** *is my cousin; Fred is her husband. They have two sons.*

There were nifty "coincidences;" strangers linked by more than just Jackson . . .

126

**. . . our son had to have surgery at one week old for a large cyst on his neck, and as "routine" as it was, we were nervous, so I know what you're going through. Our surgeon was out of UCSF, Dr. Diana Farmer . . . and she was great. I think they all are! . . .**

> · *I went to junior high with* **SUZANNE ISHII;** *she's a podiatrist and a mother of two . . .*

Within minutes of this last came the following:

**I have read all your missives. Thank you for including me. You are in the good hands of the great Dr. Harrison today and I will be thinking of you all.**

**Diana (MD) Farmer**

> · **DR. DIANA FARMER** *was on Jackson's pediatric surgery team, and apparently my old schoolmate Suzanne's, too!*

Some of my favorites were brief. Their depth of feeling transcended their brevity.

**i love you**

> · **ILANA LEVINE** *is an actor; she played Lucy to my Linus in* You're a Good Man, Charlie Brown; *a relationship we can't seem to shake.*

**My thoughts are with you . . . . . .**

**Love,
Michelle**

> · **MICHELLE KWAN** *is a figure skater, Olympic medalist, record-holding world champion, and my greatest hero.*

Entire families were rooting for the Chestnut Man . . .

. . . When we read your message I was reading it for the first time out loud to my family. There were times I just couldn't go on because I was crying and Brittany finished reading for me while I gained my composure. She (Brittany) was so touched by your message that she printed everything you wrote and all of the pictures and she made a little binder scrap book with Jackson & Boaz's names and birthday on the front. Your E-mail touched us to the bone, Jackson will always be in our thoughts as he has his little operation and on his road to health and Boaz will always be in our hearts. You guys take care, please call us if you need anything we'll always be here for you.

We love you!!

Pam, Craig, Brittany, Alyssa & Kelsey

- **PAM (LOUIE) WONG** *is one of my favorite cousins (sister of the previously mentioned respondents Brenda Louie and Stephanie Louie), and a mother. Pam and Craig have three amazing daughters.*

Does group prayer work?

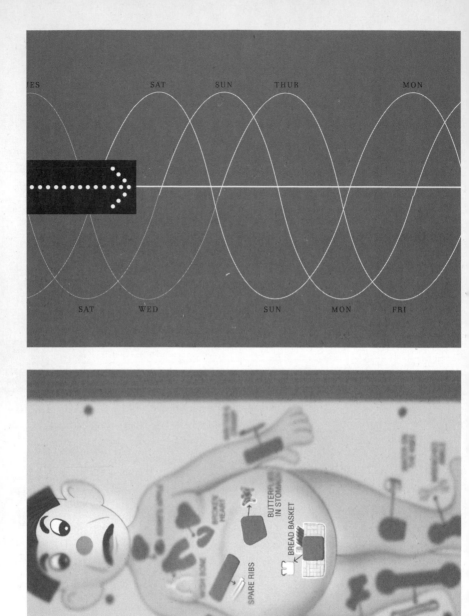

# UPDATE #3

JUNE 14, 2000
(THE DAY AFTER UPDATE #2)

*at the dining room table*

I'm giving up acting, and starting a new religion:

### << *healing through rooting.* >>

It will have nearly 200 followers. The rooters' first project, mending the lilliputian bowels of Jackson Foo Wong, is going very well. His surgery only took about an hour, and after all the terrifying possible outcomes offered to us by Mike Harrison, master pioneer surgeon (perhaps you've seen him on *20/20* . . . only the best for Our Boy) his outcome was absolutely "Choice A." Beneath Boaz's watchful eye, 6 centimeters of "bad" small intestine were located, gently snipped away, and the rest refastened (he has about 100 centimeters, so he can definitely sail on the remaining 94). He didn't need to have anything outside his body (temporary colostomy) or remove any remarkable amount of "dead bowel." Mike just sewed him all up, nice and neat, in a little incision approximately 1¾ in. (but believe me, 1¾ in. goes a *LONG WAY* across Jackson Foo Wong's belly!)

The next project is the healing. He looked pink and sweet and content last night, and they're hoping no infections, or fevers, changes in vital signs, or anything which would require going in again, occurs. Again, we just wait. Jeez, all the waiting. It's a good thing I've been in a couple of movies.

So, please, keep up the good work. You're doing *GREAT*!

**<< Rah. Rah. Ciss-boom-bah. >>**

Oh yes, and thank you, every one of you who's given him even the briefest thought. We feel your care and hope.

In the face of everything, we manage to find great joy.

As for us, Richie & I are doing great. Mark (the Jackson brother who lives in Japan) goes back home today; his timing was impeccable, but boy will we miss him. Compared to some of the other emotional events of the last $2^1/_2$ weeks, major invasive surgery on our 28-week premature infant was a piece of cake!

**133**

Check out Jackson's updated Web site, and don't forget to sign the guest book! We'll be printing it out for him to read this Christmas. You know, give him a couple of months to learn how to read . . .

http://www.geocities.com/jacksonfoowong/

our love for you all is boundless.

jackson foo,
richard alan,
&
bradley darryl
(I **ALWAYS** get the "and billing").

he list kept growing, like those weird furry things on
that episode of *Star Trek*. I constantly searched for new people to
reach out to. People we didn't know began E-mailing us and
signing the guest book on Jackson's Web site (which my brother
Barry had designed) because mutual loved ones had forwarded
Foo to them.

As always, our story brought out the best news in many . . .

**Phil and I also have some pretty good news . . . we're hav-
ing a baby in January . . . We went to see the doctor yesterday and heard the baby's heartbeat, which makes it all
real. I just hope everything goes okay. I've really wanted to
share the news with you, but wanted to wait for the doctor's appointment . . . we're still rooting for Jackson.**

- **TERI (LOUIE) FRENKEL** *is my cousin; the sister of the heretofore
  mentioned Pam, Stephanie ("Soapy"), and Brenda ("BJ") Louie; and
  now, a mother.*

. . . and spanned generations . . .

**Goodness!! This baby has been through a lot of turmoil.
Hope his condition will heal and move forward to an enrich-
ing life. My thoughts are with you, Richie and Jackson.**

**Love, Auntie Betty**

- **BETTY LOUIE** *is the mother of the heretofore mentioned Pam,
  Stephanie ("Soapy"), Brenda ("BJ"), and Teri (Louie) Wong-
  Goodwin-Miyake-Frenkel.*

**134**

Sometimes I was sweetly reminded of things going on at home that we were missing . . .

**tell jackson i know all about intestines, perforated and otherwise, and i will be there to talk to him about it all. give him a kiss for me. next year he'll be at the seder. kisses to you all. love, barbara and jay**

- **BARBARA BARRIE** *is an actor, author, and mother; with her husband, Jay Harnick, she annually hosts one of New York's most meaningful Passover seders.*

Dear friends included news about their kids, and Richie and I felt like we were being initiated into Parenthood . . .

**. . . He's been dubbed Action Jackson at our Santa Monica household. In fact, the only thing that is guaranteed to get a giggle out of (*newborn*) Isabelle are the words Action Jackson. So perhaps she's in touch with him in a way that we can't even comprehend . . .**

- **ROSALIND CHAO** *is an actor. She and her husband, actor Simon Templeman, are the parents of Roland and Isabelle.*

Many tirelessly took on the task of spreading the word . . .

**. . . I took a printout of all your E-mails to dinner and showed them that sweet, sweet picture of Jackson. Victor took them to read and I will forward mine to Blair and Scott. They all send their love. Thank you for the beautiful writings . . .**

- **DEBRA MONK** *is a Tony Award–winning actor.*

**VICTOR GARBER** *(actor),* **BLAIR BROWN** *(actor), and* **SCOTT ELLIS** *(director) are prominent townspeople living in a burg called Broadway.*

135

Like I said, we heard from a lot of folks we didn't even know . . .

**Hi there Jackson,**

**. . . Please add me to your E-mail list for updates. I've been reading your guest book and you are one very well loved little guy. Can't wait to meet you . . .**

**XXXOOO Auntie Lauren**

**. . . this is one very lucky young man, to have the two of you as parents and, from the look of his guest book, at least ½ of the rest of humanity rooting for him and loving him. It will be wonderful to be part of his life, to share in the joy (and aggravation) he brings to you and BD, to watch him grow and change, and to experience the impact he has on the world around him.**

**136**

**Love and hugs to all of you. XXXOOOL**

· **LAUREN HUGHES** *is a therapist, and a good friend of Jackson's uncle Harvey Fierstein.*

The list soon included the medical team, many of whom wrote regularly . . .

**Dear Richie and B.D.**

**I finally had the time to sit and take my time and read all of your letters. The first one brings tears to my eyes every time. I think you are both amazing and going to be fantastic parents! Hopefully one day I can visit Jackson in NY and tell him how lucky he is.**

I am so happy to be a part of the team taking care of him and whether I am at work or actually not in the hospital—Jackson will be in my thoughts.

—stacey L.

· **STACEY LEVITT** *was a fellow in neonatology at UCSF, and one of J. Foo's star doctors.*

Last but not least, three entries from Jackson's Web site guestbook . . .

Well, little one. For all the worrying you are making us Show Folk do you will be paying us back by attending lots of our rehearsals, running lines endlessly, and sitting through Aunt Julie's nightclub act ad infinitum!!! Serves you right!!!!

xoxoxoxo come home soon.
Uncle Harvey

· **HARVEY FIERSTEIN** *is my personification of The Creative Mind.*

Jackson, don't listen to Uncle Harvey—we've sat through his club act plenty of times!!! Promise us you won't think of doing one though! We all can't wait—you look like an angel and clearly are a winner!

Love Julie H.

· **JULIE HALSTON** *is an actor and writer, who indeed has a killer club act. She is one of the funniest people I have ever met.*

Dear Jackson, That's a great name to which you've added new luster. We Jacksons have been known for lots of things through the years, but courage and resilience were not among them until now. Heck, you've only been around for two weeks and you've already been on one of those small planes that neither your father Richie, your cousin Rachel, nor I would even consider boarding. If you grow up to like roller coasters, my happiness will be complete. I came to visit you for four days this past week and amidst all those procedures, wires and shift changes, one thing remained constant: your determination to keep going. You slept the entire time I was there—opening your eyes for four or five precious seconds one day—but how comforting it was to see you each visit serenely going about your business of growing and developing . . .

. . . I was there for your bowel operation. Even though I was nervous—it's my nature—I wasn't surprised that you did well. Once again it was your determination at work. When I speak of courage and resilience, I'm not just talking about you. Your dads have demonstrated true grit (who would ever have thought that I'd use those words with respect to my brother) through these tumultuous times. I didn't do badly either, by the way. The only time I got teary-eyed was each night when your fathers kissed you good night. But trust me, I would've done that even if we hadn't been in the hospital. I want to set the record straight about one thing: word will get out about how much attention and love you received from the nurses, the doctors and other hospital staff. Your father B.D. will tell people it is because you are so cute. You are cute Jackson, but that has little to do with it. Your fathers have this astonishing ability to bring other people into their lives. I've never met two people who not only bond so easily with complete strangers, but actually bring these people into their lives and make them part of their family. As one of the original members of the family, I can tell you that it is a wonderful place to be. But you will learn that for yourself soon enough. In the meantime, wel-

**B.D. WONG**

come to the family Jackson. And in the future, please stay
away from those small aircrafts.

With love,
Your Uncle Mark.

- **MARK JACKSON** *is the earth-bound equivalent to Richie that Boaz
  is to Jackson from above.*

Then, one excruciating week after Jackson played **"OPER-
ATION"** with Dr. Mike Harrison, the latter of who successfully
tweezed the bad gut from Jackson's "Bread Basket" without getting the buzzer, one of life's great everyday miracles presented us
with an **even greater**

## concretely *tangible,*

*Gift...*

139

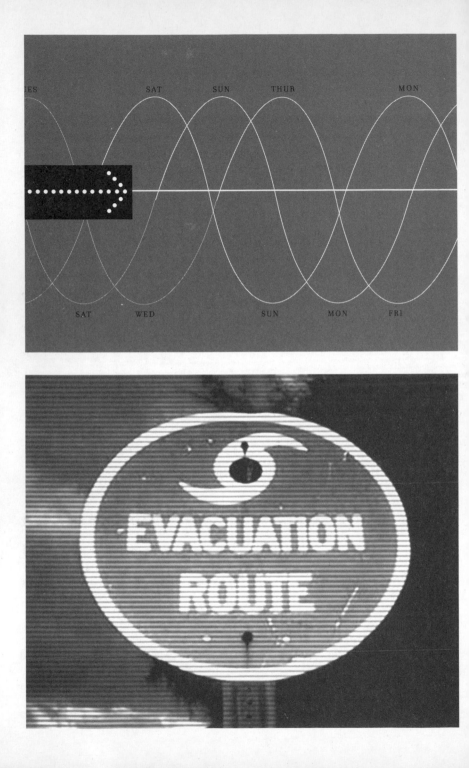

# UPDATE #4

JUNE 21, 2000
(ONE WEEK AFTER UPDATE #3)

written downstairs in the family room

## << A POEM ABOUT POOP >>
### (or "Poop Dreams")

Poop. Poop.
our son took a poop.
he furrowed his brow
and out came the goop.
not green, like a grown-up,
but black, like bean soup.
poop. poop.
Jackson Foo took a poop.

Jackson's seen quite a lot
in his young little life . . .
just two weeks on earth
and under the knife!

What they fixed was his tummy,
'twas blocked down below!
could **eat** something yummy
but not **let it go!**

They went in t' fix it,
before it turned foul
(uncle victor might sing
"You just Gotta Have Bowel!")*

But 'nough of all that!
a week we've been waiting
for signs of some "movement"
with doctors debating!

*142*

* "Uncle Victor" Garber starred in the hit Broadway revival of *Damn Yankees*, which
features the old standard "You Gotta Have Heart" misplagiarized above.

**B.D. WONG**

We waited thru Wednesday,
though **'twas** kind of soon,
but why not dump first
on this sweet spring June noon?

Would Thursday be Turds Day?
Would Friday, or Sat?
Would he "bless us" on Sunday
with a skit about scat?

> He'll not yet squeak, he'll not yet speak, he'll
> take no more than just a leak. He'll
> take his time (almost a week). We'll
> shriek, we'll freak before he's fecal.

Butt . . . (sorry)

On Monday, the Dad
(with no hair on the top)
had to fly home through Newark:
(United, nonstop).
airborne, and on laptop,
in fair, friendly skies,
this **brown** "instant message"
brought tears to his eyes:

## << [everybody!] >>

**"Poop. Poop.
your son took a poop.
he furrowed his brow
and out came the goop.
not green, like a grown-up
but black, like bean soup.
poop. poop.
Jackson Foo took a poop."**

poor richie.
he misses **everything.**

love,
the dad **with** hair on top

p.s. he really did cry.

p.p.s. a few new updates on JFW's website!

http://www.geocities.com/jacksonfoowong/

p.p.p.s. another update coming soon!
BACKSTORY: the special tale of Jackson Foo Wong's
GENETICS,

and,

**144**      **alas,**

**alas,**

**now we're waiting for GAS!!!**

(really)

the end.

XOXOX :—)

I think at this point it was pretty clear that Jackson Foo Wong had gotten everybody's attention.

So I guess the next time *you* want to get everybody's attention, you know what you gotta do.

I guess the joy that I felt caught on, via the update. Mirth (and gastrointestinal relief) emanated on both sides of the electronic equation.

By now Richie and I were coming home from the hospital and rushing to the computer to check for new replies.

**. . . to take what has been such an ordeal and bring to it humor . . . for me that is where God lives! Lucky Jackson! Lucky you twos—with and without hair! . . .**

> · **JAYNE ATKINSON GILL** *is an actor, and a mom.*

**I shudder to think what you'll do when he wins his first Tony . . .**

**Love, Mark, Karen, Rachel, and Katie**

> · **MARK JACKSON** *and* **KAREN HAGBERG** *are respectively Richie's brother and sister-in-law, and are the dad and mom of the incredible Rachel and Katie Jackson. Please note Mark says "his first Tony."*

**POOP made me poop. Literally.**

> · **DAN LIPTON** *is a musician and a writer often found at a piano on Broadway. I hope his computer was near a john.*

**Dearest BD,**

**. . . I'm so happy for you. I know this was a very important step. I know that every day that *I* take a poop is a big step for me as well . . .**

> **· (DEBRA MONK)**

**. . . I'm sure Jackson will be quite embarrassed when he's off to the prom and you reminisce about his very first poop.**

> **· TERI LOUIE FRENKEL.** *Just get me to that prom so I can say "tough."*

## MAZEL TOV ON THE POOP!!

**Julie & Bruce**

> **· JULIE KATZ** *is Richie's oldest schoolchum; her husband is Bruce Katz. They have three kids.*

**B.D. you are one sick puppy.**

**Believe you me, you'll become the foremost doctor of Poopology, color, texture, smell, quantity, and frequency. Rock on, JPoop.com. ed.**

> **· EDDIE FORD** *is a Broadway and television production electrician, and a father.*

**Hey Busta Suess,**

**I smiled and I chuckled
'Til spittle did flow
Upon reading your tale
Of how Jackson did go.**

*B.D. WONG*

146

Your rhythm was soothing
A fine piece of rap
The story quite moving
('bout a little boy's crap).

So here's to your son
And his daring doo-doo
Now the rest of us children
Can go take one, too.

Love,
Bennett

> · **BENNETT YELLIN** *is a screenwriter, and one of my best friends.*

**There will be plenty of poop in the future for Richie . . .**

**Scott**

> · **SCOTT HARRIS** *is Richie's boss, and a father. But is he talking about Richie's role as a diaper-changing dad, or his job???*

Apparently the poem brought out the "off-color" part of folks . . .

**Congratulations!!! Did you save any of it?**

**love love love steven**

> · **STEVEN PETRARCA** *is an actor. As a matter of fact, I did save some of it.*

**. . . Here is *my* pooping poem, inspired by an unfortunate incident when, while stretched out on my tummy in the drama room at stratford high school, my friend mike threw himself on top of me, and . . .**

**and it is an exercise in alliteration**

## Public Pooping

*Public pooping prevents many people from possible popu-
larity with other popular people* . . . . . . . .

> · (TERRI PURCELL)

I think I can get seven figures for the rights. Ving Rhames
to star as the poop!

JJC

> · **JOHN CAMPAGNOLO** *was an agent. Ving Rhames is an accom-*
> *plished actor who, and please don't shoot me I'm just the messenger,*
> *also happens to be Black-American. (When I said "off-color," I*
> *meant it.)*

Richie's not the only one who cried at that news. Thank you
for the wonderful update! I'm enrolling him in the Danny
Thomas fan club! Love you.

> · *This is from one of Jackson's three godfathers, who won't let me use his*
> *name! He is mischieviously referring to an age-old, mysterious Holly-*
> *wood rumor (started by someone else, I hasten to add) about the late,*
> *great Danny Thomas.*

My brother Barry and his entire family all joined in the
effort:

. . . **Everyone that got your E-mail must've checked out
the new pictures on Jackson's web site because the count is
up to over 800!!!! WOW!! See you soon!**

love you,
Doris and Barry and the girls

> · **BARRY WONG** *and* **DORIS (LEE) WONG** *are my brother and*
> *sister-in-law, and the mom and dad of Taylor, Marisa, and Jillian*
> *("Jilli"), the last of whom was three years old at this time . . .*

**We just finished dinner and wanted to tell you about something that Jilli said . . . when we were all giving thanks . . . Jilli said she was thankful for Jackson's poo!!! Out of the mouths of babes! HeeHee! Doris**

I found the continued "theme and variations" that inspired others to use Jackson's predicament to riff on their own family stories really swell, and a major feature of this unique dialogue . . .

**We all eagerly await news of Jackson Foo Fart. Isabelle is especially gifted in that department. Perhaps she could vibe him a few pointers. In the meantime . . . tell Jackson to keep up the good work. Keep us apprised of all future bodily functions. We live for that stuff in this house (Every poop of Isabelle's is rated on a scale of 1—10 by our personal excrement expert, [big brother] Master Roland. Master Roland also likes to liken the shape to a country or state). So you see, Jackson's good work has found an appreciative audience! Yay Jackson! Love to the dad with no hair on top! . . .**

**· (ROSALIND CHAO)**

By now there was a routine. Write. Send. Receive. Digest. Experience. Process. Write . . .

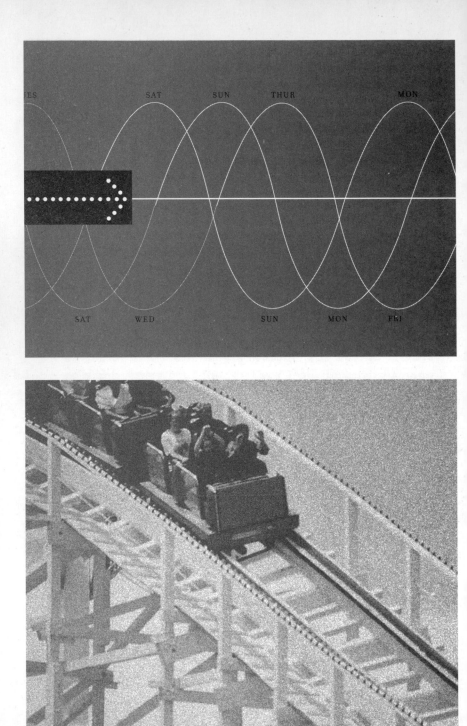

# UPDATE #5

in the living room, on a TV tray, sitting in my dad's La-Z-Boy

## << FORTY-EIGHT HOURS IN THE LIFE OF YOUNG JACKSON FOO WONG >>

**Wednesday**

**1:00 P.M. >>**

It's like graduation. After waiting for the fart that never really came, Medical Team Jackson decides that it's time for Our Boy to EAT. By the way, the Medical Team does use the unofficial medical term "fart." "Hey!" I protest (wearing a smart/indignant expression), *"I* know what *flatulence* means" . . . anyway, maybe he'll give us a little poop/fart combo out the posterior end, they say. (Again, please pardon my coarse language. I'm sure Shakespeare had a *floral* expression for the P/F combo, I guess all of the Shakespearean characters I have ever played neither smelt it nor dealt it.) Anyway, we're thrilled. It's the beginning of the big chain reaction: feeding, weight gain, extubation, crying, self-sufficiency, more weight gain, going home, more crying, rebellion, wreaking havoc, magna cum laude, Nobel Prize, grandchildren, feeding, etc. As you can see, I aim high. So feeding is a big deal for me; the sooner the better. On second thought, I want the grandchildren *before* the Nobel Prize.

**B.D. WONG**

One of Jackson's Primary Care nurses, Susan DeHaan, prepares his first meal with flair. Shauna has been tirelessly pumping her breast milk since delivery, and there's quite a stockpile in the large freezer at the hospital, like Fort Knox. Susan thaws the first little portion of it in a pink plastic hospital pitcher of warm water on which she has written "Jackson Foo Wong's Dim Sum Cart" with a permanent marker. Susan has been a nurse for more than thirty years at UCSF, looks way too young for it, and reminisces proudly about the old days, before monitors and respirators, when each baby had an assigned nurse 24/7, and all the babies were ventilated by hand, thirteen out of every fifteen minutes, with a kind of rubber bellows-like bulb. She wrapped Jackson's first poopy diaper in white tape, like the ribbon on a Tiffany engagement ring box, slipped it in a "beware: BIOHAZARD" Ziploc bag, and wrote "to my Dads, love, JFW" on the white field that says "contents." I immediately FedExed it to Richie's office in New York. Susan slides a tiny tube down into Jackson's stomach, connects a syringe, and slowly lets gravity take 2ccs of the precious elixir into his virgin belly. This is barely half a teaspoon. She will wait two hours, and draw from a syringe again to see if any milk remains in his stomach, and if it has passed, feed again. Grandpa and Grandma Wong and I are all watching this rather uneventful event as if "Thus Spake Zarathustra" was playing loudly on the soundtrack of our life (I know, a year early). Afterwards, we're hungry. We go out to lunch.

**3:01 P.M.>>**
When we return to the hospital, Sue DeHaan has already checked him, and fed him again! No trace of the first meal left in the tummy, on to the second. She even fed him fifteen minutes early, hoping to eventually get him

153

on an "even hours" feeding schedule. This place is like a Swiss train station.

**4:00 P.M. »**
Once again, my parents have swiftly driven me to San Francisco International Airport. The movie has called me down for a quick scene that kept getting rescheduled and rescheduled. You know, for movie people, they sure are nice. They let me come at the last minute (4:45 P.M. flight to be shooting that evening? Unheard of!), fly me, and have me picked up, which they definitely don't have to do. (They've "bought me" for this general time period, usually that means "stay nearby"!) If I don't make the 10:30 P.M. return flight, I'll stay in our cute little L.A. green cottage and come back to be with Jackson first thing Thursday. Shari deFranchi, the upbeat, freakishly efficient production coordinator working on the film, reminds ME that "life is more important than movies." What ever happened to "The Kid Stays in the Picture"??? Isn't Hollywood supposed to be the *antidote* to stable, mature, family behavior?

**7:00 P.M. »**
I have landed in Los Angeles and am being driven directly to the set, a truly seedy bar in the remotest portion of downtown/east L.A. How did all you ol' folks have babies without cell phones? I call Nurse Sue just moments before her 7:00 P.M. shift change. She proudly (but ever so nonchalantly) mentions that by this time, she has fed our son four times. No sign of rejection, or complication. She warns me not to get too excited. He could decide at any time he doesn't want to be fed any more, and the international preemie sign language for this would be PUKING. That would be the "roller coaster" they warned us about.

*B.D. WONG*

From the moment that Jackson was born, every doctor, every nurse, every social worker who worked with us warned us of the same thing: "Having a preemie in the Intensive Care Nursery is like being on a roller coaster." Richie's stomach churned each time: "But I HATE roller coasters." The last time Richie got on a thrill ride we were at Disney World, when I was working on the sitcom *All-American Girl* and assigned to press duties there. We were all in line for the TOWER OF TERROR and Richie adamantly refused to go on, until Jackson's Aunt Amy Hill's tiny eighty-year-old Japanese mother said SHE was going on, and shamed the nervous New York Jew. (Sigh. Sometimes I feel like I'm in a Woody Allen movie.)

Richie and I enjoy a brief moment of bi-coastal family triumph re: the feeding. When I get to the set, I quickly call the hospital before I get into the makeup chair for the painstaking application of a cowboy suntan and a week's worth of stubble. Abbie Hofstede, the first UCSF nurse to fall in love with Jackson (she set up the Primary Care team and made the fancy red "teddy bear" sign with Jackson's name and birth statistics that Uncle Barry features on the Web site) is now on duty. She has fed him once, uneventfully, and has just begun her shift, which will include monitoring his blood/oxygen saturation levels (his have been going up and down), weighing him (an entire production with all the wires and tubes), feeding him every two hours, suctioning his lungs, having gas readings done on his $CO_2$, filling out an impossibly lengthy daily report, changing countless wet (but not yet again poopy) diapers, listening (with a stethoscope) to his heart, lungs, and bowels, turning him over/taking his temperature/adjusting his bedding several times, coordinating his IV feedings, soothing me (and Richie) on the phone and in person, and voluntarily writing in the bedside diary that we brought to document Jackson's ups and downs.

I am about to be filmed smoking a cigarette, silently leaning against the side of a building, in the rain.

Before we hang up, Abbie protectively says,

"Don't work too hard."

**9:00 P.M. >>**
The abovementioned scene is under way. Like I said before, this scene has been scheduled and rescheduled many times. So the scenic department on the movie has cleverly dummied up a set on an overpass down the street from the seedy bar so they can quickly squeeze it into the shooting schedule tonight. Picture an absurdly small (fake) cross section of the roof of a building. It is sitting incongruously on the top of a downtown L.A. overpass, so as to feature the wimpy downtown L.A. skyline in the background. From a distance, it looks ridiculous. Two rainbirds are sending fake rain everywhere. The cigarette never stays lit. I am kind of bad at smoking. But everyone that knows about Jackson (and Boaz) is warm to me, and the shoot is painless. Jim Behnke is the producer who arranged for me to be flown and driven so that I could be by our son as much as possible. "More towels," he tells the wardrobe department. "He can't bring a cold home to that boy." Inexplicably, I am in and out of the scene in forty-five minutes. (This *never* happens). I don't make the Thursday-night flight, but I'm at the L.A. house by 10:00 P.M. A couple of late-night calls to Abbie confirm more successful feedings. I sail through a call or two and check my E-mail. (This last is no small task these days.) The reviews for the "poop poem" are good. I catch a few winks.

## Thursday

**6:00 A.M.»**
I am up, like, "Dad early," and throwing stuff in a bag to catch that first flight back to San Francisco. The car comes, and as soon as we are on the freeway I'm calling Abbie, to catch her before the 7:00 A.M. shift change, and I get a lousy cell phone connection. She says Jackson is tolerating the feeds well, but "de-satting" a lot. This means that the vital level of oxygen he saturates into his blood through respiration drops from time to time, and either he raises it himself, or he needs a little help; Abbie turns up the pressure on his ventilator. This is not an immediate emergency, but part of an ongoing observation: postsurgery, his lungs are not as cracker-jack as they were prior. There is an accumulation of "wetness" in his lungs, and periodic de-satting. A few doses of a medicine called Lasix are supposed to help him pee out the extra wetness, but it hasn't really been working. Again, nothing to worry too much about, they say. More watching and waiting. This makes me crazy. Enough "watching and waiting" already. The connection is breaking up periodically, but I do manage to hear that Abbie has "heard murmurs" about some such thing or other, either through other nurses, or the residents or doctors. This is often helpful, for the nurses can often tell you "on the Q.T." that your baby might be moved to another spot (so that you won't totally freak out when you walk in and he isn't there . . . sometimes it's just the little things, folks, the little things . . . ), or that an X ray or ultrasound is scheduled and when, or when that hard-to-nail-down-super-surgeon might be stopping by to check on your baby, and you can get in a question or two.

157

"Great, Abbie," I say. "Sorry, I got a bad connection . . . what kind of 'murmurs' did you say?"

"... No, I heard a *murmur* today ...

... this morning ... in Jackson's heartbeat ...

... when I was listening to his heart ...

... B.D? Are you still there?"

The bad connection morphs into a vaguely familiar
sound ...

click-click-click-click-click-click ...

... the TOWER OF TERROR begins its ascent.

So what if she says not everyone agrees they hear it?

So what if she says it's not anything to worry about, yet?

So what if she says lots of preemies have them?

I still have to call Richie.

So I do, and I emphasize all of the nonconcern Abbie
seems to be expressing. Cardiology will pay a visit today,
and we will know more then.

**9:00 A.M. >>**
Grandpa and Grandma Wong, ever unbelievably ener-
getic for people in their seventies, pick me up at the
airport (yes, again), and we go right to the hospital.
Rushing the morning scrub impatiently, I cut my hand on
the stainless-steel dispenser reaching out aggressively
for the paper towels and misjudging the distance. The
sight of my own blood makes me realize that today I
am more afraid of what is going to happen than usual.

Stacey Levitt, UCSF fellow, solid and steady as a rock, seems especially fond of Jackson. She always wears an aura of apology when explaining the challenges that Jackson faces. The morning a week or so ago that they reintubated him after trying unsuccessfully to let him breathe on his own, she came trotting down the hall as soon as we got off the elevator: "Don't be mad at me!!! I had to put it back in!!! He tried his best!!!" She makes me feel that any anxiety felt about Jackson "making it" is not just mine and Richie's, but hers as well (and so many others', actually). She softly and directly explains that by now, everyone hears the murmur, and there could be a number of explanations for it. It could be an "Innocent Murmur" (which sounds, I know, like a Jennifer Love Hewitt movie); lots of babies have these, they either go away or they don't, but they don't hurt. Or he could have a ductus, a reopening of some sort of heart valve which happens often in preemies; its symptoms often include the very "wetness" in the lungs Jackson has. "How do you treat that?" I ask, with Grandpa and Grandma Wong cowering stoically in the corner beside their grandson's isolette protectively, like two parental grizzly bears with their cub checking out a park ranger.

"Surgery," Stacey says, flatly.

click-click-click-click-click-click . . .

Stacey has asked the Cardiology Department to order a particular ultrasound of Jackson's heart called an "echo," and an examination by the cardiologist, first thing that morning. Before I know it, it's already 11:30. Just wait.

"Another hurdle," sighs Grandma Bear.

We go home and I try to take a nap, which doesn't come as effortlessly as usual, though I am bushed. In the car on the way I call Richie. I tell him that at the end of my conversation with Stacey, I somehow bravely "unclenched," and told myself that if Jackson has a ductus, he has a ductus, and if he needs heart surgery then that's just what they'll have to do. Simple. We're lucky to have them to do it. Then I told Stacey, "Yeah, but that's not gonna help Richie, huh?" Stacey and Richie and I all managed to laugh about this. In the end, I find myself somewhere in the great, gray nether-world between "unclenched" and "basket case."

**2:00 P.M. >>**
I go back to the hospital with my stalwart, steadfast parents, and Uncle Matt is there to meet his nephew.

A sidebar about Uncle Barez: I wish to write a whole update about Matt Barez and his incredible family, namely his great and giving wife, Aunt Sue, Richie's youngest sister. Her role in Jackson and Boaz's life has been sorely left out in all of these updates. So I want to pledge that forthcoming, and apologize to her for not including it earlier, and maintain suspense for those of you who don't already know. She deserves volumes of her own.

So, Uncle Matt is at the hospital where he has presented Jackson with a humongous stuffed bassett hound. In town for business, this is a chance for another member of the family to get a peek at the "Chestnut Man" (my own personal, random nickname for J. Foo). No sooner has Matt said his "so longs," when Stacey Levitt is enthusiastically in line for a chat:

*B.D. WONG*

The "echo" ultrasound technicians see nothing wrong with Jackson Foo Wong's heart.

Now, the cardiologist still needs to look at the pictures that the cardiology techs have taken. The cardiologist makes the diagnosis, and files the report. But Stacey says the tech's word is often an "unofficial" forecast of what the cardiologist will see. Besides, the tech's opinion here isn't particularly controversial; it seems real clear.

I am constantly trying to head off the shock of terrible news by anticipating it, which reminds me of routinely going to the market on the bus in Israel and numbly wondering if this is the day you'll encounter some kind of terrorism.

I sternly remind Stacey that when we were in Modesto, a technician similarly "unofficially reported" that Jackson had a "Grade 3" hemorrhage in his brain, and it turned out he actually had the much less severe "Grade 1."

In a perfectly objective line reading, Stacey replies, "Well, this isn't Modesto."

She says that she'll be leaving today by 4:30 P.M., and hopes to officially talk with the cardiologist by then.

**4:00 P.M. >>**
I finally succumb to temptation and call Stacey at the hospital, hoping to catch her before she goes. She says that she has not been able to speak to the cardiologist, but that she did call down and had the report read to her. "Normal" is what the cardiologist wrote on the report with my son's name on it.

Normal.

Now, you have to understand how difficult it is for me to have a clear head during all of these conversations, having no real relative frame of reference or medical knowledge.

"Stacey, is there anything *better* than '*normal*'?" I ask.

She gives away her amusement as she chuckles, "No."

You see, in my personal Hollywood lexicon of superlatives, "normal" just doesn't cut it. It doesn't sound *fabulous* enough. We actors prefer words like "brilliant" and "unrivaled" and "incandescent." Really, now. What's wrong with wanting him to have an *"incandescent heart"*?

Soon after this announcement, and calling Richie, I sit down at the dinner table with my parents, who continue to astound. My mom has prepared one of my top three childhood meals: tacos. I know that "tacos" probably won't sound like comfort food to most of you, but believe me, Mama Roberta knows what she's doing in La Cocina Wong. I am instantly brought back to those old days in my childhood when my parents worked 'round the clock to provide for their boys, tag teaming; back when Mom made tacos every Wednesday, because that was the day when the fragrant corn tortillas were delivered to the market from the Mission District of San Francisco, and she brought them home so fresh that they steamed up the inside of their plastic wrapping. So, yeah, tacos really remind me of being *taken care of.*

Since *my* boys were born, I vowed to try to give thanks before every meal. We never did this when I was a kid. With that in mind, I introduced it tentatively, hoping

Mom and Dad would understand this "new" thing I wished to pass on to my son. As I approach the table, they are beaming (incandescently), holding hands, upraised, with each of their own free hands reaching for mine. "Thanks!!! Gotta give thanks, first!!!"

**<< "FOR A NORMAL HEART!"** we chorus. **>>**

Oh yeah, and tacos.

**7:00 P.M. >>**
Mom and Dad and I go visit Jackson one more time. As always, he looks perfectly content, but still wet in the lungs, still the periodic de-satting. The feeds are continuing to go well, but a second poop hasn't really come, and it has been a day and a half. Frankly, I am not so worried about this, because of my own personal, leisurely, digestive m.o. Sometimes I . . . never mind. More than enough said.

On "Jackson detail" tonight is perky Jennipher Goodner, who lets me take his temperature and change his diaper, the latter of which is literally about the size of a Palm Pilot. Grandpa Wong coos to him encouragingly in English and Chinese, spoken word and song.

**8:00 P.M.>>**
In a weary act of sponteneity, I go to the "Kabuki Hot Springs" in Japantown for an hour or so of new age music and hot water. I actually feel better afterward.

**10:00 P.M. >>**
I return to the hospital, armed with Ziploc freezer bags and a permanent marker. I am valiantly determined to organize Jackson's breast milk stash, which is stockpiled willy-nilly in a corner of a huge laboratory freezer in small plastic bottles and bottle liners, with all the

*163*

other milk for the many babies in the entire four-wing Intensive Care Nursery. The milk has a limited freezer life and the nurses tend to just grab the first bottle they see. I intend to organize all the dates, oldest in the front, newest in the back, so the staff can select the milk the *opposite* way my mom taught me to when she sent me grocery shopping: *"Always* pick out the one with the most recent date," Mom said. Shauna and others have also warned me not to allow the milk to thaw, even a bit. Shauna says, "if it's even a little 'juicy' on the inside, you have to throw it out." Of course, the idea of throwing out unused milk from Shauna's cherished, finite supply makes me crazy. See, I save things like paper clips and rubber bands.

Into the night, I am shuffling, labeling, and separating Jackson's hundred or so bottles and sacks, frantically trying to keep the freezer door open as little as possible. The amount of the precious commodity stored safely in this freezer for everyone in the ICN is daunting. As I continue on my little project, I become painfully aware that every opening of the freezer door threatens the nourishment of about a hundred little lives. I begin working increasingly feverishly, sorting, labeling, bagging, dating, opening the doors, closing the doors, like Lucy Ricardo at the candy factory.

After about a half hour of working in and outside of the freezer, an alarm goes off.

The freezer has a fancy computerized thermostat which must be kept at about −20.00 degrees. When it rises to −10.00 degrees, an irritating, piercing tone jarringly signals that it is in the "danger zone."

I panic.

**B.D. WONG**

I zoom out of the breast milk storage area as if I have just held up a 7-Eleven, and nurses are running toward me down the hall like a SWAT team. "What did you do? What did you do?" they half-jokingly ask. I am not confident enough that I did NOT do something to respond glibly.

"I thought I . . . I was just . . . I tried to keep the . . . I never left the . . . I was only trying to . . ."

The freezer alarm goes on and off for the next HOUR. A nurse throws a big "DO NOT OPEN" sign across the freezer doors; another calls the twenty-four-hour 911 repair number. I begin pacing and having nightmares about all the burly, stressed-out fathers whose wives have been painfully pumping the precious nutrients to help save the lives of their struggling flesh and blood, drop by priceless drop. They are splitting off into teams and searching the halls for me, with big Dobermans and tiki torches.

**"THERE HE IS! THAT'S THE ONE! <u>GET 'IM!</u>"**

I don't feel so good. The effects of the Kabuki Hot Springs have completely worn off. The nurses are trying to reassure me, halfheartedly telling me that they had been having trouble with the freezer and that it was not my fault. Like everything that happens to me in this building every day, *I am not easily reassured.* Carmen, the nurse who righteously slapped the *"DO NOT OPEN"* sign on the freezer, says, "We'll just keep watching the temperature gauge, and see what happens. There's nothing to do yet." I think to myself, *what is this, the motto of the whole hospital??? Do we have to wait for EVERYTHING??? Can't we ever DO SOMETHING???*

**1:00 A.M. >>**
The nurses plead with me to go home. I have been
rehearsing the monologue which explains to the dads
what happened to their kid's lifesaving lunch, but it
is not my best work. It will be another hour before the
repairman has a diagnosis. I say "night-night" to my
oblivious Chestnut Man, and I drive "home," muttering
to myself like a true madman. I am so tired and so
disproportionately upset that I collapse immediately
when I get into bed. I am worried now not only about
the wetness in Jackson's lungs, but the wetness in two
thousand bottles of frozen breast milk.

*Friday*

**10:00 A.M. >>**
Shauna calls to say she is going to hit the road and
come up to San Francisco to visit Jackson and to bring
more breast milk.

Oy, don't say "breast milk," I mumble bitterly under my
breath.

The drive takes a couple of hours, so I sit down at the
computer in my pajamas and start writing this to you.

**12:00 NOON >>**
On my way out the door to meet Shauna, I notice my
mom and dad are having lunch. We have been sent tons
of fabulous food by our nearest and dearest in New York
to nourish and soothe us, and my parents have really
been enjoying some of it.

My father is eating a toasted Zabar's **cinnamon-raisin**
bagel, with a schmear of cream cheese and a
PILE OF **NOVA SCOTIA LOX** ON TOP.

*B.D. WONG*

Cinnamon, raisins, Philadelphia cream cheese, and smoked fish?

"It's *great!*" he says, like the anachronistic old smiling Chinese man in a Hebrew National commercial.

Going against the grain of everything deeply embedded within me regarding the way a Chinese son behaves toward his elders, I tell my dad that what he is eating looks "gross."

My mom shrugs and says dramatically, "I put the salmon on the *side.* I didn't think he'd make a *sandwich* out of it."

What can I say, they weren't married under a canopy.

After a quick visit to Jackson, Shauna and I are having lunch (*we* food-combine normally). I hesitantly get around to asking her how she feels physically and emotionally, and we both agree that even though it's so wonderful to visit Magic Jackson, and watch him progress day to day, we both kinda wish Shauna was still pregnant (as she still normally would be). Even though we worried so much, it sure was fun . . .

**1:00 P.M. (Forty-eight hours after the first entry) >>**
I realize that I have come to the hospital today more frustrated and worried than usual, and it's not the Charlie Chaplin Breast Milk Caper (the breast milk is fine, by the way). Jackson's condition remains the same, not bad but not great, and there isn't much to do but the proverbial watching and waiting. It's so paralyzing to me. Passive. After lunch Shauna and I return to the hospital, and I resume my conversation with Stacey Levitt about my (and Richie's) anxiety. Later, when Christine White,

another of Jackson's Primary Care nurses, hip and friendly, mentions to me how this anxiety is part of "being a parent," I gently take issue with that. Actually, not so gently.

" *'Being a parent'* is supposed to start when you bring the kid home! This is a whole extra thing! This isn't NORMAL parenting! If this was *normal* parenting, then ALL parents would have this! I didn't sign up for the 'extra credit!!!' "

Apparently stumped, she replies, "I see your point."

My victory is hollow.

I see her point, too. Shauna and I discussed this at lunch. She explained to me how you *never* stop worrying, that the fear you feel the first time he throws up will cause you the same panic as waiting for him to come out of surgery last week. That waiting for him to come home on that first night when he takes the car is no different. When he says, "What's the big deal, Dad, it's just a *safari*!" will I throw myself in front of the jetway in fits of inconsolable sobs? Have you ever seen the Discovery Channel? You bet your ass I will.

Speaking of airplanes, I flashed on something while Shauna and I were discussing this. There's an old snapshot in my scrapbook of my parents and me, boarding pass in my hand, at the good ol' San Francisco International Airport on the night I first flew to New York on a budget "red-eye" almost twenty years ago. To the naked eye, we look perfectly happy, but just a glance at it for me immediately reminds me of those last moments before I left home that first time. They both choked out what they could: she said, "Call as soon as you get there," and he swallowed and said, "Go get 'em." I remember being so amused, and impatient at their worry. Definitely feeling loved, but a bit dismissive. When I bought my first apartment, they worried. When I told them there was a Richie (and everything that that entailed), they worried. When I told them that we were going to try to give them a grandchild, boy did they ever worry.

You know, it's not just the never-ending cycle of worrying that stuns me. It is my inability, until these very moments this late in my life, to appreciate how their worry funnels directly back to that original, simplest desire, that need, to bring me into this unbelievable world, and how that worry is my constant (and believe me when I say CONSTANT) reminder of their very expensive, but unreturnable, gift of life to me. The same desire and obsessive need they have shown, which I once judged, is the one I show today. It's the desire and obsessive need I now have to see the day when I will throw myself in front of that Air Africa jetway. The desperate need to *know* that everything here and now will be all right, that that day will come.

I have never been much at prayer, but I am fast learning.

**Give. Me. That. Day.**

I promise that if I can have that day, I will gladly embrace all the worry there is in the world. I will be slave to it; my worry, as well as my actions and my commitment and my love for him, will justify bringing Jackson Foo Wong into the world. If I can have that day, I may worry, but I will not shrink from it. But give me that day.

*JUST GIVE ME THE PROMISE OF THAT DAY, GOD, AND I PROMISE, I WILL HAVE EARNED IT.*

Stacey Levitt, alas, cannot promise me that day. What she can do, ever so gently and with as much love as a doctor can professionally offer, is constantly remind me that even though he goes back and forth and up and down and to and fro, he is generally doing all right. That a bad day for Jackson Foo Wong isn't anything like a bad day for the cardiac babies, or the brain surgery babies, or many of Jackson's ever-changing roommates, or their weary, confused, red-eyed, sometimes hysterical parents. This is the roller coaster they were talking about. I thought the roller coaster was the flying from Modesto, the "code 3" ambulance ride, the potential brain hemorrhage, the intestinal surgery, the brother who didn't make it.

No, the roller coaster is the everyday ups and downs. The ventilator tube gets taken out, the ventilator tube gets put back in. The tummy is flat, the tummy is distended. One day he poops, the next three he doesn't. The strict laws of physics are unfailingly executed: if it goes up, eventually it's gotta come down. So, when I think about it, I suppose Nurse Christine is right: this IS the ride of being a parent, and during the ride, the spectacular team of doctors and nurses and surgeons and technicians scurries about, and turns the dials, and changes the fluids, and takes the X rays, and discusses things, and makes the decisions, all based upon the silent semaphore signals of the tiniest sailor at sea.

Maybe, just maybe, if they keep doing that, if Richie and I keep letting them do that, and he has the wind at his back, then maybe I can have that day.

**Won't that be swell?**

So I told Richie, no more refusing to get on the roller coaster. We have to wait in line, and give The Man our ticket, and I promise to hold your hand, I say. We are tall enough to get on, and even though there's a big warning sign, we don't have a heart condition, and we're definitely not pregnant, so we can handle the ride. We can be thankful that these days, it's a comparatively mild one, as roller coasters go. Let's just see what happens. Let's just put our hands up over our heads, let go, and

Look behind us. Everyone we love is on the ride, too.

Have you thought about . . .

. . . or called your mom and dad recently?

I bet they're worried sick about you.

please keep rooting . . .

love, bd

XOXOX :–)

I guess "forty-eight hours . . ." struck a chord in some that was more deep private, where as "A Poem About Poop" was just, basically, well, "a gas." The responses we received from this update were among the most revealing and healing, and helped me to see something that I always preach but rarely experience: how wonderful energy can spring from the well of the most challenging situations.

As I was discovering my worth as a writer, were others discovering theirs?

I'm not as big as you, BD, but I can ride the biggest horse you can send my way, drive the biggest car, and I'm not afraid of roller coasters. I've often observed that more determination gets packed into small packages than it does into the 600lb gorilla types. So, don't you worry about Sailor Jackson. He will conquer the seven seas and Africa as well. But I can't wait to see you throw yourself across the runway. Now that's a sight worth waiting for . . .

• (KARYN WAGNER)

. . . Thank you from the bottom of my own anxiety-filled soul for expressing so eloquently what it's like to have your heart walk around on the outside of your body . . .

. . . Please stay seated until the ride comes to a full and complete stop!

Peace, Anita, fellow parent

**P.S. I will give my own children an extra kiss in your honor tonight on one of the many times I check to make sure the covers are moving as they sleep and the closet is free of monsters. Oh, and I'll call my mom of course!**

> • **ANITA BRUSH** *is one of Shauna's stalwart pals, and a sister surrogate. She was there the night our boys were born.*

As usual, people reflected:

**. . . Uncle Ernie has a heart murmur. He's lived with it for 72 years.**

**Looks like this is a test of Richie and your patience and faith. Hang in there. Miracles have happened!**

**Love, Auntie Betty**

> • **(BETTY LOUIE)**

**173**

**. . . p.s., suzi has a heart murmur, and we all know how she turned out.**

**all my love, ilene**

> • **ILENE ROSEN** *is the former head of production of DRAMA DEPT. Theater Company. Suzi is her equally gorgeous twin.*

One response was from an "intended father" whom we had met on the path to surrogacy as kindred spirits:

**. . . I'm humbled by your parenting and by your parents and by your medical team and by your son. What an incredible journey you've begun . . .**

**. . . This is the week we will attempt pregnancy again. I'm attaching a photo of me with my third and (please, God), final egg donor. She and I have been able to spend several**

days together this week with doctor's appointments and we're so much alike I'm afraid the child we produce is going to be lopsided—a sugar-loving, free-spirited, stubborn, risk-taking, foot-dragging thing. We would appreciate your prayers on this, my fifth and (again, please, God) final try.

My thoughts are ever with you,

Bill

> • **BILL WALKER** *is a writer, and at the time he wrote this, a hopeful "intended father."*

Others and shared deeply personal revelations and experiences . . .

B.D.,

. . . This has been a year on the roller coaster (for me)! . . .

. . . In the middle of all this things got worse. Friends of mine lost their 18-month-old baby to some rare liver disease. The baby just died in his crib.

It took me an hour to write a two-paragraph E-mail through the tears.

My Sam came along and helped me get through this year. We will all help you get your Day!

> • **(DAVID SPAGNOLO,** *father of Sam***)**

. . . Your words made me think of what my parents must have experienced with me as a child when I was sick—constantly hospitalized, constantly in pain, constantly fighting to do everything that came so easily to all of the other children because of being forced to constantly fight to breathe . . .

. . . I will never forget the day that they had to put me in an oxygen tent . . .

. . . and the only thing that assured me during that time that everything would be OK, that the torture would eventually come to an end and I would again breathe air freely from outside that plastic bubble, was the face of my mother who never left my side . . . No matter how frightened everyone else looked . . . my mother's eyes were filled with smiles and I felt safe, and I felt her feel that I would be safe, and I felt OK.

I could feel the love coming through that layer of material, as nothing man-made could stop it—and that parental force was strong enough to help me beat the odds and to help me recover and to help me eventually get to where I am today.

Jackson knows that love, as he can feel it not only from you and Richie, and not only from your parents and relatives, but from everyone here and there and everywhere that is sending out that special energy, and cheering, and smiling as we put our hands up over our heads and ride the coaster down, together.

I love roller coasters, and I always will. Count me in for the long haul . . .

- (MARC AYRIS)

. . . I had a tough time in my childhood. And I remember being a small boy and hating myself for crying. In fact, I took pride in myself for not doing so. Thus the journey to manhood was fraught with emotional suppression.

This past week has been one of the toughest I've ever had as my wife, Jo, has, too, had surgery. To see her in so much pain and to be powerless to protect her in any way hurt me deeply . . .

. . . I, too, was waiting for my loved one to fart this week. When the long awaited PHert! came I ran in to the corridor to share my excitement with anyone who would listen. And last night the poop came . . . (what joy poop!) all meaning that Joanne can go home soon. I have experienced elements of your struggle. Though, I couldn't imagine what I would feel like if this was happening to my child.

Love is a powerful force. I don't believe your worry will ever decrease. Nor shall mine.

Today I brought your E-mail to Joanne. So I could read it to her in her hospital bed and I wept. I wept uncontrollably for some time. While Jo (who was also crying) handed me tissues. I feel so much for you and Richie and Shauna and Jackson and Boaz and your entire family. Crying this morning for little Jackson made me feel proud. And, for the first time . . . made me feel like a man. A strong emotionally connected man . . .

> · **MIKE MAGEE** is an actor studying to be a child psychologist. Today, he and wife, Joanne, are the proud parents of a beautiful baby boy, River Magee.

We heard again from Dr. Stacey Levitt:

. . . It is great to read it from your perspective . . . You are definitely right—I have a very special fondness for little Jackson—and can't wait until he is a toddler and I get to visit him when I visit (or move back to) NYC!

**B.D. WONG**

I know it is extremely frustrating with all the ups and downs "the roller coaster." But try to hang in there—in the long run this will be such a short period of his life—and when he leaves for that safari this will all be a distant and faint memory.

And keep believing that this is all par for the course and that we are all doing anything we can to make it smoother and shorter for Jackson.

And I particularly will always let you know when and if we depart from the small bumps in the ride—and if it is something to be more concerned about—try to leave the rest of the worrying to us!!!

Love

Stacey L

- (DR. STACEY LEVITT)

177

There was no turning back now, E-lectronically or otherwise.

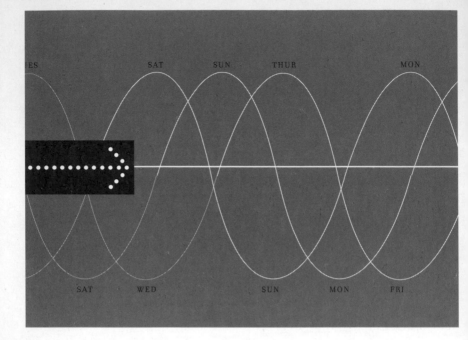

50's & 60's Hot Rock 'N' Roll

# Rockin' Pneumonia

Featuring Dr John / Sir Douglas Quintet / Huey Piano
Jimmy Clanton / Earl King / Lee Dorsey

# UPDATE #6

SUBJECT:

"A SONG FOR RICHIE"

JUNE 27, 2000
(3 DAYS AFTER UPDATE #5)

at the TV tray-Z-boy

**180**  ## << a song for richie >>

(also an update)

by b.d.

(chorus)
pneumonia . . .

pneumonia . . .

is jackson getting pneumonia?
if jackson gets pneumonia
ya want the doc to phone ya?

"of course!" you say, "but not today!
i just got over yesterday!
'cause yesterday, the play by play
was a mess of distress and dismál dismáy!"

**B.D. WONG**

you say a prayer, you say a cheer
you root next year'll be clear of fear
thank gosh the kid that ya hold so dear
is tough as a weary-free musketeer!

and it's all for one,
and one for all!
doctors,
nurses,
small and tall
out on a mission
in for the haul
holding his candle
and breaking his fall

there's wetness in his lung . . .

there's gassiness in his gut . . .

if he wasn't so goshdarn young . . .

we would all be sayin' "so what?" . . .

we would all be sayin' "who cares?" . . .

even i would be sayin' "i don't!" . . .

take a look at the booties he wears . . .

they should fit like a glove but they won't!

(chorus 2)
pneumonia . . .

pneumonia . . .

it's not so bad, pneumonia

especially when pneumonia
is NEW-monia
not FULL BLOWN-ia

see the doctors are smart
the nurses are good
they are good as they should
(as i knock on some wood)
but i feel from the heart
what you'd hope that i would
they got down to an art
jackson's chart,
understood?

(chorus 3)
pneumonia . . .

pneumonia . . .

it's a fear that's so great it could own ya
but remember it's not yet pneumonia
till the song from some fat prima don-ya

they're cautious . . .

they're careful . . .

not dumb, demigoddish, or dare-ful
can't help it when they're a big scare-ful
but at times it's a wear and a tear-ful

they know what they know
and they see what they see
but there's more than you see in a wee pree-mie
'cause a preemie can't show what he shows as he grows
he only shows highs
and he only shows lows

**B.D. WONG**

and that's about it, the highs and the lows
the ebbs and the flows, he'll wake and he'll doze
but those of us looking for more, i suppose
won't find any more than there's ten of his toes!

and THAT'S why . . .

the SCI-ENCE . . .

application (the same as appli-ance),
the what and the when and the why-ance
is tricky for these med-school gi-ants

but

they looked at the picture,
they looked at the scan;
the chest x ray of
"the chestnut man."
saw something strange, presented a plan:

anti-

biotics,

perhaps ATIVAN!

(something to help the boy sleep when he can)
"how about us?" said his dads,
"ATIVAN!
        LAND US THE NEXT VAN
                        TO ATIVAN LAND!"

before
        it gets
                too ugly
while he's still so serene and so snuggly

*FOLLOWING FOO*

they've decided to treat the big bug-ly
hope he don't get too dopey or drug-ly

and THAT'S all . . .
          they know, now . . .

getting rid o' wet lungs can be slow, now
going off the machine is a "no," now
that his lungs were just fine was a faux, now

a possible thing could explain it
it's simple and sensible, ain't it?
just hope that the drugs will help drain it
the bug has a name, please retain it:

(chorus 4)
it's
pneumonia . . .

pneumonia . . .

is jackson getting pneumonia?
if jackson gets pneumonia
i'll E-mail, rather than phone ya

let's give three cheers for the medical staff
'cause this medical staff is a staff and a half
it's because they are there that i'm able to laugh
yes, i'm able to cheer, chide and cheekily chaff

and after you cheer will you throw in a root
for the cute little foot in the baby blue boot?
to the pup who can poop (though he can't seem
     to "poot")
please send a pneumonial prayer and salute

B.D. WONG

to jackson, to jackson, a fighter named foo
and richie my sweet,
      often worried and blue:
send your love
      via phone,
          Ɛ-mail,
            face to face . . .
say " 'fore you can blink won't be nary a trace . . ."

(final chorus to richie!)
of pneumonia . . .

pneumonia . . .

you and me seen way worse than pneumonia.

if i was afraid

of pneumonia,

                    **185**

i would never have

sown ya

ta

clone ya.

i love you!

(the end)

keep those Ɛ-mails and website guestbook entries
coming!

got a message for shauna? Ɛ-mail her! (see website)

new webpages/pics as soon as uncle barry has a
day off!!!

http://www.geocities.com/jacksonfoowong/

(over a thousand hits! goin' for two!)

XOXOX :-)

Once again, closet poets "came out" . . .

**Pneumonia they can cure and that is a fact,**
**It is amazing how it is done.**
**The doctors and nurses work and act,**
**So someday Jackson and his Dads will jointly have fun.**

**OK so it is crummy poetry, but is our way of wishing you all**
**well.**

> · **PHIL** and **RUTHE BERMAN** are Richie's oldest friend Julie's parents. Many, many people Forwarded Foo to their Folks.

**Sis Boom Bah! Go Jackson, Go Jackson Go Fah!**
**(that's New Jersey for Far!)**
**With love from back east, we're cheering you on!**
**That your new little lungs will be kept safe from harm!**
**And your Dads with and without hair love you soo much . . .**

**B.D. WONG**

and with prayers, and kisses and a little bit of luck . . .
you'll be healthy and ready to come on home . . .
and none of us will ever, ever leave ya alone!

Love jayne and her boyz here in weston.

- (JAYNE ATKINSON)

Tidbits:

Well . . . kudos, B.D, on rhyming "pneumonia" with "prima
don-ya." *That's* skill . . .

—Reiko

- **REIKO AYLESWORTH** *is an actor. And just for the record, I know sarcasm when I see it.*

Thanks for the updates and tell little Jackson to get rid of
the fluid! (I can't stand phlegmy singers!)

Love,
Seth

- **SETH RUDETSKY** *is a pianist, composer, writer, performer, vocal coach, talk-show host, and television correspondent.*

Lorenz Hart better look to his laurels. Wow!

Peter N. PS I see Kevin Kline. . . .

- (PETER NEUFELD)

. . . I GIVE THANKS TO THE STARS AND THE HEAVENS OF THE
UNIVERSE FOR THE VICTORY THAT IS COMING.

Love, Rigel

- **RIGEL SPENCER** *is an old old friend from high school days, and a mother of two.*

I knew there was a musical in this somewhere. Richie was SO touched, and from the reactions of everyone else around me (at the office) who was able to "sing along" yesterday, you've again succeeded in putting a song in our step and making sure that no matter what plunge we are about to take as the ride continues on, there will always be that smile about to form at the corner of our lips . . .

- (MARC AYRIS)

New E-mails from old friends . . .

**Dear B.D. & Richie,**

What an amazing time you've been through, and how wonderful that you're emerging with your love and optimism even stronger. Your beautiful baby boy is a miracle which reaffirms all the important and vital things in life, and the sacrifice which his brother made is a testament to the power of love . . .

**Love,**
**Noah, Kathryn, and David**

- **DAVID HENRY HWANG** *is a Tony Award—winning playwright, a screenwriter, and now, with his wife, Kathryn Layng, the father of Noah and Eva.*

**Dearest B.D. and Richie,**

I turned on my laptop to check the usual porno/junk/circular/friends you've never heard of stuff and here is a tale that has everything. I remember a wonderful dinner at your apartment, and the conversation drifting around the subject of parenthood . . .

. . . but here you are . . . with this blessed bundle, this jewel of life at the centre of your world. I am so thrilled for

*B.D. WONG*

you both, as is Jill. Thank you for letting us know all about this joyous event . . .

- **ALFRED MOLINA** *is a Tony Award—winning actor. Can you hear his calming British accent?*

**Luvah Daddy, Luvah Daddy, Luvah Daddy!!!!!!!!**
**Just got back to New Zealand yesterday, which is where I left my computer . . . I've been sitting at my computer for the last two hours, cheering and laughing and crying hysterically and then cheering and laughing all over again . . . WOW! . . .**

**Ginaxoxoxoxoxoxoxoxoxoxoxox**

And then she went directly to the Web site guestbook . . .

**Dear Sweet Angel, WELCOME!!!!!! Your courage and light are inspiring to all that have heard your story. I can't wait to lay eyes on you and whisper into your tiny little ears, how beautiful and smart you are to have chosen such two adoring and nurturing parents, who happen to be armed with the FIERCEST ARMY of LOVE, aka: friends and family, on the planet. By the way, I'm your "Titi G." I keep the world safe from evil in rubber hot pants. That's my day job. We'll share secrets on chafing prevention when you get a little older. In the meantime, you have all of my love and hope and prayers. I'm so happy you're here kiddo, you're going to teach us a lot.**

**Love, Titi G xoxoxoxoxoxoxoxox**

- **GINA TORRES** *is an actor and dear friend. At this time in television history, Gina was shooting in New Zealand, earning a respectable living on one of those "Amazon War Princess"—type shows. "Luvah" is the Cuban beauty's nickname for me.*

Oh my God. I just read all the E-mails. Daddy!!!!! You are so amazing. I am so excited. I don't know what to say. I love you. Welcome Jackson! He is the luckiest boy in the world. So incredible. I am rooting. I am loving. I am so proud of you. Love, Margaret

> • **MARGARET CHO** *is an actor, comic, author, and yet another performer who has played my sister, and another of the funniest people I have ever met.*

Another "counter-date" from Roz in Santa Monica:

. . . He's a lucky guy to have you and Richie as parents . . . Try to stay away from the milk freezer though. I'm not letting you within ten feet of ours!

I love your treatise on worry . . . now that you are a parent, you will never be worry free. But it's a delicious worry. It's a privilege to worry. Even when you have nothing to worry about . . . you will worry.
My current list of worries includes . . .

Is Isabelle eating too often?
Is Roland eating too little?
What teacher will Roland get next year?
How will Isabelle react to her shots next week?
Does Simon drive too fast when he's alone with the kids in the car?
Should Roland be playing with the rough ten-year-old who lives down the street?
That's just the tip of the iceberg.

Last night I awoke with the awareness that Roland doesn't know what to do in case of a fire. And I'm not even considered a neurotic mom . . . . . I'm calm, cool, and collected!!! Worry is part of our repertoire as parents . . .

> • (ROSALIND CHAO)

*B.D. WONG*

Caregiver Corner:

**Don't get discouraged! I know the waiting is the worst part of all this—but try to remember that you are watching this little man who should still be invisible to you, swimming inside Shauna's belly. It's not as comfy for him to be out of his own private Kabuki "hot tub"—and that's what causes all the stressful events. But he's just working hard to get up to his due date, and the waiting is simply built in to that!**

**Joan (occasionally, one of JFW's nurses)**

- **JOAN BENEDUSI** *is a neonatal nurse at UCSF ICN, and one of Jackson's "primaries."*

**. . . Reading this is making me start to feel sad that I am going off service even though I will have much more free time. But I will certainly check on Jackson and come visit— at least every other day or so—**
**And of course if either of you need anything—another person to explain—etc—i'll give you my pager**
**And I almost forgot to thank you sooo much for the very nice part in the last scene of Jackson's play/life. It was an honor to be mentioned and I appreciate it. THANK YOU**

**—STACE**

- **(DR. STACEY LEVITT.** <u>*She's* thanking *me*.</u>**)**

More from the Web site guestbook . . .

**. . . We had only a small taste of the test you are enduring, but we know what it is to fight for a child. There is agony in watching the object of such overwhelming love wobble as he struggles to find the balance that will carry him on his way. But suddenly it is there, unmistakably. Don't let the wobbles get you down. This kid fights. This kid endures. He**

knows what he is doing. And he has you, my God, what a blessing. Just keep blowing on the little spark, gently. All our love, Bradley, Jane, Frances, and Jumbo George.

- (*Not since Lucy and Ricky:* Emmy-winning actor **BRADLEY WHITFORD** *plays Josh Lyman on* The West Wing, *multiple-Emmy-nominee* **JANE KAZMAREK** *stars on* Malcolm in the Middle. *In my opinion they are being modest, because they indeed moved heaven and earth to give birth to both their beautiful Frances and George as well as their newest little Mary Louisa.*)

Jackson, your struggle to get into this world and your incredible determination to stay here (dammit!) is cool squared. That and your dads' iron bond of love have made my heart sing with joy in celebrating the magnificent boundlessness of the human spirit. I am humbled to have witnessed your journey thus far. Your dads and I met in a restaurant in Los Angeles last fall, when you and Boaz were mere twinkles in their eyes. They spoke with such joy of having met Shauna and were thrilled to begin their journey of bringing you into this nutty place. The next time I saw your dads, you had just made your first trip to West Hollywood (it was about my 10,000th, but that's another posting). You and Boaz had just taken up residence in Shauna and were causing her to consume a great variety of pizzas that night. Kelly and I were thrilled to place our hands on her tummy and know that you were there. This week, we begin the same journey (once again). We pray to have half the perseverance and gumption that you and your dads have shown in guiding you through yours. While a lot of people crave an easy-to-follow plot, we all know the best stories are character driven. If they gave Oscars for life, you, Boaz, and your dads would all split the vote. Daily prayers go up for you, little one, from all across the country. You've somehow managed to expand our souls.

- (**BILL WALKER**. *We were really rooting for he and Kelly to get "pregnant"*).

**B.D. WONG**

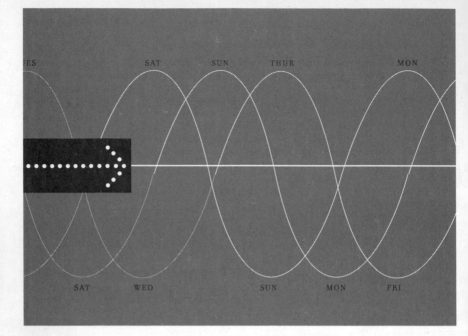

# UPDATE #7

SUBJECT:
"HARRY POTTER
*ƐAT* YOUR HEART OUT"

JULY 7, 2000
(TEN DAYS LATER)

at the TV tray-Z-boy, and in the ICN deep into the night

## << "TOLERATING THE FEEDINGS" >>
a
discussion
of
degustation
and
deglutition

**by B.D.**

Walter Matthau died today and I cut my nails.

Morbid and cryptic, but the two facts do relate.

Whenever a famous person passes, I always think that two other famous people are going to go soon after, because people say that. They say it always happens in threes. I'm not sure whether this is a show business thing or what. Do any of you who are *not* in show business know about this?

When I noticed that Walter Matthau had died, I started playing that game where I guess who the other two might be, you know, who was *eligible* to go next. Then I realized that the only way I knew Walter Matthau had died is 'cause I saw it on the "welcome page" of America Online. As soon as you sign on to AOL, there's immediately an ad for some cheap digital camera, today's headlines, and a postage-stamp-sized photo of Britney Spears and her fantastic "barely legal" body (or whoever the "body of the moment" is) that pops up to distract you from your E-mail.

***B.D. WONG***

I thought, gee, I'll have to keep watching the welcome page of America Online, to see who the other two people are going to be . . .

That's when I realized I haven't read a newspaper, or watched the news, or even talked to Richie about what's been going on in the world, for almost *six weeks now.* I haven't a clue whether we like Bill Clinton again or not, or what community Giuliani has most recently alienated, or whether Elian Gonzales is *here* or *there,* or even if anyone still gives a rat's ass. I don't know what Broadway shows are opening, what's closing, who got all the parts that I auditioned for prior to May 28, and whether those people have been fired yet, or quit. Even *THAT* I don't know (like I usually do).

Since the end of May, I have spent my days going to the hospital, sleeping, writing, and corresponding on the computer . . . and *EATING.* That's pretty much it.

**197**

Well, I did cut my nails. I was at my mom and dad's house when I did this. While I was cutting them, I realized the last time I cut them I was at my mom and dad's house, and the time before that, I was at my mom and dad's house! I thought, land sakes, how long has this been going on? How long have I been living away from my *relatively* normal Manhattan home, switching over into "crisis management mode" as easily as if I had flipped the channel from *Everybody Loves Raymond* to *Third Watch?* I have completely lost all track of time and sense of any world other than my own (yeah, so what else is new, but this is *different,* all right?). I have been wearing the same handful of T-shirts, dingy work pants, and sweatshirts since I came up from L.A. to visit my mom and dad (and Shauna) on that fateful weekend when the boys were born, with a single carry-on bag, so long, long ago. Then, I suppose my maternal instinct kicked in (boys have them, too, you know) and made this all seem like the most normal thing in the world. It isn't until now, when Jackson seems to be a little more stable and I can breathe, that I realize how crazy my life these days has become.

So let's get down to it. Sometime after our last update the doctors decided to discontinue feeding the star of this show for a while. He just wasn't quite getting the hang of pooping or farting regularly, and an X ray showed a slight edema, or swelling, in his intestines. Was the surgery unsuccessful after all? Was he having a new bout with that as-horrible-as-it-sounds *necrotizing enterocoliti*s or NEC (which required surgery two endless weeks prior)? Stacey Levitt called me on the phone herself, which she rarely does, and made sure to say, "Don't worry! Don't worry! Nothing's wrong! Nothing's wrong!" as soon as I picked up, just in case the mere sound of her voice might send me into another tailspin (which is actually not entirely inaccurate). She just wanted to report that until further notice, no more feeds, though he had been tolerating the feedings fine. "Don't *worry*, we'll just *wait*." Now, I just laugh when they say that. Worry *and* wait? Pshaw! You try it! Try doing the waiting without doing the worrying in anything that's remotely important to you. I'm sure those people in *Cirque du Soleil* can do it. They can do anything. They can touch their freaking butts to their heads. But *I'm* just a *NORMAL* person.

Then there came the "wet lungs" thing, and then pneumonia reared its uncomely noggin, and that led to the antibiotics and increased Lasix to try and get him to pee out all the extra wetness in his lungs and water-weight-gain. His breathing, though still on relatively low ventilator settings, was a little labored and he de-satted pretty regularly. Though this is not particularly threat-

198

**B.D. WONG**

ening, it's just awful to be there beside him when he begins innocently de-satting and watch the pretty, benignly emerald green light on his monitor turn into the nightmarish, flashing-siren red, with the ominous, repeating, electronic beeptone, signaling his inability to maintain supplying a sufficient amount of oxygen in his bloodstream. In the last week this has happened quite a bit. Even though the doctors and nurses are still somewhat reassuring, you just don't want to see it. Jackson's Grandpa Wong has always been hypnotized by the saturation monitor. He sits in a chair directly in front of it, staring at it, watching the digital read-out as the numbers go up and down. When it is red and the number is 79 or below, he leans toward the isolette and says, "Up up up, Jackson, you can do it!" and as soon as it turns, at 80, he says **"Hooray!!! Good boy!!! *GREEN NUMBERS!!!*"** I laugh at him, and yet, inside I feel no differently.

199

So discontinuing Jackson's feeds was really a bummer, and I have finally put my finger on why, aside from my understandable anxiety over him getting well. You see, as I sit here writing to you, I am feeling distended in my own stomach. I have done nothing but eat the most unbelievably satisfying home-cooked food at my mother's dining room table since the end of May.

Food in the Wong family is a sacred and nurturing ritual. It symbolizes the personification of the idea of a close-knit family, and of the spanning of many generations, to us. Not only am I being cooked for at Mom's house, but at my brother's, Jackson's Uncle Barry's, house as well. Barry, an S.F. fireman, is as unbelievable a cook as my mom (as well as a computer genius). I cannot properly express how important food is in my family. We sit down to a spread at an average lunch, and spin the lazy Susan until the plates and bowls are a blur. When it finally stops, the plates and bowls are full of bones and seeds and skins. Then, while we eat and talk and laugh and make fun of each other, we ALWAYS plan and talk about what to have for *dinner.* Whenever I am away from home, I sometimes forget exactly how intense the food experience is. So for our son to be deprived of the measly 2cc of breast milk he was being fed, well, that just hurts. It just 'tain't natural for a son o' mine. Sassy nurse Sue DeHaan always razzes us, because whenever we come up to visit Jackson, we are always off somewhere afterward to have some huge meal. "Don't you people do anything but eat?" she says, incredulously and enviously.

I look at my parents. My parents look at me.

"No," we shrug.

I know a lot of you are *vegans* or whatever, or if you are like dear Shauna (bearer not only of the boy but of his breast milk breakfasts, don't forget), you don't really care for food that is *not* from a chain restaurant. However, for the rest of you folk who have what I consider "normal" culinary tastes, here's what we're talking about: the first day Jackson was fed Mom and Dad and I just had to go right out for steaming, heaping bowls of wonton soup smothered in Chinese beef stew flavored with star anise, accompanied by broad rice noodles stir-fried with red peppers, jalapeños, and sliced flank steak. I already told you that on the night we found out Jackson's heart was "normal," Mom made her famous tacos. What I didn't tell you was that I ate at least five. Plus a chicken tamale. Plus a beef enchilada. My brother has cooked for us so many times, the dishes and the meals all blur into one tremendous sadomasochistic food orgy: spare ribs in fermented tofu sauce, a rosemary-rubbed pork loin roast, killer marinated Korean short ribs, steamed catfish with black bean sauce. Even his "door slammers" (his firehouse term for one-step oven meals) are so much more than your average thrown-together affairs. Then there's my mom's brother, the great Uncle Ray (a California high school culinary careers teacher, of course), and my Auntie Karen, who sat Richie and I down to a meal right out of the *Martha Stewart's Kitchen* Cape Cod Summer Episode: salmon tartare and a mountain of caviar to start, a two-and-a-half-pound lobster on every plate (the lobsters were easily bigger than our son!), sweet white corn on the cob, velvety garlic mashed potatoes, and homemade blueberry cheesecake.

I write these detailed "E-meals" to relate to you the care and calculation that went into them. They were brief episodes in my and Richie's day altruistically designed to divert and calm and nourish the most terrified and weary of souls. I highly recommend this technique. It's right up there with sending loving, bright-light-energy electronic letters, phone messages, and pep talks, like all of you out there have been doing. Between these methods, we have gathered superhuman strength. Not to mention from the delicacies and treats we have been sent in the mail! God puts love in dried figs and bagels and butter cookies, believe you me. As you might imagine, I have literally been scarfing the energy and strength from the *heart* of all this food. Sucking the life force from these generous gifts so I can breathe deeply enough to cope with all the stress. Inhaling, if you will. At least until the Chestnut Man can do a little "inhaling" of his own.

So now I'm a fat pig.

Needless to say, Jackson is no fat pig. Yet. He looks more like the *poussin* that you pass over at the poultry counter because the drumsticks are too skinny. The closest thing he's gotten to being a "fat pig" is an incredible jump in weight gain of 6 ounces in one night last week. Sounds great for a little Chestnut like himself, but everyone was somewhat perplexed and alarmed. The doctors suspected that he was gaining and holding on to an incredible amount of fluids, not only in his lungs, but now all over, and so they increased his Lasix and cut back on all his sodium.

So no more tummy food for the Foo Man, for the time being. Back to relying on the clinical hospital diet of Hyperal (it's not a Jim Carrey character, it's really a sickening-looking yellow kind of "preemie Gatorade") fed through the not-terribly-tasty I.V. tube.

**202** Jackson also started to check off of the shrinking list another set of organs waiting to be found A-OK: the other day the ophthalmologist paid a visit. He looked like the lyricist David Zippel (I am sure this is a request from Boaz for another song) and was armed with an alarmingly humorless associate and a tiny metal medieval torture apparatus which he would insert under Jackson's eyelids while he examined his eyeballs. You always know you're in trouble when the doctor says to you ever-so-casually as he washes his hands, "Have you ever seen this procedure done before?" When they ask you that, believe me, they'd rather you didn't watch. That's 'cause they don't want you to faint and slam your head on the linoleum and bleed all over the floor. They hate it when that happens. Either that or you attack them.

Defiantly, I witnessed the procedure with a macabre fascination I haven't experienced since my nephew

Joshua's *bris* (circumcision, you Gentile). Only there were no cold cuts after. Doc was looking for the blood vessels to grow to the edge of the retina, and they were almost there. "Great," I say. "Thank God! . . . Doctor, thank you *so much*!"

Then I tried to explain this to Richie on the phone:

                          B.D.
                (enthusiastically)
        Honey, the doctor said that
        the blood vessels are almost
        to the edge of the retina!

                        RICHIE
                (relieved)
        Oh! So Jackson will eventu-
        ally be able to see, right?

                          B.D.
                (pause, then)
        He said that the blood vessels
        are almost to the edge of the
        retina.

                      RICHIE
             (beat, then, confused)
        So that's good, right?

                        B.D.
              (definitively)
             *Yes.*

                      RICHIE
             (panicked)
    WILL HE BE ABLE TO SEE?

```
                    (pause)

                         B.D.
                    (enthusiastically)
            He said that the blood vessels
            are almost to the edge of the
            retina!!! . . .
```

Then, a week later, right when I got the hang of looking at the outcome of the eye exam as positive, I find out that he's due for another one. See, they don't prepare you for a *series* of eye exams. They only barely prepare you for the one that's *the next day.*

Then, they hope they won't be on duty when you find out it's a whole damn "To Be Continued," FOUR-PART MINISERIES.

**204**    **"Natal Vision."**

Last Wednesday, June 28, was Jackson's official one-month birthday. Isn't that a trip? Time sure flies when you've only got a handful of T-shirts and a few pairs of dingy work pants. Furthermore, I think it's only fair on your one-month birthday, if you've been fasting, that you should get some grub, especially when you're in MY family. The doctors agreed. The latest X ray showed less intestinal edema, perhaps because of the Lasix, or just time passing after the surgery, so they decided to start feeds again, ever so slowly. Again 2cc, which is less than half a teaspoon, every two hours, through a tiny tube going down into his stomach, starting at 2:30 P.M.

Ironically, that same afternoon my father received a phone call from a staff member at my grandmother's senior-care home on the outskirts of Chinatown. Grandma was refusing to eat! Maybe Dad would try to persuade her to accept nourishment on his next visit. Eating is of course as crucial to a one-month-old preemie as it is to his one-month-shy-of-ninety-eight-year-old great-grandmother . . .

Meanwhile, I was off on another Hollywood caper. The movie flew me down on Friday morning for a crazy day and night of shooting at a sleazy motel in the desert (a lot of sleazy locations in this movie, I know). I only overheard my father's end of the conversation from my grandma's social worker as I was once again getting ready to fly down to L.A.

My paternal grandmother (my *"Ngin-Ngin"*) is a remarkable symbol to me of my own Chinese-ness (as my mom's mom also continues to be, even after her death in 1995). The amazing sacrifices and hardships my grandmothers both endured to benefit future generations that they would never even know are as life-sustaining to me as the recipes they passed down to us. My father's amazing role as Ngin-Ngin's One and Only Chinese Son, particularly in these latest years, was the classic example of that sometimes cliché Chinese tradition: a son's life lived in deferential, respectful service to his parent. Dad was already planning his weekly visit to the feisty matriarch; this Friday morning he went with his sleeves rolled up. But the #1 Son (and only child) was unsuccessful. Not surprisingly, she dramatically and unreasonably wouldn't let Dad get a morsel into her stomach, spitting out food and throwing it against the wall. Later my dad and mom learned that doctors had discovered some sort of internal, perhaps intestinal bleeding, because she had blood in the stool in her diapers. Maybe she was refusing to eat because it was painful. It is impossible to gauge, for she has not been "all there" for many years now.

Friday, two days later, Jackson was much more easily fed than his great-grandma; his feeds had gone quietly and uneventfully for forty-eight hours. So well that at 2:00 P.M. the doctors decided to begin slowly *increasing* the volume of his feeds, 1cc per twelve-hour shift. When he got to 16 ccs, it would be considered "full feeds" for his weight. His stomach seemed strong, his intestines seemed to be healed, and his disposition was, as always, serene and tolerant. Just like his great-grandma (his *"Tai-Ngin"*), he had had traces of blood in his stool in his diapers (post-bowel surgery) but they were no more . . .

On Saturday morning, by the 2:00 A.M. feeding, they had doubled his volume: 4 ccs and counting! If all continued so sweetly, by the same time the following Thursday he would be getting the full 16cc.

**206**  Then Life did that little sleight of hand that she sometimes does which makes her such a popular party guest, and she showed everyone what she was all about.

Only a couple of hours later, at a little after 4:00 A.M. on Saturday, July 1, 2000, just as he hit his gastronomic stride, Jackson Foo Wong's great-grandmother Tom Shee Wong passed him the torch, passed away, and booked passage to Heaven . . .

. . . where the food is even better than it is here. In fact, I'm positive that Boaz was waiting just inside the pearly gates, flipping thru the skinny ***ZagatSurvey 2000: HEAVEN*** book in a dutiful Chinese great-grandson's preparation for her arrival.

I'm sure it's no accident that I was at the Los Angeles house when my brother Barry called early Saturday morning and told me this, awakening me in a bedroom

*B.D. WONG*

furnished with all of the furniture from Ngin-Ngin's old Chinatown flat. Her deco bed and matching nightstand, armoire, and chair suddenly vibrated with even more resonance than I have always imbued them with. The face in the huge portrait of her late husband on top of the armoire smirked stoically. They were together again at long, long last.

The only thing I could think to do was to light every candle in the house. Which, let me tell ya, is a lot of candles. In the living room is a painting of Ngin-Ngin's mother-in-law, Jackson's great-great-grandmother, **my** "*Tai-Ngin,*" another "tough cookie" as my dad says, and I lit the candles around her (the earliest ancestor who I have an image of), in a kind of altar. I found a small, silly old red candle, already half burned, in the shape of a heart, and it became the centerpiece of the shrine. I had thought it would put itself out after a few hours, but it burned steadfastly for so long (just like she did) that the car service had to turn back on the way to the airport (4:00 P.M.) because I had forgotten, and frankly was reluctant to, extinguish it myself. I considered allowing it to burn away to nothing, but Richie would have murdered me when he found out if I had. (Everyone at the New York office of Innovative Artists is laughing now: they all got the Richie Jackson "no more candles memo"). So I told her I loved her and softly blew it out, while the car idled outside.

I became very nostalgic not only about Ngin-Ngin and her furniture but about the tiny cottage that we have rented in L.A. since I worked on the sitcom *All-American Girl,* which all the furniture is in. It will be time for me to let that go very soon, too, I'm guessin'. It is a hideaway "bachelor's" guest house, not really a single-family dwelling. There has been so much time spent there, mostly with Richie back home in New York, my only company often our trusty Keeshond Rhodar, who was recently adopted by our next-door neighbors when we renovated our now dog-unfriendly N.Y. apartment. Rhodar *loved* being in that little green house with me! She was born in 1985, making her my "oldest living relative" (if you can count our canine friends), even including the ninety-seven-year-old Ngin-Ngin! Ngin-Ngin's passing immediately began that slide presentation of memories, and while in that house, the memories were very specific.

"Hey, Life, do some more of those tricks!"

The movie company, which as you know has been unbelievably supportive, flew me down early Friday morning to work on Friday and Monday. In the middle of Friday they decided that the person driving "my" truck in the scene to be shot on Monday would never be visible on camera. They elected to use a driving double, and cut me loose for Monday. As soon as Barry called me about Ngin-Ngin on Saturday morning, I was able to make immediate arrangements to fly home so I could be with my dad. This is the third or fourth time that the movie has serendipitously allowed real life to take precedence over cinematic. Hooray for Hollywood. Many outrageous things happened on the set, but I will restrain myself from going into them all since they don't directly relate to Jackson.

On Sunday or Monday, I called Richie on the cell phone while we're all in the car (probably on our way to go eat lunch). Richie says, "Are you ready for more bad news?"

I had not been to or talked with the hospital recently (and I hadn't auditioned for anything in a while, usually a set-up for *some* kind of actor's disappointment or another), so I panicked. I took a deep breath, and lied.

"Yes. What is it."

"They had to put Rhodar to sleep."

**<< *Oh!* >>**

Poor, sweet, Rhodar Jean, the Keeshond. My mom was very upset, and she *hates* dogs.

Seems Rhodar wasn't eating at the end, either.

---

**Boaz Dov Wong (2000—2000)**

**Tom Shee Wong (1902—2000)**

**Rhodar Jackson-Aalan-Anderson-Weill-Wong (1985—2000)**

---

I guess it really does "happen in threes."

Richie and I are planning to celebrate Boaz's brief life with family and friends during Jackson's "coming home" party. (When that may be, we still don't know.)

I'm not sure if the adoring adoptive next-door neighbors, Maxine and Wendell, always so loving and patient, will be having anything for Rhodar.

The memorial service for Ngin-Ngin happened Wednesday, July 5, the day I am writing this part, and was as kaleidoscopic an experience for me as all of these last indescribable weeks that I have spent here in this great hometown o' mine have been.

This morning I got up and tried to continue working on this update for you all. (I know it's really for ME, but please let me keep pretending it's for YOU.) I got all dressed up in a black suit that I had forgotten I had left at Mom and Dad's house a long time ago and Mom had dug out. My dad sat in the La-Z-Boy opposite mine and started talking.

First he asked me where we got the name Boaz. I had told him once before, but he really seemed to want to get the facts right. I told him it was from the Old Testament, and Boaz's middle name, Dov, was Hebrew for "peace." Dad reminisced that my older brother Brian's nickname was "Bobo," or "Bo." Bo would sometimes torture my younger brother Barry, by calling him "Barris." When Barry got older, he retaliated by calling Brian "Bois" (rhymes with Lois).

Dad had thought we had named the baby **Bois,** and that it was a Wong family inside joke!

Then he talked about Ngin-Ngin, and his sometimes difficult relationship with her. He talked about the Chinese Son, and the burdens He bears that are born from tradition. He talked about his mother sacrificing her education and working so that her younger siblings could go to school. Coming over on a boat as a teenager, working in a sweatshop knitting socks. How hers was one of the first Chinatown factories whose employees became members of the International Ladies Garment Workers Union.

Then, as his emotions sounded like they might strangle him, and I feebly tried to hold him, and he let out only what he could, I thought I could feel those burdens slowly unwinding themselves from his heart.

It may not surprise you to hear that the Wong family spent most of the day of Ngin-Ngin's memorial service

EATING. At 11:30 A.M. my parents and I met my older brother Brian, sister-in-law Cindy, and my two nephews Evan and Will, at a restaurant called Gum San (Gold Mountain), for dim sum, with Cindy's mom, "Mama Gok." Brian and family had flown in from Seattle, like a tornado! Have you ever had dim sum, the Chinese tea lunch where they wheel the carts of 1001 kinds of dumplings around and you just point and eat? If you haven't, let's just say "restraint" isn't part of it. We were so stuffed, even though I was STILL FULL FROM THE NIGHT BEFORE. How stuffed was I? Well, I was so stuffed you had to sit on me to zip me up. Here's my new code word for overeating:

**"Get the check. I'm SAMSONITE!"**

Brian's family had also already eaten breakfast at the hotel, by the way, because it was, hmmm—how can I say this delicately?—**FREE.**

211

We rolled out of Gum San (Gold Mountain) and went right to the mortuary. The service was simple, and just right. Minister Norman Fong, who officiated at Barry and Doris's wedding, set just the right tone of respect and celebration. He had asked me to sing, but not only was I unprepared, I knew I wouldn't get through it. (I was surprised. Didn't Norman remember how I choked my way through Barry and Doris's nuptials?)

When Norman outlined the family tree, and listed Ngin-Ngin's six great-grandchildren, and ended with, ". . . and the newest addition, *Jackson . . .*" I felt a bittersweet chill of consanguine validation running up my spine that I was totally unprepared for.

I had volunteered to say something, in lieu of braying through a song. So Brian (the ex-doctor), and I (the actor), and Barry (the fireman), all in just that birth order, each said a few words.

When I got to the lectern, I don't know what came over me. I was so moved by my conversation with Dad, and hearing Norman tell even more about Ngin-Ngin's life; immigrating here to the "Gold Mountain" (Gum San!), the sacrifices, working in the sweatshop, joining the union, making ends meet, supporting the family, and her tirelessness, stubbornness, and relentlessness (even till the very last moments of her life), that I changed my mind, and sang.

I warned the congregation that what I was going to sing might seem really dumb, but that I thought that the words to the song were a fitting tribute to Ngin-Ngin's heroic life:

**LOOK FOR**

**THE UNION LABEL**

**WHEN YOU ARE BUYING**

**A COAT, DRESS OR BLOUSE.**

**REMEMBER, SOMEDAY,**

**OUR UNION SEWING,**

**OUR WAGES GROWING**

**TO FEED THE KIDS**

**AND RUN THE HOUSE**

**WE WORK HARD,**

*B.D. WONG*

**BUT WHO'S COMPLAINING?**

**FOR THROUGH THE UNION**

**WE'RE PAYING OUR WAY!**

**SO ALWAYS LOOK FOR . . .**

**. . . THE UNION LABEL . . .**

**IT SHOWS WE'RE ABLE**

# TO **MAKE IT**
# IN THE U.S.A.

213

After the service, Dad looked like he felt much better. Well, if he didn't, there was one last thing that, according to Chinese tradition, would help him with those last few blues:

A simple,
    Old-Fashioned,
        Seven-Course
            Chinese
                **BANQUET.**

So at 3:00 in the afternoon, everyone who had been to the service was invited to an "early dinner"; an after-funeral "so chan," which consisted of the following:

*FOLLOWING FOO*

海鮮拼盤　鮑魚粉絲湯　脆皮乳豬　薑蔥雞　炒三鮮　松仁炒蝦球　羅漢齋

1. Jellyfish salad tossed in sesame dressing, surrounded by Chinese cold cuts

2. Abalone and Glass noodle soup

3. Roast Pig (with an absolutely celestial crispy skin)

4. Warm poached chicken dressed with slivers of green onion and ginger-infused oil

5. Sauteed snap peas, mushrooms, and scallops

6. Jumbo prawns stir-fried with pine nuts

7. Monk's Vegetables Medley

Before the meal, Dad asked everyone at each of the five huge round tables to join hands. My whole childhood we never said grace or gave thanks before we ate. It was during this miraculous summer that my family began practicing this humble and important ritual. I will always remember what Dad said, for again I received that flutter of bittersweet validation that I haven't ever felt before, and may never again.

He said, "Let us all join hands and give thanks for the bounty of which we are about to partake, and to celebrate the life of Tom Shee Wong, **and Boaz Dov Wong** . . ."

. . . whose "energy," he continued, "shines down upon us . . ."

". . . so that we can live our lives with grace, gusto, and glory."

**B.D. WONG**

This, of course, is why he was asking me about how to say Boaz's name early that morning. I am ashamed to remember that I thought he was just being "dizzy."

By the way, the man practices what he preaches.

Grace. Gusto. Glory.

One more thing: that wasn't our last meal of the day. When we got back to the house at around 7:00 P.M., my mom rushed out to get a "snack," which consisted of two absurdly heaping orders of beef chow fun, since she thought we "might be hungry."

I told her she was completely out of her mind, and then I ate three helpings. Give me a break, it was a stressful day.

As I write this sentence, it just happens to be early Thursday, at a quarter to two in the morning. I'm at the hospital, writing to you. In fifteen minutes, Jackson will finally be given that first "full feed": 16cc of 100%, grade AAA, organic, precious, unpasteurized, no preservatives added, painstakingly frozen and thawed (and *organized*), priceless, whole, hearty, heavenly, medicinal *MILK*.

Atta boy, son. There's the Wong family spirit.

So before he eats this milestone meal, let *ME* give thanks:

I am thankful for this First Full Feed.

May there always be food as long as he is hungry.

I am thankful for the gift of this child who is about to receive it.

He has made me a better man even before he has taken his first truly independent breath.

May he grow big and strong so that I may learn more about myself, about life. (I gotta hand it to ya, God, this course is pretty interesting. Sign me up for next semester; if I pass the final.)

I am thankful he is well enough today to consume it.

To his health: may it continue to improve, so he may soon spin Grandma Wong's lazy Susan with the rest of us fat pigs.

Last, but not least, I am so ever, profoundly thankful for Fatherhood.

I pray that I could

>           might

>                   will just be

*half* the father

and

*half* the son

that my own father is.

amen

**B.D. WONG**

I forgot to mention that Ngin-Ngin was old enough to be Walter Matthau's mother. Now *THAT'S OLD!*

At this very moment, Jackson's doing better and better every day. The Lasix and antibiotics seem to be working; he has just finished his course of antibiotics and his lungs look and sound much clearer. (But I may never have the satisfaction of knowing *exactly* what it was: Pneumonia or not . . . ARGH.)

"onward, Jackson rooters . . ."

Now, I am writing this last part at the hospital, where I have just held his *sixth* "full feed"!

Glug,
     glug,
          glug,
               down it goes into the tube.

Glug,
     glug,
          glug, with ***grace, gusto, and glory.***

**217**

***Chinese food, anyone?***

love, b.d.

Uncle Barry put some neat new stuff up!

*http://www.geocities.com/jacksonfoowong/*

Maybe for the first time in my life, the responses we got to this update made me feel like a real writer. I've always had a love-hate relationship with writing, but after ⟨**Update #7**⟩, I never again felt like I had something private inside me that no one appreciated.

Here are some reasons why. I have taken these out and put them back into this section of the book over and over. Yeah, yeah, yeah, it's a big pat on my own back. But my writer's confidence is also a plot point in this story, and I didn't find this confidence by writing alone; I found it by reading what others wrote:

**"you made me cry . . . in a great way."**
                                    **—joe redmond**

**"an eastern *Like Water For Chocolate* . . ."**
                                    **—walter kerr**

**"wonderful"**
                    **—me again**

**still rootin, I love you, joe**

> • **JOE REDMOND** *is a Broadway propmaster who (and I just love telling people this), is married to Elaine, a Radio City Rockette!*

**Dear B.D.—You deal with all this serious stuff like Jean Kerr writing one of her lovely good-humored 60s & 70s short essays. Good for you! Or are you STILL too young to know**

who Jean Kerr is besides being Walter's wife. . . . . By the way, I hate to break it to you, but there AREN'T any people who are not in show business. I've explored this thoroughly and I know I'm right.

L, Neufeld

- **(PETER NEUFELD.** *From Broadway manager to propmaster,* no one *will ever forget the great Walter Kerr.***)**

That was absolutely, inexpressibly beautiful.

You have the true writer's gift . . .

- **MICHAEL CUMPSTY** *is a much greater actor than I will ever be a writer. Or an actor, for that matter.*

. . . your writing is incredible. I've always known that and so have you . . .

- **LAURIE-ANN BARBOUR** *was in my kindergarten class. She is my longest friend. We literally learned our ABC's together.*

. . . Someday Jackson will have all of it to read. "My crazy dads," he'll say, "look at what BD was telling his friends when I was pulling it all together in that incubator . . ." and he'll smile, smile, smile.

So after all that talk we've jawed through, about how we both should be writing more, you're DOING it, you're writing after all, something much more valid than any damn musical comedy . . .

Wow!

Love, WB

- **WAYNE BARKER** *is a pianist and composer, and one of my best friends.*

On grandmas, food, fathers, and dogs:

1. **How do you manage to stay so cheerful?**

2. **How jealous I was to hear about all that good food! Can your mom adopt me, just for a weekend, so I can come over to your house and eat? I got homesick for Chinatown all over again. I started thinking about a certain mussels and clams in black bean sauce I used to drive all the way from Davis to get . . .**

Then, I got to thinking about how all that black bean sauce would make anyone see the better side of things. I'm sorry to hear about Gramma Wong; Gramma Hildebrande (Mom's mom) was also 98 when she decided it was time to hang up her hat. She was lucid until the last, except for a few small bouts of speaking to me in her native Lithuanian from time to time, of which I know not one word. I have her photo albums from her days as a silent film actress and I realize over and over again how little we can understand of the lives of that immigrant generation; the bravery it must have taken to rebuild a new life in a new country with a new language. I'm in awe these days of a lot of things, especially courage. Gramma Wong obviously passed a lot of hers to you . . . And just remember, when the going gets tough, the tough go eat . . .

  • (KARYN WAGNER)

. . . Thank-you also for the glimpse into Jackson's heritage as well as his future. What a wonderful gift a child could have, to have a family like this. My own children remember their paternal grandma by her Dutch songs, cooking, religion, and forwardness. It gives them something tangible to wrap their memories around. It gives them a past identity

**B.D. WONG**

and helps them to form a clearer picture of who they are . . .

> · **SUZANNE LANG**, *neonatal nurse, Modesto, California, was probably Jackson's first.*

I never had the pleasure of meeting your grandmother, but Rhodar was certainly a dear over the years—and how it got to be FIFTEEN YEARS is beyond me . . .

. . . Jesus H. Christ, after all of this, the sex talk and the don't-do-drugs talk will be a walk in the park for you guys . . .

> · **SHAWN POWERS** *is the director of education for a regional performing arts center.*

I loved Rhodar!! I'm so sorry. I remember taking care of her in LA. She was the cutest, especially when she pooped.

Thinking about you,
Jewdy

> · **JUDY GOLD** *is a comic, a writer, a comic writer, an actor, and a Jew.*

. . . Just f.y.i., this greek american from queens can relate to the food thing big time! I have shed a tear for Rhodar (who i first met in the lobby of Rubin Residence Hall in 1986) i have sworn ever since, if ever i got a dog it would be a "Rhodar" (i.e. keeshond) . . .

> · **DEAN MICHAELS I**s a *(my, our) business manager. He went to NYU with Richie.*

Dear Fahito,

. . . your account of your family and its traditions awakened a strong sense of my own ethnic roots and so if you don't mind, from this point on, at least for today, I will address you as Falafel . . .

. . . Stay as strong and funny and profoundly wise as you are.

<< I knew you'd be a great daddy.>>

I Love you and the baby, Taco

- **TARO MEYER**, *who I affectionately address as "Taco" due to an unfortunate (and alas, intentional) typographical error, is a producer, manager and mother. I would worry about offending her with this nickname, but you know how I feel about tacos.*

Thanks for reminding me of so many things . . . . . but especially (today) how wonderful it is to be part of a Chinese family.

- **CHRISTINE TOY JOHNSON** *is an actor and singer.*

. . . I share your appreciation for your father . . . I was so moved when I saw his scrapbook with every single picture and thank you note I had ever sent . . . Amazing . . .

- **MARK LEONG** *is my cousin, and now, through the miracle of surrogacy, the father, with partner Jay Nagdimon, of Corinne.*

On life, going on:

. . . yes, i've finally gotten good in the play. thank you for the sweet words. it was hard because you may have heard that during rehearsals jay had a series of strokes. it was a bad time for a while, but he is walking and trying to play tennis and is delivering once again his 35-year-old jokes, so that is progress . . .

- **BARBARA BARRIE**, *Oscar-nominated actor and Passover seder host; wife of Jay Harnick.*

I am in Oklahoma, where my family lives . . . and my grandmother died last night. Again, no coincidence that I was here with my family when this happened . . . to hear your words through the experience was such an example of the fact that we are surrounded by "noncoincidence" . . . God bless you. I will continue to look at your updates and the humor you have found beneath the stress . . . You were clearly born to be a Dad . . . With my love, Sam

- **SAM HARRIS** *is a singer, actor, and* Star Search *champion.*

We think of you and Richie and Jackson daily . . . I know he will grow because we're counting on him to babysit once we have ours (will find out in one week if we're pregnant).

I'm glad to know someone else is gaining weight as rapidly as I am.

Best,
Bill

- *The aforementioned* **BILL WALKER** *and Kelly Zeigler's prayers (and mine) were indeed answered. They are now, thank heavens, the fathers of the highly anticipated and miraculous Elizabeth.*

Your beautiful and humorous updates are wonderful reminders of the true priorities in our lives . . . If you didn't know, Andy, Conor, and I are expecting our daughter to enter into the world around Thanksgiving. Everything has been going along smoothly (Thank God) . . .

- (ADENA FELDMAN CHAWKE)

The membership still grew.

. . . Thank you for sending us the Jackson files . . . As I've been hunched over this computer reading, crying, and laughing for the past couple of hours (and I do mean hours, well spent, mind you), I am literally blown away by your little boy's amazing spirit and courage. It's as if he knows of the events that helped to bring him to you and is fighting with all of his might to spend his life loving you . . .

With much love,
Michele, John, and baby Jack

· **MICHELE PAWK** *and John Dossett, parents of Jack, are both fine New York actors.*

. . . congratulations from a surprising source! David, Kathryn, and I had a wonderful catching up supper last night, and your news was one of our first subjects. David (Hwang) forwarded your very moving (first) message today. I'm so happy for you, especially remembering how completely wonderful you were to my kids when they were little . . .

Love, John

· **JOHN LITHGOW** *is a Tony- and Emmy Award—winning actor, author, banjo player, and dad.*

Roz's E-mails were always among my favorites:

I was so moved by this e-mail that I was one big puddle of tears and breastmilk. In fact, all your e-mails have struck such a maternal chord that I practically start lactating at the sight of Hitano@aol.com on my E-mail . . .

Speaking of lactation . . . you know, if Jackson needs any extra milk now that he is imbibing . . . just holler. I could always pump out a couple of ounces a day if you would like . . . I would be happy to help.

In the meantime . . . I hope you continue to eat, eat, eat, 'til you drop. You're allowed: New parents always pig out.

New parents under stress pig out even more. New parents under stress who happen to be Chinese or Jewish . . . well . . . oink, oink. Simon's not Chinese or Jewish and he managed to outdo his new parent weight from the last baby. He gained so much weight this time . . . HIS breasts looked more juicy than mine! So . . . keep on eating . . . guilt free . . . worrying burns loads of calories.

I'm signing off so that Rol and I can say our goodnights. 'Action Jackson' is always the star of our prayers. We're sending you, Richie, and Jackson loads of 'chi' and love.

XxxooooRoz

- **(ROSALIND CHAO)**

Caregiver's Corner:

I didn't get to take care of Jackson today cause one of his other primaries was on. He is so lucky to have so many primaries but it is a bummer for me sometimes to never get to take care of him. I know he is pretty sick right now but Jackson is a fighter and will give it his best . . .

. . . Hang in there.
smiles,
wendi

- **WENDI ADELMAN** *is a neonatal nurse, UCSF ICN.*

Dropping a line from 38,000 feet . . .

Just received and finished reading this on the plane trip back from Hawaii.

Seems like Jackson continues to improve and you continue to find fascinating connections in parallel universes.

225

We had a great time in Hawaii. The only thing missing was your family. Dad was greatly relieved that the stresses of recent weeks were finally beginning to subside and he could finally get to relax.

True to form, we had numerous great meals: Roy's, Sansei Sushi, Alan Wong's, Oceanarium, Sam Choy's, Hula Grill . . .

. . . Mom and Dad should regale you with some great stories when they see you again.

Our love and thoughts are with Jackson.

Bo

· **BRIAN D. WONG** *is a former doctor, and now he's a consultant, speaker, and father. Oh yeah, he's my brother, too.*

**226**

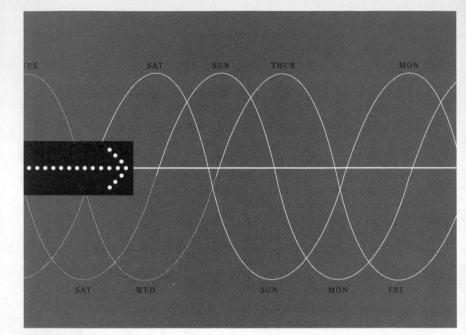

# UPDATE #8

JULY 26, 2000
(2½ WEEKS AFTER UPDATE #7)

*upstairs, downstairs, all around the house . . .*

## << "owed to Sue" >>

***the tribute, long overdue***

**230**  Which came first, the *poussin* or the egg?

To be brutally honest, Jackson still looks a little more like a "Cornish game hen" than a "Gerber Baby." Especially compared to some of the bruisers they got rooming in the Intensive Care Nursery with him. Jeez, it's a good thing they don't have ICN Inter-Wing Hockey. He'd be creamed. He could be the puck. It doesn't matter, Richie wouldn't let him on the ice anyway. Richie probably wouldn't let him sell hot dogs at the snack bar. Well, not yet, anyway. I can't say *I'm* so eager to be a Hockey Dad so soon, myself. Give me time. When I scream, "Rip his face off, son!" I'd really like to *mean* it. He *is* getting bigger, don't get me wrong. But more about that later. An update will soon follow to tell you more specifically how Jackson is doing. But now, here's an update to put even more behind the rooting. To satisfy your curiosity about what preceded the E-mail that laid upon many of you so much new information (and yet so little) way

*B.D. WONG*

back in May. You could call it "A Sister Update." Yes, here's the final answer to the question of the ages . . .

Which came first, the *poussin* or the egg?

The answer, most definitely, is **The Egg.**

### AUGUST 1998 >>

I'm glad I told you a little bit about my relationship with my grandmothers. I will always think of Boaz as an angel on our shoulders, but I will always think of Ngin-Ngin and Paw-Paw on a much grander scale. They will always be like the majestic mountains in a Chinese watercolor. Solid, soaring, always present, and reflected perfectly in the water. A solitary boatman's landmark as he winds his way through the river of life with his daily catch. Enshrouded in fog, but never ominous. You can always feel the mountain there, and it is always comforting. Because of it, you will always remember where you are, and of course, you will always remember where you came from.

By the time Grandma Leong RSVPed to that "endless heavenly Chinese banquet" (actually, that's a terribly redundant phrase on so many levels) in 1995, every family gathering until that point was planned with her attendance in mind. Every wedding, every Chinese "red egg and ginger" baby party, and especially every one of her birthdays, was an opportunity for as many of her children, grandchildren, and great-grandchildren to assemble as possible. Unlike Ngin-Ngin, my "*Paw-Paw*" (maternal grandma) was blessed with a huge family, and the fact that she was happiest only if everyone was together was classically Chinese, and taken extremely seriously (is this really "classically Chinese," or just a *grandma* thing?). It was a pain in the ass, but the family almost always got it together. We're talking about seventy-five people (give or take a few; there's occasionally a cousin's interchangeable current boyfriend). A few petty things here and there were always eventually overcome, in my opinion, in order to earn her beatific face in the middle of those massive group photos.

It was a very sad Chinese New Year in 1995 when Paw-Paw began retreating in her inequitable war with osteoporosis, and her condition was in rapid decline. She was in terrible pain, weak, had a stroke, and was well on her way to her reward, it seemed. My mom and her brothers and sisters had signed the "do not resuscitate" papers. Some of Paw-Paw's seven living sons and daughters went to her, and Richie and I got a phone call in New York saying the end was near.

But it wasn't.

Sometime that day she opened her eyes, and said . . .

"I'm hungry."

Eventually they deduced that she wasn't really "well on her way," after all. She lived for almost four more months. For those four months, she always had at least one of her sons or daughters by her side, 24/7. There was a work wheel, and a makeshift second bed was put in her room by her side. Needless to say, when a ninety-four-year-old Chinese lady wakes up and says "I'm hungry," you better start scrambling the eggs, especially when she's your mother. See, we Chinese live in mortal fear of our mothers. We're a lot like Jews that way.

Oh yeah, scrambling the eggs . . .

My mom divided up Paw-Paw's life savings, and suggested that Paw-Paw's "kids" each spend their share on some

*B.D. WONG*

kind of annual family gathering, or reunion; that's what the ol' lady woulda liked. Each family would take turns, and annually, as many people who are able would gather in honor of The Great One. So at least once a year, my family is joyfully forced to acknowledge this one thing we all have in common; our love for, loyalty and gratitude to a young woman from a village who came over to the Gold Mountain to marry some guy she never met, because her picture was in a catalog. Boy, do we think that's utterly incomprehensible today, and yet, boy, are we sure selfishly thankful she did it.

The picnic of 1998 was the first one, I believe. I was able to attend, even though my presence at these things is always undependable at best. It was a resounding success. There was an organized "super soaker" war, a Leong family trivia quiz:

"Which auntie fell out of a second-story window waving to a family friend when she was two?" (Answer: "Auntie Roberta," a.k.a. my mom) . . .

There was my brother Barry: *"Lord of the Barbecue, Master of Meat,"* and I recall there was my Uncle Ray's famous deviled eggs.

**Okay, okay, eggs.**

When I left the picnic, I was exhilarated, and surprisingly sad. We sure missed Paw-Paw. But it was a great family picnic; there was wonderful food and kids everywhere. The kids that I remember being little were big, and the kids that I remember being kind of medium-sized were, like, driving, or dating, or eating more than me (yes, it's possible). My aunts and uncles, like Mom and Dad, were aging gracefully and handsomely. Paw-Paw would have adored it, watching her family grow, and grow, and grow.

*FOLLOWING FOO*

I suppose if you're gonna leave your whole village behind, get on some lousy boat, travel six thousand miles, and spend another year detained at an immigration center where people are offing themselves all over the place; all to procreate with a *stranger*, at least you should be able to enjoy the fruit of your labor and pains seventy-five years later, even if it's from a celestial perch. Yeah, I guess that's about one family member per year. At last count, Paw-Paw would have eight kids, their spouses, and twenty-three grandkids, and **their** spouses, thirty-three great-grandkids and one great-great-grandchild, to brag about if she were alive today.

(Today, as I'm writing this, my mom is at a baby shower for one of my two cousins, coincidentally named Terry and Teri, who're each coincidentally expecting. Where do you get a wallet big enough for all those pictures?)

**234**  Yes, kids as far as the eye could see. I was feeling a little like I came to the pot luck empty-handed, because not a one of them was mine (and Richie's).

Kids and *babies,* everywhere. My own (younger) brother Barry and his wife, Doris, had just had the most recent one, Jillian, their third, and though Richie and I had always talked about kids, for us there sure wasn't a kid in sight. Certainly we'd want our kid to be born in *some* age proximity to his cousins, and to enjoy some relationship with his or her grandparents, as Richie and I had.

Tick, tock . . .

The fact is, Richie and I had *talked* about kids since we'd met almost ten years before, and knew they were always in our *future.* Where were they? I went home from the picnic having had an earth-shattering revelation on the subject:

"Guess what, honey, it's not going to happen *naturally*. We can't just expect a visit from the *STORK*, if you know what I mean. No, the stork doesn't usually make a delivery when she sees the 'Rainbow Flag' on the front porch. She'd deliver at a house with just about any *other* flag, a *SWASTIKA* even, but not that one. So if we want to do this, we have to *initiate*. We should at least look into the choices. That way, when we decide we're ready to go for it, we know exactly what we're dealing with, don't you think?"

Where was the camera? His expression of *dawning* was a Panavision masterpiece. Richie makes a particular face whenever something I say or do makes him feel like I'm not going anywhere. He will tell you that it's just love, but I'm *sure* there's relief. Relief, like Alka-Seltzer. Like Preparation H. Like Ex-Lax.

235

Yes, the face a hen makes after she lays a big one.

A big egg, of course.

### SEPTEMBER 1998>>

The research was fast. We had been terrified and dismissive of surrogacy; this was because of *Dateline*, *20/20*, and *48 Hours* ("Baby M" and all that). Come to think of it, for the last couple of years as we've been having this adventure, we've been terrified about a *lot* of things, and they were ALL on *Dateline*, *20/20*, and *48 Hours* . . . Anyway, we soon heard of an agency called "Growing Generations" which matches same-sex couples (usually men, of course) with surrogates, and straightens out all the many complicated legal and medical rooms in the "house o' surrogacy." I happened to be going to L.A. on business, and met with them, to check it all out. They managed to allay my fears about custody battles, and then taught me the different options surrogacy included. There was Traditional, or AI (artificial insemination), Surrogacy, in which one of the Intended Parents was the genetic father of the baby, and the surrogate was the genetic mother; and there was Gestational Surrogacy, in which the intended parents obtain a third party, a donor, to provide the egg, which is then fertilized in the lab by the father and implanted in the uterus of the surrogate. Got it?

Ah yes,

　　　　the egg . . .

Many surrogates and intended parents are more comfortable with Gestational Surrogacy, because the surrogate shares no genetic bond with the baby, which would only be undesirable if there were to be unexpected custody complications after the birth. Gestational Surrogacy is also much more technically difficult (like the "triple axel"). But then, there's the question of the egg.

How to shop for the egg.

Let's say we used Richie's "tadpoles." Would we try to make our baby *appear* to be ours, physically and/or otherwise?

How would we go about doing that?

. . . Well, there's always the back page of the *Village Voice*:

# FLAWLESS
## ASIAN-AMERICAN
## COLLEGE CO-ED
## EGGS WANTED

Are you a (MENSA preferred) student looking to make some extra cash for Yale Drama School? Have you played at least 4 principal roles this year in main stage productions at your school? Did you "defy your parents" and refuse to go to medical school even though your older brother is a wealthy cardiologist and golfs most of the time? Do you cook gourmet food, sew all of your own clothes, write searing emotional poetry, run the New York Marathon annually in less than 4.5 hours, and re-use your grocery bags? Are you kind to all living things, except when some jerk cuts you off on the freeway? Can you belt the entire role of Evita, in the original key, without "mixing"? Have you never had a sexually transmitted disease, or a cold?

**If this is you, we want your eggs!!!!!**

Of course, maybe it would be even harder if *I* was going to be the biological father:

# N.Y. JU.

If your parents brought you up right, you wouldn't be reading the back of the *Village Voice,* and you wouldn't be selling your eggs. Nice Jewish girls don't sell their eggs. You should save them, for later. Believe you me, a nice boy, he's gonna want those eggs. And if you ***were*** gonna sell your eggs, why do ya hafta pick the *Village Voice*? Can't you find something nicer? Did you try the temple newsletter? That's free, too, and it comes in the mail. Why didn't your father teach you that nice Jewish girls don't sell their eggs? Well, if you got extra, give us a call.

Advertising in the back of a free paper with the "Thank You St. Jude"s and the Tantric Massages didn't really sound like *our* way to start a family. Although my grandmother *was* in that catalog about seventy-five years ago. (Actually, it wasn't really a "catalog," it was probably more like an arranged marriage between families with a stranger . . . who got a picture of the "merchandise" first . . . is there a difference?) The other outside possibility, the friendly folk at Growing Generations explained, is having a sibling; a sister, as an egg donor. This is an outside possibility because for one thing, there isn't always a sister, and furthermore, there isn't always a *willing* sister.

What a concept. A son or daughter made up of our own genes. You know, we've learned so much through all of this, about the possibilities of life, about the many boundaries which are, quite simply, imaginary. Anything you can imagine, you can probably have. Unless you're, say, doing speed while you imagine it. Can't usually have *those* things. I don't suggest doing any of this on speed, by the way. Anyway, so we started looking into surrogacy, as it became less scary, more fascinating, and almost too good to be true. Just as a starting point, anyway.

239

Well, Richie and I scoured our scrawny little family trees, and on them we found one tiny blossom. It was Sue, Richie's younger-of-his-two-older sisters. Sue's egg could make that rarest of rare things happen. A baby born from Sue's egg, and my, uh . . . sp . . . sp . . . why is that word so hard to say? Whatever; *THAT* would make our child genetically ours in every way. Ahem. I hope I never have to say *that word* in a movie.

Whenever we talked about this, or even thought of it, we couldn't believe it. Boy are times a-changing.

Of course, we would be thrilled if we could have any kind of child, anyhow, anytime, anyway. But it was such exciting information that we decided to explore this scenario until it was exhausted, and if nothing came of our efforts, then we could look into all the other wonderful ways there are to have a baby.

I remember examining every muscle in Richie's face raptly, as I asked, "Do you think there's any way she would do this?"

I have always loved Sue, but I didn't really know her that well. She has two energy-zapping boys of her own, and her husband, Matt, is a hardworking dad. A pretty solid family. Would she help us to make ours? Would she be so generous, and so *modern*, that she could part with that precious, practically invisible, perfect thing within her, that thing which is innately and arguably the most personal thing she has? How would Matt feel?

Gale and Will, the founders of Growing Generations, had hinted to us that this gift is a pretty rare one. Almost always a sister has *issues*. They could be "custody" issues, or "lifestyle" issues, or maybe she "just can't stand the boyfriend" (maybe she hates his Prada sample sale outfits, for example). When I had that first meeting with Gale and Will, Will and his partner Marcellin had just had their second child through surrogacy; both were with nonrelated egg donors. If only one of *their* sisters had done this, Will was saying. What a dream that would have been, for him.

All of a sudden, I felt my relationship with Sue was not positive enough. Had I been at all helpful around the house last Thanksgiving, when she hosted the Jackson clan? Didn't I fall asleep on the couch in a tryptophan stupor, while Matt was doing the dishes, and fail to mention how much I liked her sweater-set, or how moist the turkey was? Did I eat too much, or too little? (Strike that, I definitely didn't eat too little.) Most important, what was I wearing? Would she mention that I was lazy and eccentric, or an unsuitably serious enough person to be a parent, and a tacky dresser to boot, when we asked her???

Who knows, but Richie thought there was a chance. So we decided to pop the big question.

Around Labor Day, I remember that Richie and I spent one of the last summer weekends at the beach. We were at this great house with a big deck right on the water with our best friends, Gary Gersh, Robert Perillo, and Stephen Spadaro (now respectively a.k.a "the Godfathers III, I, & II"). It was late morning, and we were languishing through breakfast: one of Robert's delectable frittatas. Richie and I told them what we were thinking about. I was afraid that we weren't ready. Well, okay, **I** was afraid that *I* wasn't ready, to do this. To have a baby. I always thought I'd be wealthier, or have my own TV series, or an Oscar, or have jumped onto a careening schoolbus and single-handedly saved fifty elderly, blind nuns on their way to Atlantic City and been canonized by the pope for it, before I became a father. I sat on the deck, looking out past the beach, enjoying the peaceful roar of the Atlantic Ocean with my friends, unable to imagine ever giving it all up. But when Gary pointed out that none of *our* parents had their own sitcoms, or medals of honor, or pads of money by the phone to write messages on when they had *us*—they just pulled it together and *made it work*—I suddenly saw the situation a completely different way. For them, in fact, times were much, much harder . . .

**241**

"We have to ask her right away."

I savored the rest of my "free man's" indulgent Sunday morning meal: the *New York Times* Sunday crossword puzzle, a deeply quiet conversation with comrades, the Atlantic Ocean, and Robert's comforting frittata: fried cubes of potato . . . a sprig of fresh basil . . .

. . . and eggs.

It was the last weekend of the summer.

### OCTOBER 1998 >>

Gale and Will at Growing Generations had said that in working with surrogates and egg donors, ageism is definitely exercised. A woman who already has her own family (no first timers, please!) who wants to carry a child for a same sex couple, and who is in her early twenties, is a pretty rare find, but they indeed are always looking for just that, and a woman who is going to give that gift of life in the form of her eggs should ideally be of a similar age. Once a woman reaches her mid-thirties, they said, the chances of her eggs being able to fertilize outside her body, or withstand the many processes that this all entails (freezing and thawing for example) go way down. When Intended Parents are looking for prospective donors, they always discourage a donor over twenty-nine. There's no huge risk or danger, but it is tricky and costly. Anything that increases the chances is preferred. The exception is having a donor who is a sister. This, they said, was such a special, and such a celebrated phenomenon, that they could actually encourage a donor who was older, in order to embrace this treasured situation. Sue was about to be thirty-seven. They warned us that chances were slim she could produce many eggs (the more eggs you get, the more tries you'll have) or that they would "take," but they definitely suggested we see it through. Their attitude about Sue's age was completely different, bathed in the warm, golden light cast by her relationship to Richie, to us. So they encouraged us to ask her. If she declined, there were other options. If she said yes, then we should take full advantage of every moment, and start the process right away. This way, we would obtain her eggs when she was as young as possible, fertilize them, and freeze the embryos, and this would buy us as much time as we needed to find the right surrogate, get our emotional act together, or save those nuns. Frozen, they'd be good for about five years. That's better than Häagen-Dazs.

October 10 is Sue's birthday (10/10: a lucky day on the Chinese calendar, and our niece Taylor's birthday, too). Richie suggested we drive up to Connecticut where Sue and Matt and the boys live to celebrate her birthday with her, take her out, and go for it. She sounded excited and accepted the invitation; being a hardworking mom leaves little time or energy for treats such as this. We decided to meet in New Haven, not too far from her town in Connecticut, where we could stroll the campus at Yale, and have a nice lunch.

On the two-hour drive up, exhaustively "discussing" every possible scenario, I recall I drove Richie crazy. This, as you might guess, is not an uncommon occurrence. I drove him so crazy that finally, he gracefully and quietly suggested that I do all of the talking and explaining and asking myself. So I rehearsed it, and he gave me direction (". . . that was okay. Start again from the top, and this time, try to make me *believe* it . . ."). Then we spent the rest of the drive trying to guess what she was going to say. I don't think we really thought we had anything to lose, but we had to keep reminding our-selves not to get caught up in the *possibilities*. That this wouldn't be our only chance. There were other ways. We were just on the beginning of this magical treasure hunt. Furthermore, how wrong and how damaging it would be if we were to hold it against her for saying no! We declared our love for her, no matter what, and eagerly drove toward New Haven.

When we found her at Yale, she was, as always, bright eyed, and I felt secret joy just being near her. She has a kind of wide, Julia Roberts—esque grin, and sparkly clear blue eyes. Part of my joy was what I was experiencing; Richie and I were so darn happy since we decided to multiply. But also, Sue has an energy which is positive, and *easy*. I think she has a very stressful life, having two such active boys and all. But you'd hardly know it.

**244**   We had trouble finding a decent place for lunch. It was obviously the first weekend of the school year on cam-pus or something, and there were a bunch of smart but confused-looking kids and their proud but confused-looking parents wandering around. Everybody was look-ing for a place to eat. For some reason a lot of places were closed, or just lousy-looking. We tugged on the door of one place just as a young woman and her folks strolled up, and asked us if it was opened or closed. Richie whispered incredulously, "I think that's Claire Danes. Could that be Claire Danes?" Richie thought he remembered that the wonderful young actor was going to Yale, so we decided it was her. I stepped forward cockily.

"Hi, Claire, it's B.D. Wong. We met at an ABC network thing when you were in *My So-Called Life* and I was in *All-American Girl,* remember?"

"Oh. Yeah. Hi." She wasn't exactly thrilled to see me. Perhaps her cover was blown. She was probably trying to be a student and all, not a movie star. Does the name "John Hinckley" ring a bell?

Sue had the hang of it: "Who's she?" she asked.

We proceeded down the thoroughfare with the Danes, like Hamlet, and it seemed like we were all going to just go to the next open restaurant we could find. Claire mentioned a Thai restaurant, so we walked with them to check it out, casually trying *not* to seem like we were going to just glom on to her family, and sit down with them at their table, waving chicken satay sticks and chattering incessantly: "Ooh Claire, darling, *you're so funny*! Could you pass the dipping sauce? . . ."

The restaurant looked okay. We all walked in and, again, Richie immediately recognized the people at the very first table in the dining room! It was Frank Rich, who had once written some really *nice* things about me in the *New York Times* Arts and Leisure section, with his wife, Alex Witchel, who had once written some really *nasty* things about me in the *New York Times* Arts and Leisure section. I am so wigged out over this peculiar paradoxical phenomenon that I never know how to act when I see them together, and I always short-circuit. (The last time I ran into them was at a Broadway opening night, when I enthusiastically pumped Mr. Rich's hand on the red carpet and brightly said, "Hi, Michael!" completely and mortifyingly mistaking him for Michael Chiklis, a.k.a. "The Commish," who I had *ALSO* met at the same ABC thing when Claire Danes was in *My So-Called Life,* but I digress . . . ) Again, we kept our distance . . .

They were just like all the other excited "grown-ups" on the campus and in the restaurants, with their kids on their first weekend of Ivy League. A room full of fresh-persons and their parents (including Juliet with Lord and Lady Capulet), the Danes, the "Ritchels," and oh yeah, two guys over there in that booth about to ask the sister to "please pass the eggs."

As soon as we ordered, Sue says, "So, *what's up*?"

She asks this *pointedly*, almost *accusingly*, as if to say, "Come on guys. You can't *really* be here to celebrate my birthday, can you?"

As if rubber-stamped on each of our foreheads was the question ***"GOT EGGS?"***

Was I that transparent, or paranoid?

246

Richie almost did a "spit take," and then he turns to me, smugly, the man who so generously suggested in the car that I do all the talking, with a presentational, leading, let's-give-the-kid-the-floor kind of smirk, like Ed Sullivan:

## "Ladies and Gentlemen ...
# THE BEATLES!"

What followed from me in this monumental conversation can only be described as *PRATTLE.* As I am writing this, I ask Richie what he recalls about this day. He remembers rehearsing and bracing ourselves for any outcome in the car. When I ask him what I said in the Thai restaurant, he matter-of-factly says,

"I just remember that you went

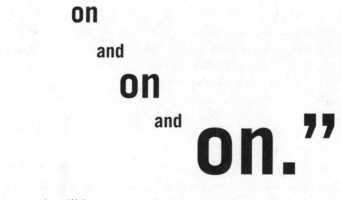

**on**

and

**on**

and

# on."

Of course, it will be no surprise to any of *you* that I went on and on and on.

# THIS IS WHAT I DO.

I go on and on and on. I'm going on and on and on and on right now. Someone, stop me. Where are the AOL Word Count Police? I have several unpaid tickets. There's probably a warrant.

However, mind you, I got all of the points in:

EGG PROPOSAL: OUTLINE

I. Introduction
  A. Happy birthday.
  B. How are the kids?
  C. What's new with us:
  1. Richie, work.
  2. B.D., work.
  3. We're planning to start a family.
II. Starting a Family
  A. Why: It's getting late.
  B. How: We've been looking into it.
  C. What we've found out:
  1. "Growing Generations."
  2. Surrogacy is not such a bad idea.
  3. We're thinking of having a woman carry our baby.
III. How That Works

  A. She probably wouldn't be the genetic mother.
  B. She would carry the baby from someone else's egg.
  1. We could find a stranger for the egg.
  2. We could ask someone in our family for the egg.
    a. B.D. doesn't have any sisters.
    b. Richie has 2 sisters.
    1. Linda is older.
    2. Then there's *you.*
      a. You could say no.
      1. That's okay.
      2. We wouldn't hold a grudge.
      b. You could say yes.
      1. We'd be thrilled.
      2. Ya hafta have a lotta shots.
      3. Ya hafta do it soon, 'cause they say you're (gulp) old.
     a. Whaddya say?
     b. Did I say "Happy birthday

**B.D. WONG**

No one interrupted or spoke during "The Ovary Mono-logues." Richie's cell phone and beeper did not go off, and Sue did not attempt to open any candy wrapped in cellophane during the entire performance.

There are always a handful of words and phrases throughout any saga in your life that you will remember with absolute crystalline clarity, and these words or phrases lie in the center of your memory of the particular episode that surrounds it, and help trigger it. I've probably written to you about nearly all of my majors, for there are few. I remember my dad giving thanks after Ngin-Ngin's memorial service: ". . . Grace, gusto, and glory." I remember Kari Carper, the nurse, saying, "Crap" after she checked Shauna's cervix, like it was five min-utes ago . . .

. . . and, whenever I need to be buoyed by the possibil-ities of the human heart, by the undramatic heroics of people who don't think of themselves as heroes, by goodness and love personified, by simplicity, or the sibling bond, I just have to remember looking across the table into the blue eyes of both Richie and my sister-in-law Sue, in that rather average Thai restaurant in New Haven, with Frank Rich who wrote something nice, and Alex Witchel who wrote something nasty, and Claire Danes, who thought I was stalking her, all present yet oblivious to probably the most seminal (sorry) event in my life to date, which was actually occurring as they sat right there, breathing the same air as me, when Sue (Jackson) Barez said the words,

**"I'd do it in a second."**

The sister sentence, which followed, is equally stirring:

"I *knew* you were gonna ask me that."

Apparently, there *were* traces of ink on our foreheads, and Sue said she had wondered over time whether we would ever ask her this question. Readable or not, I am still in awe over her acute vision.

Thai food never tasted so good. Even mediocre Thai food goes great accompanying a conversation effervescent with dreams and ideas. Sue felt it was only fair to have a conversation with Matt, and when we left her, Richie and I were giddy and electrified. Don't ever forget those times in your life when the atlas seems to be laid out before you, open to just the page of the very place you wish to visit. It's essential to devour those moments with everything you are made of, stealing the hope from them while you can store it, for they sure will help to get you through those times when the streetlights seem to be out along the shoulders of your darker highways. Take it from me.

As Richie and I drove home, the two hours raced by. When we got home, there was a message from Sue on the answering machine . . . Thanks for lunch . . . I talked to Matt . . .

**"I guess it's a go!"** she said, with her inimitable simplicity.

So now you know the specific origin of our little, *hard-boiled* bundle of dynamite, and his beloved big brother.

### OCTOBER 1998—DECEMBER 1998 >>
The time from Sue's birthday of that year until Christmas flew like Santa's reindeer. Sue immediately took Rudolph by the horns, and called all around to make the arrangements to get the blood tests, and the meds, and the appointments in her area, herself! The time line of the whole process was coordinated with her menstrual

cycle, which came right up over the hill like a San Francisco cable car, so we jumped right on. Growing Generations hooked us up with Dr. David Smotrich, a fertility doctor they were working with in San Diego, who would eventually do the procedure that would ultimately produce the embryos. Sue went through five or six weeks of shots and appointments, complete with annoying side effects, all the while constantly saying "aw, this is nothing," and before we knew it she was ready to fly to San Diego with Richie for the procedure.

In November, I went to Skokie, Illinois, on the first stop of the out-of-town tryout for *You're a Good Man, Charlie Brown,* which was coming to Broadway the following February. In the middle of a hectic, typically grueling rehearsal period, in which we made numerous changes to the musical during the day and performed a different version of the show every night until we got to New York, I was making arrangements to go to a Cryo-Laboratory about forty-five minutes away, to perform *my* particular role in the science fiction comedy thriller *Skokie Chokie.* Sorry. Ouch. I use humor to mask my discomfort.

So, I walk into the lab and the first thing I—

## WAIT!!! NO!!!

You don't want to hear about this.

**I AM NOT TELLING YOU ABOUT THIS.** Believe me, this is a huge sacrifice I am making, not telling you this part, because it's even better than the "Contest" episode of *Seinfeld.* But I have to save *something* for David Letterman.

Maybe it'll have its own track on the uncut DVD.

What I *will* say is that if you're ever in the position I was in, it is very difficult to explain to the stage manager of your big Broadway musical exactly *WHY* you have to rent a car and drive from one little nowhere town outside of Chicago, for forty-five minutes, to another little nowhere town outside of Chicago, on the morning that your big number (in which you suck your thumb and dance with an animated baby blanket) is being re-lit by the lighting designer, *without* using the word "sperm." (There. I said it. I hope you had film in the camera.) Jim Harker, stage manager par excellence, was very accepting of the explanation that I had a "nonthreatening medical urgency." That's pretty good, huh? Actually, after the required "abstinence," that became painfully accurate. (Remember when Kramer throws the money on the counter and says, **"I'M OUT!"**?)

Anyway, when I got back and fellow cast member Auntie Ilana Levine (who was actually *in* the "Contest" episode of *Seinfeld*, but I digress . . . ) came out of the hotel and caught me grinning in a huge, bright red pickup truck pulled up at the curb (because that's all that was left at the car rental place and, besides, I was hauling a huge load of testosterone) she simply *HAD* to know what was up. So I spilled a few beans. So to speak.

Basically, the point, when all is said and done, is that Boaz and the Chestnut Man were miracles born from the efforts of four principal people.

None of us have ever been all together in the same room, city, or state.

That Christmas, I wiggled out of an appearance with the Peanuts Gang in the Detroit Christmas Day Jubilee Parade, or some such nonsense, and flew home to meet the Wong family in San Francisco. Richie and Sue flew to San Diego, where Dr. Smotrich was to perform the procedure, on December 25, 1998. Jews. Don't they know you hunt for eggs on *Easter?* Richie and Sue had four days of good old-fashioned brother-sister quality time, decadently went to the movies twice in one day, and ate the best French toast they ever had at a place called Mimi's. They sure know what to do with eggs down there in San Diego. Richie and Sue's time together, as well as the experience they were sharing, strengthened their bond.

At a specific time the night before the procedure, Richie had to give Sue the final shot that would activate the entire process. It had to be given at an exact time, at an exact spot, or the whole six weeks of meds could have been a big waste. This responsibility paralyzed the poor dad-to-be. He made the nurse at the Smotrich Center use a Sharpie to put a treasure map—type "X marks the Spot" on Sue's heinie.

It worked.

Dr. Smotrich was able to harvest twenty-eight eggs from my "over the hill" sister-in-law (a twenty-two-year-old who was harvested earlier that morning at the center produced seven). I love that choice of the word "harvest." That it was.

*Bountiful.*

Of those twenty-eight, fourteen fertilized successfully into embryos.

Of those fourteen, seven thawed successfully the day of Shauna's embryo transfer.

One miraculously split after implantation, and those two "halves" became Boaz and Jackson Wong.

As I draw this installment to a close, I'm moved to reflect on the "spirit of the donor," which is constantly swirling around my life these days, like the Downy Ball, evenly distributing the fragrant fabric softener of generosity into the rinse cycle of my life. Is it just these days, or is it always and I'm just too self-involved to notice?

Shauna Barringer, who, like General Electric, brought "good things to light." My gratefulness to Shauna for her hospitality and courage will never fade . . .

My parents, who continue to waive the room, tax, room service, phone, laundry/valet, car rental, and gasoline bills without so much as a flicker of guilt in return. My father *still* fights over every single restaurant tab whenever Richie and I go out to dinner with them. Not to mention their *emotional* support . . .

Got any idea how much a computer consultant or a Web designer costs? I have no idea. I would be afraid to look into it, but Uncle Barry (the dear fire-fightin' brother o' mine who lives in San Francisco) has taken care of all that. Not to mention cooking, cooking, cooking, and sharing shifts on the shuttle service to and from the airport with Mom and Dad . . .

As for Sue, I know she takes seriously what she has done for us. I know she fully comprehends the ramifications of it. That's why it is so astounding to me that she is so peacefully *low key* about it. Shauna and her girlfriends serve up heaping portions of "Surrogate Pride"; they righteously and rightfully wear their maternity clothes like a marine wears a bulldog tattoo. Brother Barry has a monopoly on computer knowledge (as well as cooking for twenty-five expertise), and he has his own prideful ways of showing it. My parents act out of tradition and form as well as love; never complaining seems part of the job. But Sue's pride is like the sweet smile of a child just before she has been told she has done "a good thing."

If Sue is particularly pleased with herself, it must be private, for she never solicits attention, or presumes praise. So her contribution glows quietly. Radiantly. Twinkles, mischievously, from Jackson's enormous, now steel gray, eyes. The doctors and nurses say Jackson's eyes may be blue, like Richie and Sue's (it's hard to tell yet). Until recently I thought, how odd that a son of mine wouldn't have brown eyes, how less of a son of mine he might seem! How shamefully misguided those thoughts were. For if I can look into those splendid, trusting eyes every morning, and see Sue's *oculi azure* twinkling back, what a divine, constant reminder of that quietly powerful gift (to not only Jackson's life, but to mine and Richie's) that will be. It is unlikely that I could ever forget how she, indeed, "did it in a second." But to see it perpetually winking back at me every moment of every day, well . . . that would be a pretty neat reminder, yes?

Shamefully, I have felt helpless and flaccid in properly expressing my gratitude to Sue. Jackson is so far away from her, and she hasn't had that blessed meeting yet. So until I can do it right, I am once again using this bizarre platform to express my most intense of feelings. Given the amount of people that have now accumulated on this E-mail list, I suppose this is the electronic equivalent of renting the Helen Hayes Theater on Forty-fourth Street and Broadway in the Big Apple and demonstrating my love and elation and gratefulness to you, Sue Jackson Barez, by getting up on the stage in front of a Standing Room Only crowd, which is cheering just for *you*, and singing your praises backed up by the New York Philharmonic and the Radio City Rockettes; brought to you by the kind folks at the Egg Advisory Board.

Years from now, when Jackson grows nice and big and finally ready for hockey season and no longer resembles a Cornish game hen, I can't wait to sit him down, with your little brother Richie, and we'll show him pictures of how tiny he was, tell him about our journey together, and explain to him the facts of life, as our little family knows them:

"Which came first, Dads, the *poussin* or the egg?"

"The answer, Jackson, most definitely, is The Egg."

The incredible,

**256**

***bred*-**able,

***EGG!***

Thanks, Sue. That's all, yolks.

*http://www.geocities.com/jacksonfoowong/*

thanks for sticking with me. with us.

you won't have to wait too much longer to find out how he's doing, and it will be clear why it's taken so long.

go team.

**B.D. WONG**

The *Golden Goose* replied:

**B.D.—**

**A simple "Thank you" would have been fine.**

**It was a beautiful letter. I love you and Richie very much and seeing what wonderful parents you are and are going to be makes me especially thrilled to have been part of the process.**

**Love Sue**

> • **SUE BAREZ** *is, well, someone who requires no introduction. You bet she's a mom.*

**. . . Just wanted you to know that I read your entire letter (on my father's computer) . . . I think you can understand why I decided to skip the eggs for breakfast this morning. I went right to the cereal course . . .**

> • **(MARK JACKSON)**

**And Richie and B.D., you may have heard by now that I'm pregnant! . . . You may also have heard, since our folks seem to be passing the news around, that Nancy is pregnant! And she's due about the exact same week as me. I'm just thrilled to think that these 3 little second cousins, Jackson Foo Wong, baby Nemeth, and baby Metcalf, might have the opportunity to grow up knowing each other . . .**

**Love,**
**Shari**

> • **SHARI METCALF** *is Richie's cousin, and a mom! Nancy Nemeth is another cousin/mom.*

. . . just back from a week out at 425 Ocean where i sat on your old deck and pondered my navel while deciding between SPF 4 and SPF 8. to think, on that very deck you had some of the first conversations about starting a family—i am awestruck, and just a little embarrassed.

kisses & love
dean

• (DEAN MICHAELS)

People had suggested by now that Jackson's story become a book. I will skip over all of that self-congratulation (for the most part):

Dear dear guys. Are you going to box these E-mails? Like Jane Austen? Love, Neufeld

• (PETER NEUFELD)

Besides, I was very nervous about such suggestions. Did they all love my necktie because I really was a snappy dresser, or was I just your average slob, and they just hadn't ever seen me comb my hair and wear a suit before???

Stacey's corner:

HEY BD

. . . I am sitting in my lab crying! I am so happy that Richie has such a great sister.

. . . I know (Jackson) is still desatting but he will grow out of it. He is doing so well in so many ways. I was so happy that he nipples well and that is not an issue . . .

. . . I am only in the lab this month (but I am visiting Jackson at least 2 times a week) and then on call next month again. I miss seeing you both and Jackson—but I did get to feed (him) this am!!!!!!! (Highlight of my day)

-stacey

Because of a sneaky little feature on AOL, I could always tell if someone had opened our E-mail, and I would often be secretly disappointed when someone didn't reply. There were hundreds who Followed Foo silently, and I got used to this as time went on. But there *were* a few folks who I wondered why we hadn't heard from by this time . . .

After I read the following, I forwarded it to Richie with the following message:

« "Some things are worth waiting for." »

Dear B.D.,

My apologies for not having written sooner. The fact is, given the intensely personal nature of what you (and Richie) have been going through, my impulse has been to resist interfering with even the most generic expression of goodwill, for fear that it would assume a level of intimacy which, despite my great affection for you, might feel a little too close for comfort. As much as I'd like to say otherwise, we simply don't know each other that well. On the other hand, an event like this, I realize, catapults one into a realm of existential immediacy that transcends conventional propriety. So, at risk of transgressing real (or imagined) boundaries, let me say that, with each bulletin from the front—melancholy, funny, spirited, rallying, sometimes buoyant, sometimes exhausted—I've found that my heart aches for you, less out of sadness than out of amazement and wonder at the discovery of who you are. I can't pretend to understand what it feels like to have lost a child; nor can I truly imagine the gargantuan reserves of strength that must inevitably be drawn upon by the custodian of a child who is, at present, in so vulnerable a state. What I can say is this: I am tremendously proud to know you, and you should be aware that your life and the lives of the members of your family (especially Jackson) occupy my thoughts and prayers in a far deeper way than the incipient nature of our friendship might suggest. Here's something you don't know about me: if I can be of any help, now or in the future, you have only to ask. Those are not hollow words. In the meantime, I send you, Richie, Jackson, and Boaz all my love, and can't wait to meet the new addition to the family in the months ahead.

Much love, David

· **DAVID HIRSON** *is a playwright. Shame on you for not guessing that.*

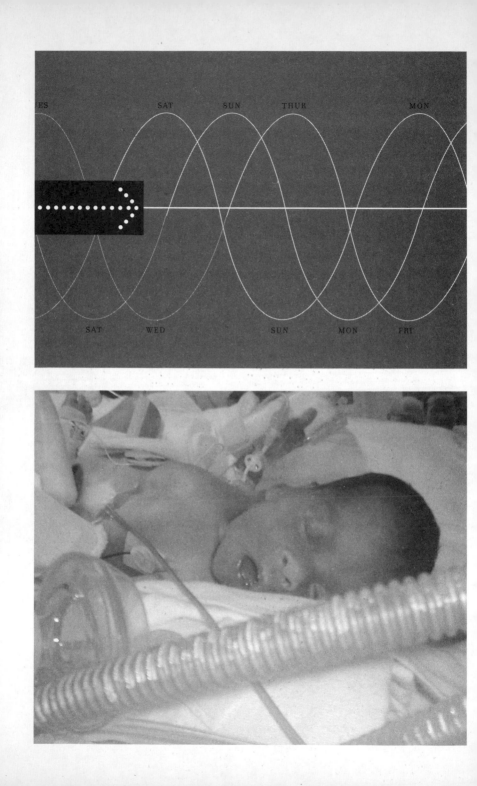

# UPDATE #9

SUBJECT:

"NEW NO MORE TEARS FORMULA"

OR

"YANKING THE HOOVER"

AUGUST 11, 2000

(MORE THAN 2 WEEKS AFTER UPDATE #8)

in San Francisco and New York, on land and in the air

# SURVIVAL
## — OF THE —
# FATTEST

as told by ME.   J. Foo, fool.

first, I was afraid. i was petrified. it was dark and there was
Boaz, shrinking, by my side. he said "it's time to hit the road," he
said "it's time to see the light," he said "no matter what should
happen just make sure you fight the fight."

and now i'm here. it's pretty clear: the place i've ended up is
bright and warm and free o' fear. was he the one that got me
here? was he the one? and now he's gone! but i can feel him
right beside me singin' songs to egg me on . . .

"go on, now GO."

"you will survive."

**B.D. WONG**

"turn it around now."

"i can't be by you anymore."

he had all his life to give, so i'd have all my life to live. i will not stumble. i will survive.

hey, hey.

     hey...

# HEY!

i think my asian-american dad with hair on top is gonna explode.

265

i mean, he looks like he's gonna actually blow up sometimes. i'm more with it now, i open my eyes more n all that, so i notice it now. all right, i can't really SEE anythin yet, but you'd be surprised how much ya can pick up when you're just lyin there. n i'm gettin the feelin dad's always all wound up. you all have known him a lot longer than i have, plus for most a my whole life i been kinda out of it, so i'm not sure <u>why</u> he would be fixin ta explode now, when things are a little better. but he is. so i'm takin over. he's kind of a control freak, i don't know if you ever noticed that, but he says i can get away with a lotta stuff other people can't, when it comes ta him. so he's lettin me take over, for a sec. just this once, he says.

jeez, where ta start? wow. a lot's happened since tai-ngin died. i don't get ta go anywhere, cause they still got me here all hooked up ta monitors n all that. but like i said i hear stuff.

*FOLLOWING FOO*

let's see, i think where my dad left off is that he was in san francisco with me, n my other dad WITHOUT hair on top (w/o h.o.t.) was in new york for a while, when i had another one a those really annoyin eye exams. y'know, one minute you're catchin some perfectly good Zs, n the next minute, dang, feels like some clown is shovin his car keys up under ya eyelids. excuse me, son. do ya mind? i'm tryin ta sleep here. anyway, my dad comes in the next day, n dr. roberta keller, she's called a fellow, she tells dad that the dude came ta examine the old peepers n told her i had this thing called "stage one r.o.p." that means the blood vessels in my eyeballs are developin slightly abnormally or somethin, on account a cause i'm a preemie n all. a coupla weeks before that, the docs told my dads everythin was goin fine, but now all of a sudden they say "stage one."

roberta said it's probably nothin ta worry about, but you shoulda seen dad's face. i can always tell when he's real uptight but he can't really yell. he says that's how i look when i'm de-sattin. see, he'd just walked inta see me (both my dads always hafta get all geared up for that) n he wasn't expectin any special new info, n he tried ta explain ta roberta that it wasn't fair that they didn't even give him the heads up i was even gonna HAVE a second eye exam, cause like he wasn't really ready for it. don't even mention the "stage one" part. he says, "you should have warned me about this!" but he says he felt like a real dweeb as soon as he said that, because both my dads are mostly just real scared i'm gonna be blind or somethin, n he got mad that he wasn't able to PREPARE for them ta break it ta him, in case the news was bad. you gotta forgive my dad. he's an actor. he's always preparin. he prepares ta go check the mailbox.

oh yeah, so that was the week i started those full feeds, remember? that was pretty cool. everybody was makin a big deal about

266

that. i said, whatever, y'all. ya shove it in a tube n it goes down
inta my stomach. big wow. so anyway, they said my lungs were
wet, but of course they'd given me everythin in the medicine
chest ta dry em up so i could breathe better. that was cool, cause
they had told my dad it was workin, n they were gonna try ta
extubate me that week, n of course my dad told my other dad in
new york, n they were all jazzed. ya know, about takin the tube
out. oh yeah, they sure got MY vote for that. anytime, fellas.
ya know, ya gotta be pretty tough for intubation, if i do say so
myself. it ain't for babies. i tried rippin it out a buncha times with
my bare hands, but they always caught me n put it back. killjoys.
n they're actin all surprised at how strong n smart i am. gimme
a break. YOU wanna just lie around with a vacuum cleaner hose
down your throat, lady? i don't think so. i would say it out loud,
but ya can't exactly talk over the hoover, if ya know what i mean.
ya know i can't hear ya when the vacuum cleaner's runnin kinda
thing.

my dad with hair on top was real disappointed, cause they were
talkin about extubatin me on this particular day, n that was the
day he was flyin back ta new york for a while ta work. oh, that's
another sore subject. he really tore himself up over that. he says
he's been on this TV show for four years, kinda sittin around on
his butt hopin for more more more ta do, n then they write him a
really juicy story n i'm in intensive care. of course he complains
but he loves it there. so then he says, he guesses that's the way
it's supposed ta be. we'll understand later. it's so corny when he
says that "bodhi tree" stuff.

so he was supposed ta leave one particular afternoon, but he
changes his flight till first flight out the next mornin, thinkin
he'll have more of a chance ta be around if they yank the hoover.
the doctor on call that day isn't as ballsy as the french guy,

dr. poulain, who is both my dads' favorite guy. so the new guy
says he's gonna play it safe n just wait till the next day. dad
was so over this doctor. we'll call him "dr. personality" cause
HE DOESN'T HAVE ANY. he's not fun like dr. poulain. plus he
doesn't have the super smooth accent. but dad feels okay about
missin the extubation, cause everybody said i was doin so good,
n so he says HEY ta me that night, n gets on the plane real early
the next mornin.

it really takes only 5 hours ta get ta new york, ya know, but of
course he has ta call the hospital as soon as he gets in the taxi
on the way home from the airport, just ta find out how i'm doin.
he's plannin ta call later in the afternoon too so he can hear them
takin the tube out over the phone. he loves that stuff. he tape
records everythin, ya know. so one of my primary nurses, chris
white, was assigned ta me that night. n she answers the phone
all like tired soundin.

well, as it turns out, of course, she's not just tired. i was there.
she's afraid ta tell my dad that while he was on the plane i
spiked a fever. outta the blue. don't ask me how, all of a
sudden i'm just hot, okay? then i guess he asked her what
does that mean, cause i heard chris tell him that they think i
got a PNEUMONIA again. dad's almost positive she's got me
mixed up with one a the other inmates here. you know, some
SICK kid! wrong. she tells him it's gonna be the same ol' drill.
lung x rays, watchin n waitin, n antibiotics. of course, they just
TOOK ME OFF the antibiotics from the LAST TIME they thought
i had pneumonia like the day before. n by the way they never
really said whether it was freakin' pneumonia or whether it
wasn't. so they put me on new ones. today's
special: freakin' antibiotics.

B.D. WONG

this is crazy, dad is thinkin. we were all ready ta yank the
hoover! oh, n here's the clincher: no more food. back to the
gross yellow i.v. aw, man, i just got to full feeds! zounds. this
place is like wimbledon, man. make up your minds, people. but
the main thing is, no extubation. dad says it felt like when ya
try ta hop outta the car n you forgot ta take your seat belt off.
oh well, at least i had it on for the ride, he says.

so my dad went home ta work on the jail show. he was totally
in shock, cause he hadn't been home for almost 2 months,
or slept in his own bed n all. but he says he had a surprisingly
good time at the set, cause everybody was really cool, n they
hadn't seen him since me n boaz jumped ship. he said for a
buncha criminals, they could be pretty sweet dudes. they
only double cross, n murder, n sodomize each other non-
consensually on TV.

269

meanwhile, gramma n grampa wong n uncle barry n auntie doris
n uncle bo n auntie cindy n all my chinese-american cousins
were flyin ta hawaii. it was like a wong family vacation ta celebrate my grandparents' 50th anniversary. the big "hawaii 5-0."
that's pretty awesome, even ta me. i still don't think it's as cool
as gut surgery when you're 2½ pounds, but it's pretty cool. my
dads were supposed ta go too, but way back when they were
plannin it all they thought shauna would be gettin ready ta spring
me n my bro right around now, n they didn't wanna be out
snorkelin, lookin at all da pretty fish, while shauna was screamin
her head off in modesto. boy are they laffin about that now. i'm
like 2 months old already!

dads decided that they were gonna switch places, n dad w/o
h.o.t. was gonna come out ta be by me now, while my other dad
was doin the jail show. so dad w/o h.o.t. flew ta san francisco

with gramma jackson, who—how can i say this without soundin fat headed?—just can't stand ta be away from me. basically, my dads had like 3 days together in new york. asian-american dad drove jewish-american dad ta the airport, n then asian-american dad dropped in on my godfathers robert, stephen & gary at the beach. that was nice for him, cause he was so stressed out about ...

# PNEUMONIA 2:
## just when you thought it was safe to go home

... n he scratches his skin all up when he frets. so he said the sun was great for him n all the marks he made on himself over the last coupla months. he took all his clothes off n laid out for a bit. but he said he couldn't really relax. he kept callin here at the hospital, n eventually he talks ta roberta keller, the fellow who took over for stacey levitt after the rotation. roberta is totally cool, but she has bad luck when it comes ta me. whenever she's around, i get some mysterious thing they can't figure out. then she's the one that's gotta tell my dads, "gee, i'm not sure what's happenin." so she says she has no idea what this fever thing is. but she has a guess that i got a yeast infection. yeah, yeah. ya know what? i've heard it all by now. save ya breath. i'm still gettin it from the other kids in the nursery. monsieur monistat. very funny. it's in my LUNGS, okay?

well, of course, my dad asks, how do ya get a yeast infection? n roberta says "from antibiotics." n then my dad asks, how do ya TREAT a yeast infection? n roberta says, "uh, with antibiotics."

*B.D. WONG*

welcome to my world, people. welcome to my world.

the good news is that i didn't have another fever since the first
time early that mornin back when dad was flyin home, but
roberta's still pretty concerned, which is why she cancelled the
extubation, n the feedings, n put me on more antibi's. if you
wanna know the truth, my dad thought that i was just missin
him, since i was doin so good when he was here, n then, POW,
i fall apart as soon as he's out the door. of course, he thinks
EVERYBODY falls apart as soon as he's out the door. he does.
anyway, i cannot really confirm or deny i DID fall apart for any
particular reason. it's like a secret pact we ICN kids have. ya just
don't wanna give away your power. get yourself a copy of "the
art of war." just a suggestion.

my dad without hair on top got here in san francisco just when
my other dad was comin back into manhattan from the beach.
so what if i started feelin better as soon as i saw dad w/o h.o.t.?
so what? can ya blame me? everyone was so psyched that i was
de-sattin a little less, n my lungs were clearin up from whatever
mushroom factory was growin in there, so they started feedin me
again, with the feedin tube. YES!!! both my dads were bummed
we couldn't be together, but i felt lucky. mostly, i was happy for
the chow.

then thespi-dad went to work another day on the jail show again.
he said if he couldn't be with me, at least he finally got some
good scenes. i said to myself, oh no, dad, that is SO "postcards
from the edge."

then the next day, he says he cleaned up our house. my other
dad said, don't expect much, he's been threatenin ta do that for
12 years; he thought this was another false alarm. but this time
he sorta really did it! ta tell ya the truth i'm kinda proud a this,

cause it was like this thing he never felt good about, the whole time my dads've been together, the mess that is, but here i come n he rolls out the red carpet.

plus, they had our apartment redone a coupla years ago, n my dad's always wanted ta enter it in a contest in a magazine. so he spent all day cleanin n' throwin stuff out so he could take pictures. he really is a complete nutcase sometimes. i mean, now of all times he's takin pictures of our apartment ta enter a contest in a magazine. n he has the nerve to say he NEEDS ta do this, cause it's like the end of one thing n the beginnin of another. n he'll never get to it once i come home n mess everythin up n there's like wall ta wall fisher price.

my wacky social worker, stephanie berman, who is a new york jew like my dad (they're the best kind) said don't bother cleanin up. don't organize. put the baby in a drawer. just let it go. it's life! after she said that, my dad stared at her like she had a big hairy foot growin outta her forehead. my dads just love her. n i'm thinkin to myself, please be quiet, lady, i don't wanna live in no drawer. n watch where ya wave those hands. you gotta sick kid down here. anyway, it doesn't matter. when my dad wants ta do somethin, basically he kinda goes deaf anyway. so he turned up the stereo n went for it. he says it was a great day, cause a the cleanup n cause he talked ta my other dad a buncha times on this end, n i was totally flyin. i got it totally together as soon as my other dad came ta be with me! coincidence? supernatural? get this: if you can believe it, they decided ta extubate me the next day! match point, "J-WO."

so the next day my dad was all ready with the tape recorder by the phone in new york for the big day. my other dad who was with me told him that they were gonna yank the hoover at 11:30.

n he was all pumped cause at the chinese restaurant his fortune
cookie said

> No one knows what he can do until he tries.

. . . so at 2:30 sharp new york dad flips on the tape recorder, n
calls my bed on the speakerphone.

everybody is so primed ta see me fly without the net, especially
me. my jewish-american dad n his jewish-american mother were
there, n dr. "frenchy" poulain n nurse chris, n the respiratory
people, n everyone's waitin with baited breath, no pun intended,
on account a cause, well . . .

let's just say everybody loves me.

i'm so sorry, we ALL know it's true.

they can't help it.

can you?

hey, i'm a SYMBOL.

yeah, that's it.

i'm a SYMBOL of everythin anybody's ever wished on a star for.

before they yanked it, they took my temperature, which was
aces, n changed my diaper. then everythin got real quiet. my dad
in new york is leanin over the speakerphone on the counter talkin
inta the phone n the tape recorder. he says, "what's happenin?
is it out already? keep talkin. i'm tryin ta tape here!"

273

i was kinda snoozin, n i was gettin ready for the big event, but when my dad who was with me said, "i don't know. his belly's all blown up like in modesto n there's blood all in his diaper," even i was surprised. then all of a sudden, nobody was talkin about extubation anymore. hey, wait a minute, i'm goin. come back. what about the dam hoover? i can do it, i can do it! what about the fortune? doesn't anybody believe in fortune cookies anymore? but nooo. nobody listens ta fortune cookies OR me, dammit. they SAY they take alla their cues from me, but nobody ever listens ta me. so the surgeon who did the surgery on my gut like eons ago, who my dad says is right outta M*A*S*H, comes down n looks at me, n i get another x ray. it's a good thing babies can take a lotta x rays. i've had a million of em. then all of a sudden, it's all about my bowels again! i'm thinkin, weren't we done with all that? do we have ta be talkin about bowels, n bloody stools, n constipation, n suppositories n necrotizin' gastroenterocolitis all over again? i'm tryin ta eat here! y'know, ya just haven't lived until you've heard a buncha experts discussin whether your colon has a "stricture" or not. none a them can tell whether i got some serious thing that they gotta operate on again, or that maybe i just need some kaopectate junior. my dad in new york, meanwhile, hangs up the phone, n looks around, just in case he's on candid camera. this time, he said it was like tryin ta jump out of a speedin train, n your raincoat gets caught in the door. oh well, at least it kept my clothes dry, he says.

i wish i could say that i had only that one bloody diaper, but i had a few more after that. oh yeah, one more thing. take a wild guess. yup, NO MORE FOOD AGAIN. now THAT got my ass up. if i could talk, i woulda been yellin at roberta the fellow, like john mcenroe.

274

**B.D. WONG**

# "Aw COME ON,

## you IDIOT!

### That was IN, man!

# THAT WAS IN!!!!"

i toldja it's like wimbledon.

can you believe they put that damn tube thing down into my
stomach again, the one that just sits there n sucks out the extra
air, n checks for that disgustin green stuff n all? i mean, i ain't
the only one who thought that was old news. ya know, it really
bites it big time when you go ta the vacuum cleaner rental place
ta return your hoover, n just as you're about ta get it on the
counter, the salesman says, "hey, guess what, we're having a
RENT ONE GET ONE FREE SALE today!" n before you can say
EUREKA, he shoves another one down your throat! so yeah,
now i got two tubes again.

so my dad in new york is gettin all busy buyin film ta take
the pictures for the contest, n fancy soap for all the soap dishes.
he really got into this, cause he was tryin ta keep movin. he
wasn't really ready for how awful n guilty he'd feel bein away
from me. i'll say it one more time. what's so surprisin? i'm the
bomb, that's all. i'm just the bomb.

the next day was not my favorite day. in case you haven't heard,
i'm not real crazy about the suppositories they give here. oh

yeah, like the other kids ARE. no sick jokes, please. let's all be
grown-ups. y'all almost blew it with the yeast infection thing.
let's just say the nurses have ta pin me down n hold the damn
thing up there until it melts, or i could put somebody's eye out
the way i can shoot it back at 'em. n because of my gut situation, of course, they're givin me the ol' silver bullet like crazy.
well if ya think that's bad, try havin a BARIUM ENEMA. yeah,
that's about as yummy as it sounds. well, let's face it. just
about anythin with "enema" in the title is about as yummy as
it sounds. "blueberry enema." "entenmann's enema." "public
enema."

so basically they shoot this nasty glow in the dark stuff up
your ass, so when they x-ray you they can see the whole
wonderful world of disney up there. this is fine for the people
who get ta watch the show. but for the CAST, it's like, well,
it's like HAVING AN ENEMA.

anyway, the x ray said none a the goop leaked outta bounds,
so ta speak, so they didn't think that my surgery went bad, or
that i had ta have another one or anythin. that's a big whew.
what sick little elf put the blood in my diapers, though, they
don't know. surprise, surprise. they HAD been spikin my milk
with extra calories, though, so maybe that was it. you know, dad
w/h.o.t. says those body-building extra protein drinks always
make HIM all bloated n constipated, so he never has em. that's
why he's so scrawny. maybe that explains it.

they were doin the "let's feed! let's extubate!" rap before i even
had a chance ta make em a nice glow in the dark diaper. n by
this time, everybody in my family knows the song by heart. but
my dads weren't exactly singin along. they both hate surprises,
when it comes ta stuff like this. n there were so many false

alarms (at least 3 total when it comes ta extubation) that they started assumin somethin would always come up. i couldn't deal with all the tension, so i just caught some Zs through most of it. so then my dad in new york just started snappin pictures of our place, n he snapped n snapped n snapped from 3 in the afternoon till 11 at night. then he rushed down to a professional photo lab that's open till midnight so he could get the pictures by the next day, cause he was flyin back ta see me. now, he says he musta been really buryin himself in the project ta DEAL. you know, ta COPE. it's like when he tried ta do dewey decimal in the breast milk freezer. it was somethin he could do, while everybody else tried ta figure out what was best for me. what's best for me? that's easy. i'll tell ya what's best for me. could i get another budweiser please? n who took the remote?

my dad in new york was doin a million things before his flight back here. he went to the gym, n he picked up the slides for the contest, n he got himself ta the airport in time, which he's always really bad at. since his flight was at 3, n they were gonna yank my hoover in new york at 2:30, dad figures he can "see" my extubation by phone, even though he's bummed he can't do the speakerphone tape recordin thing.

so let me set this up right. my dad's been waitin n waitin for me ta try ta breathe on my own, right? sure. of course, they both have. you ALL have, right? admit it. first he had this thing about bein there in person, ta kinda witness the event. then when that didn't happen, n he had ta leave town, he settled for tape recordin the speakerphone, n then THAT didn't happen, so he finally settled for listenin to it on the cell phone at the airport. so he gets all his stuff done, n he rushes to the airport, n he gets his seat, n he calls the hospital on the cell phone, ta hear

the big moment. the nurse that answers is some cheery assed
new chick we never had before, n the first thing she says is

### "guess what!
### your son doesn't have a
### BREATHING TUBE anymore !!!"

well, i knew that was a big fat mistake on this end as soon as
i heard miss priss say it. but that's cause i know my dad. any
other mom or dad woulda been totally hooray, n picked her up n
like spun her around. well, he tried ta go easy on her. i mean,
how was SHE supposed ta know he was treatin my extubation
like Y2K or somethin.

he says he THOUGHT he was feelin okay about it, once he was
on the plane. he did his little emotional checklist thing. but when
he got here, he started feelin really grumpy, all cause he missed
a dumb little extubation. he's walkin down the hall with my other
dad n gramma carol, n he comes inta my bay ta see me, n the
people are all smiley in his face n goin

### "welcome back! welcome back!

## isn't it terrific!

# he's breathing
## on his own!"

B.D. WONG

278

but of course, he only hears

"where the hell have you been?"

# "WHERE THE HELL HAVE YOU BEEN?"

*"HA, HA, you missed it!"*

### "some dad."
# "YOU SUCK."

but he tried ta snap out of it. he WAS pretty happy ta see my face, for a change, without all the paraphernalia. n for us preemies, breathin on your own IS a big deal. all i had left was a little tube across my nose, blowin me some o's ta help me out a little. they went right ta the little tube across my nose, n skipped right past the C-PAP, which is like a clunky in-between breathin tube. i was pretty proud a that.

the next day my dad spent almost the whole day on the computer writin. he had to write this big ol' essay for the contest, ta go with the pictures, n if you can believe it he actually thinks he has time for this. so he's writin like crazy, especially cause ya had ta get it to the post office by THAT DAY. he's a lunatic. most of you don't know exactly what kinda lunatic he is. like, if it's 11:55 on new year's eve, he'll say, "do we have time to make the sphinx out of LEGO before the ball drops?" and of course he's totally serious. my other dad just gets outta the way now when dad w/h.o.t. says that stuff. after 12 years, there ain't much ya can do. if ya get outta the way, n maybe egg him on a little, 9 times outta 10 there'll be a pretty nifty LEGO sphinx in the living room by midnight. aiight, 12:15 . . .

i was breathin pretty good that day. i de-satted a few times, ya know, just ta keep people on their toes. so they talked about MAYBE puttin me on C-PAP—the clunky nose tube that helps expand ya lungs—but that's hard when ya had stuff goin on in the gut like me. it blows air inta your stomach. come on, no fart jokes. gross.

dad w/o h.o.t. took my gramma carol outta the house, to leave the special projects meister alone. she couldn't believe all what dad w/h.o.t. was doin with the contest. my dad w/o h.o.t. got on the phone n called all around ta find out the latest pickups for fed-ex n the post office so insane dad could keep writin till the last minute. then he just got outta the madman's way. he explained ta gramma his technique with my other dad. light the fuse n run for cover! whatever ya do, don't tell him NOT ta do whatever he's tryin ta do, unless he's gonna get hit by a bus or somethin. so they came ta the hospital ta see me, n crazy dad was on his own.

the last postmark at the post office was at 8pm, n by the time dad wrote all afternoon, n drove ta uncle barry's house ta print it out, n got directions from the internet, n was on the road to the post office, it was past 7:30. he had ta drive out to the boonies, too. gramma carol was buggin.

but drivin like the madman he is on the way there, he realized that life was changin from the way he knew it. every day it was

changin more and more. i was changin everythin. he always
knew that would happen, n he wanted it, but he also just wanted
ta do this one last big thing first. if he didn't make the deadline,
it would really bum him out after all that work.

when he got ta the super-size post office, it was 7:50, n the
door was open, but it was empty inside. the big gates on all the
windows were all rolled down, n there was nobody there. there
was still like 10 minutes, n the mail slots were right there, but
of course dad didn't have stamps, or an envelope, or tape, or
staples ta send all the stuff with. then he thought he could get
stamps outta the machines, n he had money, but he had no
way ta seal up the old used envelope he had been usin ta carry
everythin around in. even though this kinda thing happens ta
him ALL THE TIME, this time he was more upset than usual.
he ran out inta the parkin lot, all sweaty n breathin hard, n
asked some random person if he had a stapler. the guy laughed
in his face. "aw, i left mine at home," he said. oh yeah, very
funny, my dad is thinkin. redneck. is it so outta the question
that he'd have a stapler? don't answer that. be cool, y'all. he's
my dad.

he ran back inta the post office n he was practically hyperventi-
latin by now. just this one thing, he wanted ta do just this one
thing before he brought me home. which you n i both know is
totally bogus. there are a MILLION things he wishes he could
do before i go home. ya know, he's pretty good at acceptin all
the crazy stuff that God throws his way. that's dad's thing. he
just doesn't always like the ORDER that God throws it in! but
right now, this was the most important thing in the world. he
started kissin the contest's grand prize universal home gym
that doesn't fit anywhere in our apartment good-bye. he almost
starts cryin.

then this man walks in with a buncha packages. dad says it was real strange, kinda like stephen king or the twilight zone, cause it was like just 8 n this one dude just strolls in with his arms all fulla packages, n sets 'em down like all relaxed n all. my dad starts babblin, he says does the guy have the exact correct time n would he happen ta have a stapler n he thought there was supposed ta be a window open they told him there'd be a window open why isn't there a window open, n does he have change for a twenty?

n the guy talks super slow.

n he says

"how—much—postage—do—ya—need?"

n my dad says

"sixdollarsixdollarsixdollarsixdollars"

n the guy says

"oh—i—have—six—dollars'—worth—right—here"

n he pulls out these six one-dollar stamps n gives em to my dad.

and my dad says

"ohmygodthankyouthankyouthankyouthankyou"

n he throws money at the guy.


*B.D. WONG*

n then the guy says

"do—ya—need—an—envelope?
i—got—extras—out—in—the—car."

n my dad says

"ohmygodthankyouthankyouthankyouthankyou"

n then the guy slowly looks down at his watch, n back up
ta my dad's face which is all twisted up n de-satting.

n the guy says,

"aw,—ya—need—ta—get—
this—out—tonight,

—huh?"

n my dad says,

"yestonightyestonightyestonightyesyesnownownow!"

n the guy stops, n looks at all his packages, n says

"tell ya what—"

n then he grabs one a his OWN packages

n he holds it up

n he says

"THIS one doesn't need ta go out tonight"

n then he just turns it upside down n spills all the stuff in it out onta the counter, n hands my dad the envelope!

"here . . . take . . . THIS . . . one"

speakin of stephen king, my dad is lookin like CUJO right around now, n he SWIPES at the envelope, like he hasn't eaten in weeks n it's a bag o' chips or somethin, n he shoves all the papers n the slides in it, n he scribbles the address down on it, n slaps on the stamps, n licks it with his foamy mouth, n he pulls the big hatch open n shoves it in, n it slams shut n goes echo echo echo echo.

n dad thinks but he's still not sure that it just then turned 8 o'clock.

284

dad never got the package guy's name.
he says betcha it was boaz.

the next mornin gramma carol flew back home ta long island. it sure was nice for me ta have her around, even if she worries too much. it's a jewish thing. you wouldn't understand.

that day i de-satted more, which is such a blast, cause then you get ta watch everybody hoppin around like popcorn in boilin oil. it's a barrel o' laughs. abbie, my original primary care team nurse, is totally cool, so i let her do this thing called "sigh breaths" with me. every four hours she blows air inta my lungs with a hand squeeze thing, ta help me expand my lungs.

but then late that afternoon, abbie calls my dads at gramma n grampa's. she really covers all the bases, that abbie, so she's

callin ta tell them that they're gonna put me on the clunky
C-PAP. she says she doesn't want them ta be surprised.

everyone's actin like it's a big step backward. i'm laffin. ya just
gotta keep it interestin, ya know? okay, i admit it, i messed with
abbie. i just wanted ta see how low i could de-sat before somebody did anythin. she passed the test, abbie did. she got the
ol' hand ventilator right out, n started pumpin away. way to
go, girl, i'm thinkin ta myself, while i'm lookin up at her through
the mask, all like vulnerable n cute n all.

actually, this was a big miscalculation on my part. i didn't think
they would go n actually give me a whole new breathin tube!
which is a pain in the ass. n it's a lot harder ta look adorable
with it on, even for me. but it's still fun. what's a little discomfort? don't try this at home, folks. you're talkin to the master.
i'm so good i got 'em ta start feedin me again.

285

later my night shift nurse karen grass explains ta my dads a
lotta technical stuff which they both eat right up cause she
knows so much. they're real suckers for all that garbage. i hate
it when they act like this is all happening TO me. we all know
who's in charge here. so i put on a little show for em n de-satted
a buncha times.

then karen shows my dads a way ta feed me called "venting."
that means she leaves the feedin tube open instead a corkin
it up, so that air n gas n spitups can come up in the tube,
n she said "i think he'll like it. most babies do." that was a big
mistake, her sayin that. aren't we so sure of ourself, nurse
grass, i'm thinkin. soon as she's done with her little ron popeil
"set it and forget it" demonstration, i gave her n my dads a nice
little de-sat fireworks show. my poor dads. they don't really
deserve all the grief, but i can't help it. power. it's better than

morphine. n i should know, i'm an ex-morphine user. don't worry, i'm clean now.

late that night my dad went to pick up gramma and grampa wong at the airport, cause everyone was comin back from hawaii. they were on united, which means in other words they were **3 HOURS LATE**. my dads have been flyin a lot on united lately, n nowadays they're **ALWAYS** late, or cancelled, or at a different gate than they said they would be.

anyway, my dad said that my grampa looked swell. the trip was right after tai-ngin died. it was just what grampa needed. tai-ngin was sick for so long, it was the first real vacation grampa's had in years. grampa said "it was like therapy," which is a crack-up cause my dad says grampa thinks that "therapy" means the same thing as "spa." if he only knew. anyway, he looks so happy these days. when he comes ta visit me, he gets so goofy. btw, have you ever seen a 77-year-old dude parasailing? you gotta see uncle barry's video. grampa loves bein airborne.

dad called karen ta find out how i was at around 2am. the whole operation here is 24 hours, which is right up my dad's alley. he's so into kinko's n the all-night home depot. he says there's nothin like color copies or wood filler at 3am. my other dad is the total opposite. he doesn't like stayin up late OR any kinda **STORES**. it's true. sometimes night owl dad comes ta the hospital real late ta visit me, when it's nice n still n quiet, n it's just us dudes. dad says the only thing that would make it better is if they had an atm n a take-out window. then we could shoot the breeze with some poker n buffalo wings.

karen was all peppy when dad called, cause i backed way off the shenanigans. she said i was doin great, but i was just

plannin my next big performance. guess showbiz runs in the
family. speakin a that, my dad was finally gonna do his last day
on the movie he's been doin since right before me n boaz put on
our chutes n ejected. they been just swell ta him down there in
L.A. but then the jail show wanted him too, in new york. jeez,
you'd think my dad was michael caine or somethin. not. my dad
likes workin, but this time it bugs him. he just doesn't want ta
leave me. i have that affect on people. hey, i'm sittin on truth
here. once gramma n grampa n dad w/h.o.t. were late ta go ta
the airport, all on accounta cause i just opened my eyes n looked
around a little. do not be afraid. come into my web.

right before my dad went down ta L.A., i tried not ta mess with
him too much. i had a new lung x ray, n i made sure it was nice n
clear, so he wouldn't feel too bad duckin out. they were talkin
about teachin me how ta use the nipple soon (hoo-boy lemme at
it!), so he was nervous about missin all that. and he felt a little
nervous when he told everybody that i was pale, did i need a
transfusion or somethin, but everybody else said, "you're crazy,
he looks like his old bad self."

sometimes he thinks he's paranoid.

sometimes they make him feel paranoid.

n

sometimes he actually IS paranoid.

n the poor dude never knows which one it is.

so actor dad leaves me ta take care of agent dad, n does the
last day of the movie in L.A., flies ta new york (ON TIME on
AMERICAN!), n works two days on the jail show.

287

*pack up the luggage la la la*
          *unpack the luggage la la la*
     *which town is this one? la la la*
               *hi-ho the glamourous life*

meanwhile it was time for me ta help teach the nurses how
ta nipple me. sometimes, it takes these gals a while ta get
the hang out of feedin me n my pals right. they will SAY that
preemies take a while ta learn how ta suck swallow n breathe,
but actually, n i hate ta be crass, ya gotta make em feel
useful. no sweat, i say. who's first?

nurse sue dehaan is the veteran. dads are nuts about her. she
sewed me this awesome quilt, so she's real creative (that's
why w/h.o.t. digs her), plus she's super sarcastic (that's why
w/o h.o.t. digs her). she was also the first one ta ever feed me,
way back when, so i thought she would be a good person ta
train on the ol rubba titty with.

one afternoon, when she was fixin ta feed me, i woke right
up and stared her down, n i gave her the ol' "go for it, big
mama!" i'm really good at this, so she thought it was her
idea. she melted a "shauna-sicle," warmed up a bottle, n
i grabbed some nipple action like a pro. by the time i was done
she was convinced i should get a lil more, once a day.

meanwhile, back in new york, dad was sayin "damn!" cause he
didn't wanna miss seein me "chompin at the bit" the first time.
he's been feelin a lot like a bad dad these days, not bein here
n all. he even says "B.D." stands for "bad dad." so once they
decided ta put me on the nipple once a day, he decided ta come

288

back ta be with me for the weekend, even though he could only
get away from the jail show for 48 hours.

anyway, dad says i been talkin so long you must be fallin asleep.
he says i should read ya a bedtime story. this is a good one:

b.d.

&

the
terrible,
horrible,
no good,
(very bad)
weekend.

a bedtime story by b.d.
*(with apologies to Judith Viorst).*

illustrations by Gustave Doré

it was a terrible, horrible, no good, very bad weekend.
my baby's in the hospital in san francisco.
but my boss said i had to work in new york.
he said i had to work on THURSDAY.
he said i had to work on FRIDAY.
*AND* he said i had to work on MONDAY!
"but my baby's in the hospital," i said.
"too bad," said my boss. "you have to conduct the prison
ecumenical mass on monday, cause that's the only day we can
get the muslim reverend Said, a rabbi, and Luke Perry."

"okay," i said, "but i'm going to feed my son with a nipple over
the weekend in san francisco and not even a bunch of hostile
but God-fearing prison inmates can stop me."

when i called my baby's other dad Richie, he said "nurse sue
gave him his first nipple."
"but *i* wanted to give him his first nipple!" i said.
"i know. i missed it too, dear," Richie said.

it was just the beginning of a terrible, horrible, no good, very bad
weekend.

on friday after work i drove right to the airport. i hadn't seen my
baby's other dad Richie in a long time. but he had to get back to

**B.D. WONG**

his job, too, so he came back to new york. HIS airplane was gonna *land* in new york at 5, and MY airplane was gonna *take off* from new york at 6:30. i called him with my porta-phone in the car on the way to the airport. it was 5:15. he was in a car, too, on his way *from* the airport. i didn't get to see him. i missed him. he's so nice to me.

it was already a terrible, horrible, no good, very bad weekend.

when i got to the airport, i did a smart thing! i saw a flight leaving a whole hour earlier than mine on the tv screen! i ran to the gate, and the lady was closing the door, but i said please, and she let me get on! i was so smart, because i didn't have any suitcases to check. when i sat in my seat, i called my mommy and daddy in san francisco with my porta-phone. "guess what! guess what! pick me up an hour earlier," i said. "let's have a yummy dinner together!" we jumped for joy. i was so smart. i was the last person to get on the plane, and then they shut the door!

then the plane waited on the runway for 2 hours.

it was a UNITED.

sometimes they have lasagna, but this time they only had beef and chicken.

i HATE beef.  i *HATE* chicken.

i shoulda flown ALASKA.

especially on such a terrible, horrible, no good, very bad weekend.

292

my baby's other dad is so nice. he called the hospital to make sure to tell them i wanted to be the one that gets to use the nipple to feed our baby. you can only do it once every 12 hours, otherwise the baby gets too tired. "of course, of course," they said.  my airplane finally landed after midnight. my mommy and daddy and i all went right to bed. no yummy dinner for us.

that's cause it was turning out to be a terrible, horrible, no good, very bad weekend.

when i went to the hospital in the morning, nurse abbie said,

"i nippled your son this morning!"
"what do you mean?" i said . . .

. . . "*i* wanted to nipple my son."

**B.D. WONG**

"sorry," she said. "nobody told me."
"but you can only nipple him once every 12 hours!" i said.
and she said, "don't worry! you can nipple him late tonight and
then tomorrow twice, and after that!"
"argh. i'm leaving tomorrow." i said . . .
. . . "i wanted to do it EVERY TIME! i only have 48 hours!" . . .

. . . "*i* wanted to, *i* wanted to, *i* wanted to!" . . .

. . . "ME ME ME!!!"

**"sorry," said abbie.**

she really was.
she could see it was a terrible, horrible, no good, very bad
weekend.

i didn't have any clean underwear,
and i didn't have any clean socks.

all my shirts had stickers on them that said "ICN VISITOR."
when i peeled them off, everything got all gooey.

my gums hurt.

i couldn't stand my hair, but i had to keep it for my JOB.

even $i$ couldn't look at myself in the mirror naked anymore.

when i can't look at myself in the mirror naked anymore, it's
gotta be a terrible, horrible, no good, very bad weekend.

i wanted to nipple my baby, because i wanted us to be close.
the smart people say that the best time to get close is when you're
nippling, and looking at each other, and smiling.

we nippled on saturday afternoon.
and we nippled early sunday morning.
and we nippled on sunday afternoon.
but he never opened his eyes.

**B.D. WONG**

never, never, never.
well, almost never.
i had to fly back home on sunday afternoon. my airplane was
at 3:55.

my son opened his eyes at 2:40.

my mommy and daddy and i were all late for the airport.
we just watched him and watched him, and before we knew it it
was 3:00.

grampa sure can drive fast.

especially on a terrible, horrible, no good, very bad weekend.

when we got to the airport, my mom and dad dropped me off. i
ran inside, and looked for the tv screen to find out what gate my
airplane was at. where it usually says the time, it said

# "CANCELLED"

"oh, no," i thought. "i have to go to work tomorrow in new york
at 8:30 in the morning!"

"that's okay!" said the nice man at the ticket counter, "good news! there's another flight that leaves at 10:00, and goes ALL NIGHT until 6 in the morning!"

"oh, boy," i said.

what a terrible, horrible, no good, very bad IDEA.

i shoulda flown ALASKA.

that night, before i went back to the airport, i did another smart thing. i called the airline, and the nice lady gave me my seat number! and then the nice lady told me that the airplane would take off on time from gate number 72. "lucky you!" said my mommy. "72 is right by the x-ray machine!"

(my mommy knows the whole airport just like our own house.)

then my mommy and daddy drove me to the airport. "i'm going in with you this time," my mommy said. we went to the tv screen. "hooray!" we said. "not cancelled!" then we saw that the gate was not gate number 72. it was gate number 86.

"oh, too bad," said my mommy. "THAT one's real far."
so i got on the long conveyer belt.
and i got on another long conveyer belt.
and then i got on ANOTHER long conveyer belt.
and then i walked, all the way down to gate number 86. but there was nobody AT gate number 86! "how come?" i thought.

then i went back to the tv screen, and it said gate number 72 again.

"grrr," i said.

B.D. WONG

so i got back on the first long conveyer belt.
and then i got on the second long conveyer belt.
and then i got on the THIRD long conveyer belt.

and i walked all the way back to the x-ray machine.

when i got to gate number 72, the mean man at the counter said i didn't have a seat number. "you didn't reserve a seat," the mean man said.

"yes i did," i said.

"no you didn't," the mean man said.

# "YES I DID," i said.

"how?" the mean man said.

"on the phone," i said.

"oh, the PHONE?!" the mean man laughed. "*THAT* doesn't work!"

i wondered if it was too late to fly ALASKA.

when i got on the plane, everybody had an empty seat next to them, EVEN ME!

until right before we took off, when the man with the briefcase rushed on and said,

"i'll take THAT one,"

and he pointed to the seat next to MINE.

then, everybody had an empty seat next to them, **EXCEPT ME.**

"am i the only one having a terrible, horrible, no good, very bad weekend?"

when i got off the airplane, there was just enough time for me go home, park my car, brush my teeth, and go to my job.

unless i got lost in new jersey.

which i did.

they have a big freeway there that goes to a lot of places. but there's always a big cement thing in the middle of the road, and everybody on the OTHER side of it is going where YOU want to go.

but i found my way.

after 90 minutes.

then i got into my town. when i almost got home, my porta-phone rang.

"hi, it's andy, from your job," said andy.

**B.D. WONG**

"i wanted to make sure you got in okay."

"that's so nice, andy, thanks. i did. but i—"

"great. we want you to come to work earlier."

"*grrr,*" i said to myself . . .

. . . "okay, andy, i just have to go home and brush my teeth. i've had a terrible, horrible, no good, very bad weekend."

"that's too bad," said andy.

"why can't you brush your teeth HERE?"

"*grrr,*" I said to andy.

"okay," i said, "but i have to drive my car home."

i was sore, but i felt better when i saw my baby's other dad Richie. it seemed like such a long, long time since i'd seen him last.

"what's the matter?" Richie said. "have you had a terrible, horrible, no good, very bad weekend?"

"uh huh," i said . . .

. . . "i didn't become close to our son, and my gums hurt. united airlines won't stop kicking me. i don't want to be an Executive Premier Gold Card carrier anymore."

and then he gave me a hug, like always, and he said just the right thing, like always. he said that we'd have plenty of time to become close to our baby. years and years. yeah! i thought. years and years! "you should have seen him for fifteen minutes when he opened his eyes!" i said. "they were the best fifteen minutes of my whole life."

and then he said, "see? maybe it wasn't so bad after all!"

and i thought, "you know, it really wasn't!" there are LOTS of worse things that can happen to you! especially on an airplane!

and then he reminded me that some weekends on some airplanes are just terrible, horrible, no good, very bad weekends . . .

. . . some weekends are just like that . . .

. . . even on ALASKA.

**B.D. WONG**

well, gang, what more can i say? my dad worked on the jail show
almost that whole week. this time my dads got ta be together 4
days, not 3. n my old man was right. i WAS pale. they gave me
a blood transfusion the next week, just like he predicted. ain't
he a genius?

n then, he came back here ta san francisco on one a those
dumb-ass we're-late-because-of-the-weather-not-because-
we're-on-STRIKE-or-anythin united flights, ta be with the REAL
star o' the family.

you guessed it. that would be yours truly.

n he's been here ever since.

but that, amigos, is a whole other story.

i'll let HIM tell that one.

301

peace.

oh yeah, thanks for all the rootin'.
that's really cool of y'all.

i will survive.

J. FOO 2 U

http://www.geocities.com/jacksonfoowong/

i'm workin on uncle barry ta get more new stuff up.

keep checkin!

One.

**Dear Richie and BD,**

**I feel as if I am watching life unfolding before me and I am grateful to be included to read . . . of this remarkable journey. It's funny how journeys go, they start out as one person's and become many people's. It's the great gift that the universe gave us humans. When you start walking down a path you never really know how many wonderful new sights and sounds you will experience or how many friends you will meet along the way. This is the Hero's journey and Jackson Foo has met adversity and met friends who have helped him through it and gone to unknown places and like the hero has come back stronger and wiser and made all of us a little stronger and wiser too.**

**What a wonderful life! What a joy to see it unfold.**

**Sending you strength and love and best wishes for Jackson to be a little bigger and stronger and safer day by day. He is sooo lucky to have you!!! and your extended family!!!!!!!**

**Erica**

· **ERICA SCHWARTZ** *is a Broadway production stage manager.*

302

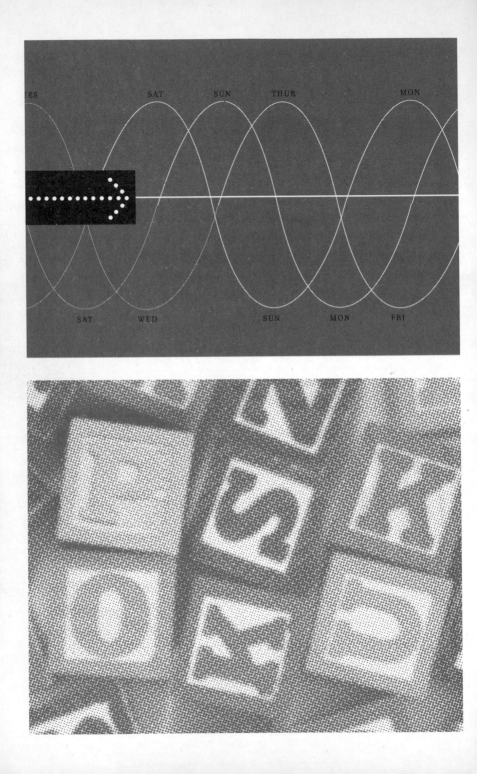

# UPDATE #10 (A,B,C)

SUBJECT:
## "THE TRIP-TYCH OF HIS LIFETIME"
(originally sent as a three-parter)

SEPTEMBER 3, 2000
(MORE THAN THREE WEEKS AFTER UPDATE #9)

San Francisco, and other points east

## << "THE ABCS OF THE ICN" >>

**ICN**
*intensive care nursery*

**Nursery:** the place in a house appropriated to the care of children.

The definition of the word "nursery" has evolved for me. I remember wanting to spit up, just like Jackson, when I first saw the nursery set for the movie *Father of the Bride Part II* (and it wasn't because the directors later abruptly removed the character I was playing from that particular scene as if he were an unwanted diaper mishap on the gorgeous Bellini rug). It was the Hollywood idea of what a nursery should be. A pretentious sprawl of pastel rocking horses and sumptuous yet impractical fabrics; no diapers, no bottles, no gnarled tubes of Desitin ointment. I go further: there was neither an oxygen tank, saturation monitor, nor amber IV drip anywhere to be seen. This movie fantasy of how the privileged baby lives, this "come on, you would have a nursery like THIS if you could afford it" attitude

*B.D. WONG*

depressed me, and this was way before I ever realized that I could actually have a child of my own; before I had a chance to have personal opinions on the subject. When the nursery was revealed in the movie, shot in all its idyllic dusky sunlight, golden, yummy as sherbet, manipulative lullaby tinkling away over whimpering strings, the movie audience gasped—of course the desired response, and a reaction I found nauseating. All that well-earned San Marino money cannot buy the warmth, welcoming, nurturing, nourishment, joy, and safety every child needs. I thought this even back then. But now . . .

The Intensive Care Nursery at UCSF, where J. Foo has spent all but five days of his nearly three months, has no imported plush giraffes or mellifluous Alan Sylvestri score, but for the Chestnut Man, in all its postwar, funky San Francisco institutional charm, it does have all of those other necessities that money *can't* buy. It has gliding chairs that don't glide anymore, rickety swings with spindly broken legs, and NOTHING aesthetically pleasing to the eye (with the notable exception of a majestic San Francisco view). But there is more magic there than all of the hand-turned European four-poster cribs and embroidered receiving blankets in every baby boutique on Rodeo Drive. Granted, it is everyone's job to inspire the mysterious phenomenon of healing there. There is also much anxiety, much fear, much despair. But permeating the air there, amid all of the sanitized surfaces and clinical behavior, is the distinctly comforting aroma of hope, and for me, the triumph of merely *attempting* to conquer the daily myriad of medical obstacles in the nursery far outweighs the stench of grief ever sensed there, and Richie and I have smelled both. This fragrant hope comes not from the no-nonsense interior design of the nursery itself, but from the souls who work there, and from their passion

307

to cure, their commitment to ease, and their willingness to spend every hour of every day LEARNING about both. How thankful we are for this. We had always been told from several sources, "go to a teaching hospital," and now i know why. Rather than that overpriced set of antique baby blocks in the Hollywood nursery, there are, at the top of an ordinary building on a blustery hill in San Francisco, the building blocks of Life, and they spell out the monograms found in the textbook which guides a premature infant on his perilous way. Only once a student like Jackson has mastered each of these infan- tile initials may his weary but grateful parents bring the scholar home . . .

## J.F.W'S ALPHABET

N E C,

C P A P,

I V, M R I,

E K G, M B M,

R O P, C P R, R N,

Etc.

*B.D. WONG*

**necrotizing (gastro)enterocolitis**

This is the condition which was the impetus for Jackson to be transported from Beautiful Downtown Modesto to the hilltop on Parnassus Street in San Francisco on Friday, June 2. Wasn't Parnassus the mountain where all of the gods, those in dominion over all fate, lived? NEC was the reason for that surgery that everyone made such a commotion over, during which they removed and repaired his entire intestine, and then stuffed it all back in, willy-nilly, like Richie's sock drawer. Apparently it was restuffed in a sufficiently orderly manner (NOT like Richie's sock drawer). Richie had bristled when one of the residents referred to the process of painstakingly perusing each centimeter of bowel (in order to find the bad part) as "rummaging":

"My son's intestines are being rummaged," Richie would say . . .

"We flew him all the way up here for RUMMAGING?"

Today, Jackson manufactures the "Grey Poop-On" with dependable, uh, regularity. Suppositories are given minimally, usually by a new nurse who is not familiar with his cavalier evacuation itinerary. During my latest stay here in San Francisco over the most recent weeks, I have become adept enough at changing his diapers through the obstacle course of monitor wires so as to avoid that "explosion at *le factorie dijon*" effect which often seems to occur as soon as the sphincter is exposed to the air and the knees are pulled up to slide in the fresh diaper. The other day he hosed down the wall of the isolette a good foot away from him using his own good ol' #2, with me feebly looking down from the outside of its Plexiglas ceiling, as if the pump on the curry vinaigrette dressing dispenser suddenly was malfunctioning disastrously; I'm standing there with the empty salad plate in my hand going, "Um, can somebody get the manager?" Thank goodness for the sneeze guard. It protects the customer, too, not just the food.

Then I joyfully reminded myself:

### *"lighten up!*

## *HEEZA POOPIN' "*

NEC: Chec NEC off your list.

# C P A P

### *continuous positive air pressure*

When Jackson was finally extubated, they really went for it and let him fly without a net of ANY kind, like a cold turkey flying to Ft. Lauderdale for the winter, or the littlest Wallenda. I believe he lasted about twenty-four hours this way, but needed to work a little harder breathing than a person of leisure who lies around all day and has people feeding them and changing their clothes and cleaning up their personal messes should have to. So they put him on what is called a nasal cannula, which is that simple tube that goes across the nose, with the two prongs that go into the nostrils, like that old lady you see at the grocery store who is dragging an oxygen tank around on a hand truck behind her, but you are smiling and pretending it's not there, while you chat about whether the broccoli smells bad or not.

*B.D. WONG*

Then he had that little dip, when Abbie had to hand-ventilate him, so they upped his assistance to CPAP. CPAP differs from the nasal cannula in that in addition to the oxygen it gives him, it also gives air PRESSURE, which helps keeps his lungs from collapsing. This collapse (atelectasis) has always been one of the major gremlins responsible for his inability to saturate a high enough percentage of oxygen into his bloodstream. The CPAP got him back to de-satting much less often.

I gave Jackson one of his first baths, you know, actually in a tub with water, not just a wipey-wipey thing, during this time when he had the CPAP. They will sometimes actually disconnect a baby's CPAP for the duration of the bath, to make it easier to put him in the water. They were pretty confident that Jackson could last without it, but just in case they had the bag and mask at hand for what they call "blow bys" (I'm not touching that one); they basically just blow oxygen into his face if he de-sats until he gets the numbers on the monitor back up.

I was just as UN-confident about my ability to give him a bath as they were confident that his breathing would be okay through it. This is apparently not uncommon with new ICN dads. If you are a faithful Foo Follower I'm sure you can easily imagine by now what I would be like giving my son a bath . . . how, shall we say, *"thorough"* I might be. I just wanted to follow all the steps they taught me, okay? So cut me some slack, it took a little more time than your average infant bath. I was *learning*. It took so long that for some reason I had to rush off just as it was done, either to the airport or something, and so I left Nurse Abbie with the straightening up after. But during the bath, I distinctly thought to myself, "Gee, he's doing really well off the CPAP . . ."

When I checked back in with Abbie after I had done whatever it was I rushed off to, she told me that I had taken so long with the bath, and Jackson had done so *swimmingly*, that they never put the CPAP back in. He was just sailing, and it was time again to see if he was ready for a longer cruise.

You see?

## ALL GOOD THINGS COME FROM OBSESSIVE/ COMPULSIVE BEHAVIOR.

Another example of the good old-fashioned arbitrary medical treatment I was telling you about:

> DOCTOR:
> "He needs it he needs it he needs it he needs it."

> NURSE:
> "But Doctor, it fell out, and he's doing fine."

> DOCTOR:
> "Did I say he needs it? No, he doesn't need it. Leave it out."
> NURSE:
> "Yes, ma'am."

Jackson eventually went back onto the old lady nasal cannula, where he is now, but CPAP?

See CPAP. See CPAP done.

*intravenous*

The IV was one of the first gifts Jackson received at his "stability party" at the ICN in Modesto (and oh, what a *marvelous* party that was) and, like CPAP, he has danced a flirtatious tango with it ever since.

An IV line doesn't stay open for very long in the vein where it has been installed, so every few days Jackson would have the bizarre tube and its accoutrements protruding from a *different* part of his body, moving around arbitrarily from body part to body part like the "hokey pokey" (except that you mustn't shake it all about). Originally he also had an IV for bloodwork, but because he was obviously going to have a lot of traffic on *that* highway, with blood gas levels taken constantly and quite a few transfusions, Stacey Levitt skillfully installed a more permanent "spaghetti line," which does *not* collapse after a few days, and makes a bee-line right to his heart. I am a lot like the "spaghetti line," actually. I always try to make a beeline right to his heart, and I can usually go at least a week before collapsing.

313

One morning, when I came to the nursery and presented myself for the ritual of Nurse Abbie's daily report on his condition, I couldn't help but notice a truly bizarre bandage and plastic medical-looking thingie protruding asymmetrically from the top of Jackson's HEAD. Jackson just lay there, benignly oblivious to it, as if he had just got it from the Henri Bendel Millinery Salon yesterday, but was already totally *over it*.

I became, from the beginning, really keen to picking up the nurses' vibes. I can tell immediately when I walk into the room if there is something wrong or not, and Abbie is chattering away about how he is doing and not saying a word about *le nouvelle chapeaux*. Looking back, I must have reached a point of numbness which allowed me to not fly into immediate hysteria about *Mystery Science Theater* sticking out of my son's head, because Abbie never forgets *ANYTHING;* she is so superhumanly trustworthy. Yet I am periodically glancing down at it, whenever she is not looking, until she finishes her progress report and turns away. At this point, there's only so much intentional deep breathing and nonchalant shifting of weight from one foot to the other a person should have to do, I feel. So I said, as casually as I could (I'm an actor, you see), "So, uh, Abbie, I guess that's a 'new' thing, huh?"

Abbie wheels around as soon as I say it and says, "Oh my GOD! I'm so sorry! I forgot to warn you about that! It's just an IV! It's *NOTHING!* We ran out of arms and legs! Please don't worry! It's not coming out of his BRAIN! Most parents say, 'what's that thing coming out of my baby's brain?' But it's *not* coming out of his *BRAIN!!!*"

Sweet Abbie. We were both laughing, and I said, "Don't worry, Abbie, I know you'd tell me if you needed to hook something up to his BRAIN, duh!"

Then as we laughed, I turned to the isolette to look at him, all those things sticking out of him. So dependent. Abbie turned back to what she had been doing when I came in.

**"Wouldn't she?"** I asked my reflection in the Plexiglas.

The point is that the many tubes and wires that have at times made Jackson look like a broken Pinocchio on

**B.D. WONG**

some futuristic Gepetto's workshop table have slowly become less and less. He's much more of a cordless model these days . . .

As he has fought his various gut wars, he went on the IV drip for nourishment and off it at the drop of a, yes, hat. Eventually he went from the feeding tube permanently to nippling from the bottle, and suddenly, that hat was LAST season's sensation, and already a collector's item.

Once he began nippling, he never had a use for the repogel, the tube in his stomach which let the air out and checked for bilious substances, ever again.

As his blood pressure stabilized, he *eschewed* the direct lead to the BP monitor, having less frequent readings taken by hand instead.

So the spectacular "multimillion-dollar stage production" of wrangling all that extra stuff in order to simply *hold* the Chestnut Man (which Richie and I only enjoyed on rare occasions), eventually was more like a little magic show in somebody's backyard. Pretty soon, people were lining up to hold and hug and protect a boy who had only one tube, a cable, and three tiny little wires left coming from his tiny swaddled bundle.

None of those are IVs.

IV: N/A.

## magnetic resonance imaging

No, they're not just for grown-ups anymore. It seems so long ago that Foo had all those brain ultrasounds to search for blood in his little ventricals. It seems so long ago that they said, "When he gets ready to go home, we'll give him an MRI, which is a much more sensitive test and will show more of what's going on up there than the ultrasounds have." That will be the final word on the situation in the Jackson Foo Wong Air Traffic Control Tower. Could anything have changed by the time he had this "final" MRI? Could this ultrasensitive test reveal new horrors, which would prolong his stay and treatment at UCSF? Have I been squeezing his tiny soft spot too hard as I zealously feed him?

### 316 *NO! NO! NO!*

Findings: Grade One bleed. The most minor classification. Fellow Roberta Keller cautiously yet optimistically states that long term, there *should be* no neurological problems. The damage that the supersensitive MRI picked up is very slight, and located only in the parts of the brain that rule motor function. No intellectual challenges expected, except with his dads in a few years, when they try to help him with algebra. At the very worst, Roberta straight-shoots, "he may be a bit klutzy." This minor damage is relegated to the lower extremities. "At the very worst, maybe he won't be a ballerina, or a tap dancer," she says.

"We'll see about *that*," replied "Papa Rose" . . .

I'm sure he'll be swell, he'll be great, gonna have the whole world on a plate.

**B.D. WONG**

Move over, Savion Glover. Smile, baby.

MRI: MysteRI solved.

***electrocardiogram***

This is not the fancy name for a heartfelt message
sent by wire. After one noteworthy, stunning episode
during which Jackson's sat monitor showed he was
de-satting down to the 20s (we always want it at least
above 80) which you'll hear about a little later, he
began having what they call "transient bradycardic
episodes," during which his HEART RATE would lower,
and *THAT* monitor would flash red. For two and a half
months, that number never turned red. Now, all of a
sudden, his heart rate would lower as far as the low
60s, when it was usually well above 100 or even 130,
and this was rather puzzling.

317

Puzzling because simultaneously I was being forced
by everyone around me to begin thinking in terms of
Jackson being well enough to go home. He had begun
nippling regularly, and at higher volumes, and gaining
weight, and his breathing was more stable, and eventually he had his nonthreatening MRI. But these alarming
"bradys," as they are nicknamed, made me incapable
of being able to embrace his proximate discharge, let
alone find joy in it. I chose to interpret everyone's
enthusiasm as an inability on their part to take him
seriously, and therefore to take *ME* seriously. Yeah,
it's always about me. In part, I was unwilling and unable
to relinquish his status as a character in the ICN soap
opera who deserved only the sexiest story lines. But I
was also afraid and trained to expect that something

inevitably would prove their enthusiasm premature. That always happens.

So after a Bunch of Bradys, the cardiology department paid a visit. They had no better explanation than I for these dips, and they were not terribly severe, but they *were* uncharacteristic and deserved investigation. So they looked up his old "echo" exam records (taken back when Abbie heard the murmur) and ordered an EKG. I was told at this time that some kind of opening in his heart could cause these bradys, oh brother, but that his history did not indicate that this was likely.

Indeed, the EKG was squeaky clean.

As time goes on, I sense the doctors and nurses worrying less and less about the de-satting and bradying. I resist joining them in this, opting instead for the Aurora Greenway from *Terms of Endearment*, *"MY DAUGHTER NEEDS HER PAINKILLER NOW!!!!!"* approach, which doctors and caregivers find so easy to work with. But even I cannot deny that his episodes have become less alarming, that his de-sats and bradys are gradually losing their bite, and that he no longer needs "stim" (-ulation) to "make the numbers green again" (that's the high-tech-nique of poking him with your finger like the Pillsbury Doughboy to make him breathe). So when the doctors announced that a week without significant de-sats or bradys would make Jackson a likely candidate for liberation, it took me and Richie at least the same amount of time to grasp their edict with a positive perpective.

Then the day finally came where I never looked at the monitor, because it never called me . . .

EKG: 'E K'n Go.

**B.D. WONG**

***mother's breast milk***

As I write this, I've been in San Francisco on this trip for more than three weeks, and Jackson has been slowly mastering the art of the nipple. He has gone from taking a bottle in about forty-five minutes to his current record of about eight minutes; his volume has gone from that 33cc "full feed" to as much as 80cc. Where he was once rather inept at sucking, swallowing, and breathing simultaneously, he has now started connecting the dots, allowing "green" to triumph on the sat monitor over "red" more often. Now he chugs the ambrosiatic nectar like a frat boy at a Saturday night kegger, complete with the drink-soaked T-shirt collar, the residual spill out the sides of the mouth, and the glazed expression of ecstasy.

The other night a new nurse came on and began to thaw some breast milk. She tiptoed up to me, and meekly explained that there were no bottles of milk in the "yellow bin" in the freezer.

Remember the Breast Milk Freezer incident of 2000? Well, the yellow bin is the container which I had hysterically labeled

### JACKSON FOO WONG:

# TODAY'S MENU.

### USE MILK FROM THIS BIN ONLY!!!!!

Yes folks, there were five exclamation points. Next to it, in which most of the other milk was stashed in neat little dated, zippered freezer bags, was a larger blue bin which screamed,

*FOLLOWING FOO*

## "DO NOT USE MILK FROM THIS BIN.

## USE MILK ONLY IN THE YELLOW

## 'TODAY'S MENU' BIN TO THE RIGHT"

with a big obnoxious arrow pointing to said yellow bin.
I made these signs with three-by-five cards and black
marker, and I would go in periodically and transfer the
oldest bottles from the blue bin to the yellow bin. This
was all because Shauna had pumped so much milk that
when we went home, I didn't want to be bringing home
the older stuff, and the nurses could not be expected
to keep track of all the dates for me. Plus, it's also
because I'm completely insane.

**320**     You can classify all of Jackson's nurses in one of two
categories: either they are cautious and fearful of the
milk situation, and of my reaction to it, because by now
everybody knows what a "mad cow" I am; or they are
laughing their asses off at me about the milk behind my
back, covering their eyes, opening the freezer door, and
grabbing whatever the hell is in front of them anyway,
regardless of the signage.

So by the time this new nurse gingerly told me that
the yellow bin was empty, I had worried exhaustively
about so many other things that I just looked up at
her slowly, with a quizzically furrowed brow, paused,
and monotonously said, "Oh, that? Oh. Gee. Um, don't
worry about that. Just take it out of the blue bin.
We're not doing that anymore. I mean, *I'm* not doing
that anymore. But thanks. I'll go take down those
signs."

**B.D. WONG**

So that crossroad was kind of the pivot point at which I turned away from the merry path of denial and protection I have been skipping down for months now.

Invariably a nurse you pass in the hall or another parent says, "He's getting ready to go home soon, isn't he? Aren't you excited?" But I can't just reply, "Yes, I am. Isn't that great?" Instead, I stiffen like an ironing board, smile falsely and say, "Gee, really? Hmmm, wouldn't that be nice." Part of this is the superstition of speaking out of turn before Fate. Was it all that "twin enthusiasm" prebirth which caused God to bellow, "Wait a minute! **NOT SO FAST!!!**" in His best James Earl Jones?

Mostly, I can't accept that such a traumatic situation could rectify itself so quickly, especially since my own trip of comprehending him as a well baby is apparently not a nonstop flight, with quite a few layovers. I don't think I am afraid of the responsibility of taking over the care of him. You know I long for that. I just can't believe that someone so tiny could negotiate corners so abruptly, with no training in the Olympic event of corner-turning. Yet the nurses who have been on vacation, the doctors who have rotated to the lab and returned, and the family and friends who have made a second visit after weeks away all say, "I can barely recognize him . . ." He is gradually making the awe-inspiring transformation from a sickly fetal creature to a small but unmistakably human cherub; steadily drawing the ivory growth serum from the tiny bottles as if he knows that the life force within them can force him to life.

The other day, Fellow Roberta Keller ran by me the name of the formula we would be switching to if/when Jackson ran out of Shauna's milk. Sure enough, two mornings

321

ago, nurse Karen Grass thawed the last two miniature bottle liners full of Shauna-licious. Two and a half months since she began pumping, this landmark in nourishment for Jackson, the end of the chapter titled "SHAUNA'S BREAST MILK" represents the tremendous span of Shauna Ann Barringer's herculean contribution to my life. The gift of her maternal nourishment is just a small symbol of that much greater gift she has given, a gift which can *never* run dry.

Yesterday afternoon, for the first and perhaps the only time, Shauna sat in one of those rickety old gliding chairs in the Intensive Care Nursery on Mount Parnassus with Jackson Foo Wong on her welcoming lap, and ever so tenderly, and ironically, fed him from a bottle filled with some of his first taste of "Enfamil 22" formula. At the transcendent sight of the *über*-madonna (who once only dreamed of bearing a child for some couple who couldn't) as she fed the fruit of her labors, Shauna's accompanying girlfriend Kendis (a surrogate herself very pregnant with another two guys' twins) burst into joyful sobs.

MBM: Good to the last drop.

## R O P

### *retinopathy of prematurity*

**The *EYE THING*.** There are four stages of ROP. When J. Foo had his first eye exam, his eyes were pronounced "immature," which meant that it was too early to tell whether or not the blood vessels in his eyes were developing normally or abnormally. Two weeks after that first, he was declared "stage 1." For each of the next three exams after that, he has been "stage 2." What the hell does all that mean? Beats me like a Finnish spa attendant. I do know that laser surgery isn't prescribed until "stage 3," and that blindness isn't really an issue unless it's "stage 4."

There has always been a *lack of focus* to Richie's and my understanding of the whole Eye Thing. The ophthalmologists seem so disconnected from the day-to-day comings and goings of the nursery. They never tell you when they are planning to examine your baby. The specialist invariably breezes in and out whenever you are feeding the meter or running out for coffee, like the cable lady or the guy delivering your new sofa. "Sorry. We *were* here. Call for another appointment." You are never able to talk to her or him unless you put the effort into tracking her or him down. It feels like someone comes to explain things to you for just about every other department. But "re: retina," Richie and I are always *in the dark.* Richie has a particular phobia over the whole eye issue, even more so than he had over Jackson's brain and heart exams; perhaps the lack of human contact is the reason why.

Jackson was scheduled for his latest eye exam last Thursday. If it were found he had become stage 3 or 4 at this exam, laser therapy or surgery would be required, and we would go into extra innings. This really gave Richie agita. Roberta Keller said that scheduling exams every two weeks like this is a sign that it's usually not particularly urgent, but Richie was still uneasy. It is always the dad who is home in New York who suffers the most from disconnection, from fear, from paranoia. I made the mistake of saying that a "bad" eye exam was the only thing which could postpone Jackson's possible discharge, giving it all too much weight.

I tried to tell Richie not to worry or be confused, which of course served to worry and confuse him, and so we went back and forth like Abbott and Costello in a routine called "Foo's on First," until Richie had a kind of "conniption fit" which he refers to as

### *"THE UNRAVELING."*

We are both so unsure of whether we would feel better if Jackson was completely well and therefore going home immediately, or *not* well, therefore demanding that this immaculate care continue.

But whether Richie and I were ready or not, last Thursday Dr. Good, the ophthalmologist, came and once again declared Jackson "stage 2." He said Jackson could see (God willing) an opthalmologist in New York instead of Dr. Good again, if we were home in two weeks. This was good news, but it still left the whole eye thing up in the air . . .

Two weeks?

A fortnight?

I had secretly hoped Dr. Good would come up with some complicated, non-sight-/non-life-threatening diagnosis which would keep the doctors from using sentences with the words "discharge" or "release" in them, so that I could keep Jackson at UCSF forever.

I mean, if you're not going to tell me he's 20/20, I would be perfectly content if the Wizard took off in the hot-air balloon without us, leaving me in these tacky ruby slippers, tightly clutching my little Toto in this Technicolor fantasy for all eternity.

**B.D. WONG**

But he didn't. After all, let's face it, there's no place like home.

ROP: Resolution-opathy of Postpone-ity

**cardio pulmonary resuscitation**

## << CPR, ACT ONE: WATCHING THE VIDEO >>

One day while Jackson was having a little lunch on me, literally, Nurse Abbie wheeled out a humongous television and VCR, audiovisual nerd that she can be, and popped in the "Infant CPR" video. "You should watch this if you're going to take him home soon," she said, "and you should sign up for the class, too."

"Well, actually, Abbie," the evil little voices in my head chimed, "we're NOT going to be taking him home soon. Whoever told you we were, pray tell? You see, we're NEVER taking him home, if *I* have anything to say about it. Come to think of it, Abbie, perhaps *YOU* should watch the infant CPR video, since *YOU'LL* be taking care of Jackson until college. Oh, and Abbie, who do you hafta know to get some Pringles around here, huh?"

Of course, rather than repeat what the voices were saying (advice: don't do it), I nodded inanely, and watched the video, while I knocked some gas outta the Chestnut Man, and held him upright to keep his reflux at bay.

It was your typical instructional-type video, circa 1979, in which, rather than have the female narrator look directly into the lens of the camera the usual way, some brilliant director had the inspired idea of having her address various random, nonspecific places OFF-camera, in order, I believe, to create the effect that she was addressing an entire CLASS that you (lucky, lucky you) were privileged to be enrolled in. However, as you watched the tape all by yourself, it just made you feel like a total *ass*. The result was more like being forced to have a listless conversation with an uninteresting woman sporting an outdated hairdo at a cocktail party, during which a stream of people she finds more compelling than you are entering the room from various doorways around you. It really played to my low self-esteem.

Plus, there is something downright surreal in an instructional video about saving a baby's life, literally breathing the life back into a child, when the infant depicted is a plastic doll with a perpetual O expression, like the baby version of a blow-up mannequin from some sleazy adult bookstore. It's just not very motivating, not to mention unsavory. It's hard to take seriously. Maybe if we got to KNOW the CHARACTER of the plastic doll as a PERSON, then we could *ROOT* for the plastic doll to "make it" . . . but *no*. I frankly found the dolls employed in the various vignettes of the video missing a certain HEROIC quality. Not to mention that one plastic doll with an O mouth is no different from the next, with the possible exception of the occasional doll *à la negro*. The O mouth is far from the most expressive facial feature, pardon my honesty.

The performances by these babies were all rather lifeless. I wanted to shout, "Don't bother! *IT'S TOO LATE!!!*" Call me critical, and grumpy. I was also irritated with Abbie for not providing popcorn.

**326**

**B.D. WONG**

Of course, there's no other way to demonstrate these techniques. Yet it's absurd watching a bad female actor dressed as a housewife calmly kneeling over a Cabbage Patch Kid, closing her mouth over its polyvinyl nose and mouth, breathing, and counting while she pokes down into its hard little chest with her fingers. I found it preposterous.

*Or was I just worried about*
*actually ever having to do this?*

The video is designed to teach you to think of a quiet afternoon in your living room, alone with your infant, during which some delightful event creates a need for you to resuscitate your child by massaging her heart and breathing air into her nose and mouth, as an everyday, domestic event, like baking Toll House cookies from scratch. The video had an unpanicked, antiseptically relaxed air about it reminiscent of a nuclear evacuation film hosted by Mr. Rogers. It underlines all the important points of infant CPR, including what you need to know if your child is choking.

Every parent of an ICN infant must take the infant CPR class, and the class is one of many things which the nurses check off your list (like whether you've been briefed on your child's meds, or learned how to bathe him) prior to your discharge.

Oops, pardon me, prior to **YOUR CHILD'S** discharge; Freudian slip.

So, with my own little lifelike doll tucked beneath my arm, I'm thinking, Gosh, that could be us. I might have to actually do this someday. With his "chronic lung disease/de-satting/bradycardic/whatnot" record, I really need to know this, don't I? The realization that Jackson's LIFE would soon be in our hands, and no longer in the safe haven of the hospital, began seeping sneakily into the water-damaged, cobwebbed, termite-infested attic of my mind.

Then they got to the choking part. To dislodge an obstruction in the airway, turn the baby over and strike her on her back with the heel of your hand. Up until this point in the video the actors had all intentionally behaved in a nonalarming, torpid manner, devoid of any semblance of tension or distress. But I was so shocked to see the video mom strike the heel of her hand repeatedly into the doll's back with brute force, **ONE**
**TWO**
**THREE**
**FOUR**

**FIVE TIMES,** that I was shaken and stirred into a sickening reality. Looking down at the Chestnut Man, who was munching adorably, I could only imagine him smashing like a tiny overripe pumpkin if I were to do that, with all the strings and seeds and slimy stuff going everywhere. God, this is awful. Not all of the underacting in the world could any longer obscure the desperation you must feel when you have to resort to using such force on your baby, and all it would take is an unchewed garbanzo bean or a disenfranchised button from the cuff of a talent agent's dress shirt to do that. Sigh . . .

"Abbie, where's that phone number to sign up for the class?"

Teacher, do I really have to read the book? I saw the movie.

CPR: CPRL punishment (for dolls).

**B.D. WONG**

## INTERMISSION:
## A FATHER'S FINAL FIT FROM THE PHOBIA OF FREEDOM

Richie and I always felt that when Jackson was ready to go home, the arc of his recovery would have been logical and obvious and climactic, ending like the triumphant last movement of an exhausting, multimovement Mahler symphony. I assumed that when it was time, Richie and I would both be as emotionally primed as Jackson was physically. I assumed that OUR healing would correspond neatly with our son's. That OUR healing would come BEFORE his . . .

Once again I was absurdly mistaken.

A few weeks ago they told me that Jackson was being moved from the West Wing to the North Wing, and that he was being taken out of the isolette and would now live in an open bed. Within the West Wing he had been moved many times, like a marble in a game of lightning Chinese checkers, but goin' north was different. The entire nursery is still called the Intensive Care Nursery, but they refer to the North Wing less alarmingly as "special care," and as a "step-down" unit. Most parents would be thrilled at this. Right?

I was stricken. One of the main reasons for the move was Jackson's extubation, for they do not deal with the more complicated looking-after of intubated babies up North. But I was unprepared for Jackson to be placed in a lower-maintenance classification, to part with some of our favorite specialized nurses (like Abbie), to be geographically farther away from the doctors' office . . .

and to receive less attention.

329

As for the isolette, he WAS holding his temperature better, which was the main reason for him to be in one. Gosh, it would be easier to hold him, and to bathe him, and to watch him grow.

*"Oh, all right,"* I said, shuffling my feet and looking at the shiny floor. Go ahead. Put him in the open crib. But as for moving to the North Wing, he just isn't ready for that. No way. He's very sick. He really needs specialized observation.

"What do you mean he needs to share a nurse with TWO other babies? What happens if he has a big de-sat, and needs blow-bys or needs to be hand-ventilated with the bag and mask and she is wiping some other well baby's ***ASS?***"

In the irritatingly composed manner that they all seem to have mastered, they replied that yes, they knew he was still having a few de-sat episodes, but there's always the second nurse in the bay, who also has three babies, and the two nurses always cover each other. In the case of an absolute emergency, they specifically said, there's always that "code" button on the wall, which everyone responds to in an emergency. They hastily added, "That will never happen."

***W o n n n d e r r r f u l l l .***

Goin' North, in the convertible, not the hard top. This was a big big deal. Not for him. For ***ME.***

One day Richie and I said, "Something's wrong. We're not appreciating this right. Maybe he really is getting better. Maybe he won't be in the hospital forever. We should be enjoying this."

**B.D. WONG**

I guess I am in a perpetual state of resentment these days, I'm ashamed to say, because none of this, and I mean not one major part of it to speak of, has ever gone the way I thought I wanted it to. None of it has been under my rule. For a self-confessed fiend whose favorite hobby is *control*, this adjustment has been like playing Helen Keller in a first-class production of *The Miracle Worker*. I've thrown porridge and milk products all over the walls at the end of the first scene in a theatrical tantrum, the likes of which have never before been seen on any stage, and even after Annie Sullivan wrestles me to the floor, and punches and kicks me in the head with her turn-of-the-century high-button boots, I *still* don't get it.

This relinquishing of control has been the nucleus of what has been unquestionably the most empowering and fortunate aspect of these last two years. The cool part, if you will. To be forced to learn that you are at best your favorite character in the video game of life, and that once you drop that quarter, the meteors that shower your way, as well as how much power they have to render you helpless, are not of your choosing. If you get good at mastering the joystick, you can dodge and whiz past the androids. If you do get zapped, you might still possibly survive; maybe eventually enter your initials under "Top Scores." But please don't think that twenty-five cents buys you a brand of fun of your own mastery. That twenty-five cents is only for the privilege of playing. Besides, it's not FUN if it IS of your own mastery anyway, right? Yes, Jackson. Video games once used to cost a quarter.

So Jackson got to meet a whole new cast of characters in the diverse forms of five roommates, and I begrudgingly settled in with a perpetual crabby expression on my face. Whenever the slightest thing occurred which gave me the impression that the nurse was overextended, or that Jackson's condition was too intense for this laid-back, California step-down thing, I immediately found one way or other to sneer, "See, I told you he doesn't belong here. When are we going back? Could you hold the door open? *I'll* push the crib."

Eventually, of course, I chilled. It all actually forced me to submerge myself in the day-to-day learning of how to take care of our boy. Soon after learning how to nipple, together, I was measuring and warming and feeding with an actual devil-may-care attitude, throwing over my shoulder to the nurses opinions about how much I think we should give him at any given feeding. Then I graduated to learning about his five medications, and soon I was juggling the meds, the feedings, and the baths like a plate spinner from some Communist country. Just get me a unicycle and I will wait in the toilet paper line for you.

So long, West Wing.

It was a grand term, President Bartlett.

Tell Abbie we will miss her.

### << CPR, ACT TWO: SEEING THE DEMONSTRATION >>

A couple of days later, it was a bright, sunny Saturday. The sun streamed into the North Wing of the Intensive Care Nursery optimistically, and I was trying to bask in the glow of Jackson's progress. I was making progress, too, becoming pretty comfortable giving him a bath and drawing up the five medicines to go with his feedings every twelve hours. Good ol' Sue DeHaan, the ICN war vet, was Jackson's day nurse, and she firmly and cheerily and amusingly was nudging me out of the nest, testing me by making me do more and more things on my own for Chestnut. Her energy matched the peerless San Francisco weather on the hilltop that day, crisp and confidence-inspiring; the colorful scrubs which she had sewn herself were equally merry and encouraging. I was even beginning to grasp the concept of our impending independence.

Then something awful happened.

Sometime around five in the afternoon, the second nurse on duty in the same bay, Julie, took her break. Sue would cover all six of their babies while Julie was briefly out. I was feeling pretty great, bathing our son. There are a few times here and there when I know he is my son for sure, and one of them is when I dunk him in a tub of warm water, and softly cup handfuls of the bathwater over the top of his sweet head. He makes a goofy, blissful face that I have seen not only in the mirror, but on my father.

As per my rigorous training, the milk bottle is soaking scrumptiously in the hot tap water, and the cozy flannel receiving blankets from the warmer are waiting to surround his helpless body reassuringly. I expertly transfer him to the open crib, and diaper him up, always making sure there's warm cotton printed with duckies snuggled around His Dampness at all times. I quickly reconnect all his monitor wires, and Sue prepares to show me how to give him his one reflux medicine that doesn't go in the milk. Given a half hour before he eats, it is a kind of antacid; it is simply squeezed from a tiny syringe directly into his mouth.

Because we were a little late with the bath and because I'm taught to do everything bang bang bang, one chore right on the tail of another, Sue is poised with the syringe as I am drying him. She sits him up, and shows me how to squeeze out the contents of the syringe, not into the back of his throat, but into the side of his mouth. Sue confidently gives the syringe one, two, three little squirts, and doesn't baby him with a pacifier; he misses not a drop. He actually appeared to savor the sticky sweet tonic, making a tiny smacking sound and sitting still with a kind of smirk on his face, which cracked us up.

Then we noticed that he didn't open his mouth again; that it stayed tightly shut.

All of a sudden, his oxygen saturation level began dropping dramatically, causing the monitor to beep and flash red. It is preferred he saturate from about 88 to 94; 100 is peachy. Below 80 is when the numbers flash red, but Jackson hasn't really de-satted below around 68 in a long time . . .

**99**

**92**

**88**

**81**

**80**

**79**

**B.D. WONG**

**79**

**79**

**79**

**79**

**79**

**79**

**79**

**79**

**79**                                                                    *335*

**79**

As soon as it starts beeping and flashing,
you always hold your breath

to see if it will go *UP*

*or DOWN . . .*

**79**

**79**

**79**

**79**

**75**

**75**

**75**

**75**

**75**

**74**

**73**

**72**

**71**

**70**

Sue, ever used to this bratty preemie behavior, always knows exactly what to do (you may recall that she's the sassy nurse who has been working at UCSF, in the ICN, for more than thirty years). She always just springs into action, nudging the baby to get him to stabilize his breathing, and starts talking tough love, without missing a beat.

"Oh, come on, mister, you can't get away with *THAT* now. Not with me. You're getting too old for this nonsense. Let's see a little breathing, pal."

**68**

**66**

**64**

**63**

**62**

**61**

"Come on, J. Foo, you're freakin' your dad out, here!"

**59**

"Come on, honey, breathe for me! Breathe for Dad. I
can't take you home if you're gonna keep doing that!"

**57**

"This ain't funny, J. Foo. Mister man."

**55**

"Sue, is he okay?"

**51**

**47**

**46**

**42**

**37**

**32**

**31**

**30**

Sometime between the 60s and the 30s, Jackson screwed up his face and started making this straining sound, which I thought was good. Crying was usually a sign that his breathing would soon stabilize. Besides, they are always teaching me to watch his color, and when he cries he turns nice and pink. He did, he turned bright pink!

**338** Then he turned red.

Then he turned burgundy.

Then he turned purple.

Then not only his face, but his entire *body* was as *BLACK* as the
        darkest,

            richest

                **EGGPLANT.**

**29**

**29**

**29**

**29**

**29**

**29**

**29**

There was a noticible shift in Sue's energy when Jackson
turned that horrifying shade of *aubergine,* and he hit
"29." She swiftly carried him over from the bathing
table to the crib, laid him down, and when the usual
nudging, poking, and tickling did not activate him to
unclench his mouth, which was drawn tight like a vise,
she grabbed the bag and mask, which was nearby in
the event of an emergency, and began hand-ventilating
him forcefully. The hollow sound of the bag inflating
and the rubber bulb pulsing and rhythmically emptying
in Sue's fist was artificial and sickening. I stood watching dumbly, for it was obviously an inappropriate time
to ask questions, and yet it took every ounce of restraint
to refrain from panicking. I did not want to seem hysterical, but he had never been so unresponsive. After
an eternity of hand-ventilating, maybe fifteen or
twenty squeezes, Sue became aware that Julie was still
on her break. Aside from little Jackson, Sarah, William,
Koshawn, and the Gonzales brothers (Ernesto and
Eduardo), Sue and I were the only people in the room.
Then the boys flanking Jackson's crib, William and
Koshawn, began wailing simultaneously, adding to
my agitation and confusion.

339

Sue was completely focused on her task, which became more and more intense as Jackson's sat monitor stayed in the upper 20s and lower 30s. However, I had no real indication yet whether she had things under control or not. Then, never taking her eyes off him, in a voice that sounded oddly collected, she said, "B.D., could you just do me a favor and go into the next bay and ask someone to come in here and help me?"

I had been waiting patiently for some indication that Sue had things under control, but her question immediately shattered any confidence I had assembled.

It wasn't until I looked back on these moments that I realized I was paralyzed. I did not wish to appear overwrought, or overdramatic (just like the night of the birth). I guess in my actor's head that alarm went off, saying, "Don't overdo it." I was also relatively paranoid that I had been too challenging to the doctors, the nurses, and the staff about Jackson's state of health, that I had been too grumpy and so unwilling to celebrate with them that I didn't want to gild the lily. So rather than run into the next room and shriek, "Please, help us, it's . . . it's . . . **MY BABY . . . *STAT!!!!!*"** I just bumbled and fumferred.

"Uh, okay, I don't know what you mean. Who should I get? Where should I go? Who do you mean? What do you need?"

As soon as I replied, so ineptly, she realized she had wasted the time it took to ask and answer.

"I'm so sorry. I should never have asked you to do that. Forget it . . ."

**B.D. WONG**

"But if you need help . . . just tell me what to do . . . what should I do? **WILLIAM, PLEASE! BE QUIET!!!**"

When I heard myself snapping at a defenseless newborn infant, I realized I was wound up as tight as a roll of the Iron Chef's first-place sushi. Then, never dropping a stitch as she was hand-ventilating the tiny, still Jackson, trying to turn his condition around, she said,

"B.D., I'm just gonna do this . . . I don't want you to be upset. This is just an easy way to get someone in here. Don't get upset . . ."

Then she reached over and swatted the red "code" button on the wall.

The same button that, when I complained that there were too many babies to each nurse in the North Wing/Special Care, they said, "Well, there's always the code button. But you'll NEVER need *THAT*."

Rewind: the day we flew from Modesto, Nurse Andrew used exactly the same tone: "Don't worry. The traffic is just bad, that's all. We're just going to hit the siren . . ." Mirror images?

Suddenly I was in a Nazi Air Raid B movie, and the Allied storm troopers were on the scene. They came from every doorway and every entrance into the room.

"Everything okay in here?"

"What's going on?"

"Sue, need help?"

*FOLLOWING FOO*

"What ya got?"

There were residents and fellows and respiratory thera-
pists and nurses, at least a couple of each. Sue rattled
off a quick summation of what had occurred and the
highest ranked, Fellow David Loren, the quintessence
of the Nice Jewish Doctor your mom wants you to meet,
began making suggestions.

My perspective of this scene was like someone's
account of their own out-of-body experience on some
cheesy show hosted by William Shatner. I stood a few
paces back from the crib, mostly to give the doctors
room, possessing an adult, quasi-aerial viewpoint.
Aside from the view, I remember telling myself not to
make any rash judgments about what was happening,
ask questions, or disrupt the proceedings in any way.
So silently, I just watched them. Watched the monitors.
Listened to their docspeak. But the mass had descended
completely, so I could no longer see the boy who I was
so mad about.

Rewind: and the day Jackson was flown from Modesto
I sat curled up in a ball in the ambulance while the team
did its thing . . . I couldn't move. I couldn't ask questions. I couldn't see him. Parallel lines?

A fantastic nurse named Catherine, who I've never been
lucky enough to have assigned to Jackson but who
always asks about and visits him, and who I was friendly
with, was one of those who answered the call. As there
were plenty of cooks actively working over the stove,
she instinctively took the task of studying the sat
monitor and reading its findings aloud, so they could
keep their focus on the baby. That is when I heard a
term I hadn't heard before:

"He's bradycardic . . .

still bradycardic . . .

he's still bradycardic . . ."

It wasn't until much later I learned that this meant his heart rate had dropped dangerously low.

The doctors continued to talk about what to do, and Cathy, taking up all of the tasks not directly related to resuscitating the baby, came over to me—still standing stiffly, staring at everything like a zombie. At some point during this I got a glimpse of the baby, who was dark as midnight moments earlier, and by this time the blood had completely drained from him; and as if there was a midnight eclipse, his entire body was literally as white as the preemie-size diaper he was wearing. This further confused and frightened me. Cathy softly put her hand on my shoulder, as they pumped and prodded and pondered and prescribed.

**343**

"How are you doin', Dad?"

I have a very jovial, chatty relationship with Cathy, and I remember her addressing me, and I remember having a whole dialogue with her going on in my head, including a few appropriate responses to her comments, but honestly, nothing would come out of my mouth. I was just standing fixed in the middle of the room, staring.

"It'll be okay. Pretty scary, huh?"

Pretty scary . . .

You know, ever since I was a little boy I have been a crier. To this day I can cry at the drop of the hat; I am a lot like Jackson's Grampa that way. Through my tears I can still hear my mother saying to other grown-ups, "Oh, he's just so *sensitive*." Over the years, there are a lot of very specific things that set me off. But one of the odder things that always gets me going is when someone actually validates my feelings. When I hear another human's voice echoing the emotional voice buried in my heart (the way Richie had hoped that I would when he had the "Unraveling"), something gets triggered. It's just that fellow traveler thing that causes something to move within me. So when Cathy came over and casually said, "Pretty scary, huh?" as if we were objectively watching the Rodney King video, or some OTHER person's baby having an attack, it was soon high tide. Surf's up. Flash flood. I backed into an empty glider, fell into it, and kept staring. All I could do was keep concentrating, and willing, bearing down, focusing on, straining toward HOPE, the way I (and Richie) have been for months now. Even more than I did the night that Boaz and Jackson were born, and Boaz disappeared into the little window, the only time I ever saw him alive. Even more than I did the day they wheeled Jackson down to pediatric surgery, and wondered if this was my last chance to see *him* alive.

Because by this time, I could taste it.

See, he is my son. He has nicknames. He has a personality. He has likes, and dislikes, and facial expressions, and mannerisms. We have a relationship. I know him. It is impossible to think about letting him go again today, after all this time. After everything we have been through together. No matter what I say I have learned from this incredible experience. No matter how much I tell myself, and others, how important it is to learn to let go. None of that matters right this very minute.

344

**B.D. WONG**

Please don't make me say good-bye again, God. I guess I'm not ready after all. I confess. Call me a liar, or a hypocrite, or a man without a spine, I don't care, but I'm not ready after all. I'm only human. And I am his father. And we need each other. Please, God.

**Give. Me. That. Day.** *Please.*

I just kept squeezing and squeezing my guts, hoping to wring out drops of hope, mustering as much of it as my soul could press out. Soon I was brimming with hope, and then I was drowning in it. Then, all that surplus hope began streaming from my eyes, and before I knew it I was clenched and perspiring and just like a little teapot short and stout here is my handle here is my spout when I get all steamed up hear me shout tip me over and pour me out.

While Sue and the doctors gave Jackson terbutaline, the kind of medication you give to someone having an asthma attack, Cathy tended me with tissues.

Rewind: I realize now that I hadn't cried at the hospital since that first night months ago in Modesto when I first saw Boaz, and there again, a nurse was pressing tissues into my hand. Bookends?

I didn't have much to say aloud, because there was so much going on in my head. I was thinking, mainly, three things:

First, I was thinking how furious I was at the doctors who had been teasing me, taunting me to get ready to take him home. How cruel their joke was, how amateurish, how irresponsible, how unprofessional. Clearly we should not have been moved North, in a bay where even Super Sue could not handle what happened alone. How disappointed I was in them, for I had found them so brilliant before. What a fool I felt like for trusting them.

Second, I was thinking how not one thing I watched Sue do, the entire time she worked on him, not the blow-by bag and mask, not the studying of the brady monitor, not the terbutaline, NONE OF IT remotely resembled anything I'd seen on the CPR video, or anything I could do at home, by myself. Abbie makes you watch the video to learn how to resuscitate your child, in case something happens at home. But this was an official hospital situation, with expert, offical, specialized hospital procedures and resources. If we had been at home baking Toll House cookies from scratch, there obviously wouldn't have been enough time for 911; surely he would've died. I wouldn't have known the first thing to do with him if he got like that at home.

**346**   Which drove me right around the block again to my first thought. How could you all even talk about bringing him home? Just look at him!

Third, I had brief, fitful flashbacks, which were at first hard to place. There's a certain style of Agatha Christie movies that were made in the seventies and are among the first movies I ever saw and loved. At the end of the movie, when Hercule Poirot has gathered all the eccentric suspects, and he is piecing it all together, they always flash-cut to images from an earlier part of the movie—a closeup of someone's face as they said that particular thing which now resonates differently, a once meaningless but now pivotal prop—just split seconds of images, and eventually it all starts coming into focus.

Rewind:

*B.D. WONG*

Jackson hadn't looked that violently purple-black since
he was pulled from Shauna's womb, "topped off" with
Boaz's red blood and perilously close to death.

## DO NOT TOP OFF. DO NOT TOP OFF. SHUT ENGINE WHEN FILLING. NO SMOKING.

Then, halfway through this episode, when Jackson
"drained" completely, white as Ivory Soap, he haunt-
ingly resembled his identical twin brother, who came
briefly into the world pallid and limp, even closer to
death than his brother. The black, and the white. A sort
of symbol of the "yin and yang" of all of these blessed
events of the past few months. Blessed in both their
goodness, and . . . whatever the word for the opposite
of this kind of goodness is.

347

Again, I was driven around the block, but this radius
was a grander one. Here I was, coming Full Circle, like
the round driveway in front of the hospital that Grampa
and Gramma and I are always trying to scam for a parking spot. As I reconnected to the images which brought
me to that very moment, collapsed in the old glider in
this remarkable hospital, I felt at once drained by our
journey and yet so undeniably lucky. How lucky I was
to be able to make these comparisons. How lucky I was
to NOT be home at this particular time, baking Toll
House cookies from scratch. How lucky I was to witness,
and benefit from, this endless ongoing quest to protect,
to save every human life possible in this magnificent
institution. How lucky I was to have amazing health
insurance. How lucky I was, and how lucky Richie was
to NOT be there! For when Nurse Sue and the other
gamblers finally stepped back from the craps table,

there was our boy, not really looking any the worse for wear, and "the winner," to boot.

I try not to exaggerate. The entire episode took not much longer than the time it has taken you to read its description. I don't think Jackson ever "saw the light" (stage 2 ROP or no) or anything like that. But even Seen-It-All Sue could not underplay the operatic nature of this episode. Days later, I overheard doctors, while making their rounds, referring to Jackson's event as "impressive." Yes, that's my boy.

Sue and the others eventually came to the conclusion that Jackson's attack was a "bronchospasm," which the doctors eventually convinced me was a random incident, not something directly related to his lung condition (though that was hard for me to believe). Cowboy Jackson. Takin' a ride on the ol' spastic "electric pulmonary broncho." They also claim that his continued "bradys" after this event (remember, I hadn't even heard the term before this) were also a coincidence. Oh well. More of the infuriating nonscience of medicine.

What deals I tried to cut during this "bronchospasm" so that I might eventually get my dander up and bring him home . . . just like the deals I cut during the "transport turbulence." So that I might have that day when I will throw myself in front of the Air Africa jetway when he is twenty-four; that carrot so many people at the hospital were dangling before my disbelieving eyes. How elated I was, relieved, when he was obviously completely unperturbed by his ordeal afterward, like Linda Blair in the last scene of *The Exorcist*: ". . . She doesn't remember a thing . . ." What an incredible trip this is. Yeah, yeah, I know, I know, don't say it . . .

**B.D. WONG**

348

## << *WELCOME TO PARENTHOOD.* >>

I signed right up for the Infant CPR class.

CPR: Controlling Parents Reprimanded

 , etc. >>
### *registered nurse, et cetera*

If Jackson is so inclined and desires it, may he someday
have as much female attention as a man as he has had
in the first three months of his life. So much for "but
what about a woman's influence . . . ?" Believe me,
he's started out with more feminine doting than he
would have with an automatic garage door opener to
the Playboy Mansion. There would be no such thing as
too much praise for the remarkable people that we have
met on this incredible odyssey. But if too much praise
*were* to be given, this would be the time to give it.
Acknowledge, personalize, immortalize. Speak now.

### BECAUSE WE'RE GOING *HOME.*

Believe me, I am even exponentially more all a-twitter
at writing this then you are at reading it. Yes, the bradys
and the de-sats came, were seen, and were conquered.
J. Foo eventually passed the five-day "no flashing red
lights" test. There isn't a caregiver's task I haven't
learned how to do. Like the title of one of the more
bizarre, obscure AOL chatrooms, Jackson is "Fat and
Gaining." First he crossed that four-pound mark, and
held steady. Then he reached two kilos . . . the next

*FOLLOWING FOO*

milestone weight. They always told us two kilos was an acceptable weight to go home with. So yeah, he's readier and readier, and you know what?

I'm tired of fighting.
I am ready as I will ever be.

"Richie, get a plane ticket. By the time you get here, your son will be just about ready to come home."

Within a couple of weeks, many events occurred which helped sharpen the obsidian arrowhead pointing our way back to the East Coast. For weeks Richie (still in New York) and I had been struggling to determine a date when he would fly back out to San Francisco, in preparation for us ALL traveling home to New York *as a family*. We finally picked a weekend he would fly, hoping Jackson's forecasted release wasn't postponed, which would waste Richie's paternity leave. If it was at all possible, we wanted as much time together at home as we could.

Here are some of the reasons WHY the date that people were all predicting seemed too soon to Richie and me. For example, it took me a while to figure out that I was learning to give Jackson all these various medicines in order to prepare me to give them to him *at home*! I always assumed in the back room of my mind (which we all know is poorly lit, and down a very, very long hallway) that I was just *helping* the nurses with his care; it didn't sink in to me he'd still have to take all this crap once we got out! It made perfect sense to me that you get out of the hospital when you're better, and if you're better you don't need medicine anymore. Being deeply entrenched in a program of five different medicines seemed incongruous with holding your own. I had to get over THAT one pretty fast. His lungs were fine, but he still needed the medication. His reflux was in check, but not without the medication. Yup, twice a day, four medicines measured and mixed with his meals. Four times a day, another reflux med given a half hour before the feeding. Got it? Okay, now add another person to your team. Sleep in shifts. When you wake up and he goes to sleep, how do you know which medicines he's been giving and which medicines he hasn't been giving? Are you double dosing? Are you not dosing at all? Is your partner dosing while you doze? Or worse, are either of you dozing while you dose? What dosage of dozing does it? Which dosage of dozing doesn't do it? Exactly what are the dosing do's and don'ts? Do watch that dose, it's a doozy. Swing your partner, don't be slow. Allemande right, and do-si-do.

The other thing that disappointed Richie and me was the doctors' rumblings, eventually more and more decisive, that Jackson would have to go home hooked up to an oxygen tank, probably for the first few months of his New York life. The doctors explained that it just wasn't worth keeping him in the hospital another month, if it were only for the oxygen. Richie saw it differently.

"I was hoping we could bring him home without all the extra stuff. You know, all better. *Triumphantly*. That's so disappointing. It's like limping home after the battle."

After all this time, we were still looking for that closure, that "That was when he was sick, but this is now that he's NOT" kind of demarcation. Hello? Where have we been this whole time? There is no "Mason-Dixon line." The war is ending, boys. Shake hands and come home, why don't you?

This has all been about acceptance, no questions asked. I had so easily calculated a flawless life for Richie and me, with two scrumptiously adorable, healthy, identical twin girls or boys. I hadn't planned every detail, but I just assumed it would all go the way *I* wished. How godlike of me. How presumptuous and entitled.

You can perfectly organize all the breast milk in the freezer; you can even keep the freezer from breaking down, you can narrowly escape the Attack of the Irate Fathers. But you sure can't guarantee, when all is said and done, that you'll have ANYONE TO FEED when you come crawling out of your hiding place afterward like a cockroach emerging from the ruins left by an A-bomb. So if I've tried to do anything as I've continued on my own snail's journey from boyhood to manhood (with fatherhood somewhere in between) during these last few months, witnessing this miracle, it has been to remember as often as I can what a gift really is.

Does a TRUE gift come with the little *gift receipt*, in case it's not "just right"?

Richie and I had a huge disagreement many many months ago, before Shauna went into preterm labor, over having a party, a shower in anticipation of our blessings. My mom, who tends to put her quarter's worth in whenever she can (actually, if you really wanna know, sometimes it's a dollar's worth), overheard that we had sealed up the invitations we were about to send out inviting some New York friends and family to our home sometime in June. She became unusually upset. "You can't throw yourself a shower," she said adamantly. "SOMEONE HAS TO DO THAT *FOR* YOU. YOU JUST DON'T DO THAT. THAT'S ASKING FOR PRESENTS." Richie and I argued, because he assumed my mom was just being controlling, and besides, we needed so many things, and because even way back then, we were both so terribly stressed out (though we had no idea at that time what stress *really* was).

**B.D. WONG**

"You can't throw yourself a shower." (Wasn't that a hit Kaufman and Hart play?) A true gift is not something you are allowed to ask for. I've always thought, through the entire process of monitoring "our" pregnancy and subsequently monitoring Jackson's ups and downs, that if I could just have a child, I would be grateful, no matter if the baby were somehow compromised or handicapped in any way. I tried so hard to be so open-minded, so open and loving. I thought that somehow would make me deserving.

But maybe even that was not enough. Surely, most people say, "I want a baby: baby, please," and more often than not, nine months later, boom, there indeed is a wish apparently granted. Richie and I were always so proud of ourselves that we felt we were aching for children for all the "right reasons." We said, rather smugly, that all couples who want children should have to fill out the forms we filled out, write the essays about WHY, take the blood tests, put tons of money in escrow like we did.

We should not have concerned ourselves with "other couples." I'm not insinuating we were punished, far from it. It just happened so NOT the way "it was sup- posed to." I won't speak for Richie, but I am infinitely better for that. I feel so much more powerful. Ironically relaxed. I can see so much farther, even though, as you probably can guess, I will still *always* miss Boaz, and always wonder "what if . . ." But on those serendipitous moments when I feel this beautiful surviving boy peer- ing into my soul with those limpid, sinless, premature retinae, I also see Boaz there, and when I do I feel ready to face anything. For that courage to face every new day before us, on this wacky, bumpy thrill ride which will bring Jackson Foo Wong safely, eventually, finally to our Hell's Kitchen doorstep; for THIS perhaps above all other things have the three of us been truly, majestically blessed. Truly, majestically beholden.

So as far as the "triumph" Richie once felt we were being deprived of, there isn't a towering bully or microscopic bacteria (or reflux medicine or oxygen tank) that can take away from Jackson Foo Wong an iota of that victory he deserves upon his homecoming. His tolerance, his resilience, his strength, his will, his tranquillity, his ability to accept, his desire to stay with us all earn him the ticker tape parade of anyone's dreams. Don't they? With Stars and Stripes. Forever.

So, magically, a San Francisco lighthouse finally cast its ferocious beam through the mist, guiding my weary way, and I dragged myself up the foggy shore of Pacific Ocean Beach, sopping wet, just as Richie's plane was landing. I did not have to search for a new attitude with much scrutiny.

Jackson's Auntie Doris, Wife of Webmaster Uncle Barry, flew into a frenzy planning a shower (to my mother's delight) with San Francisco friends and family, squeezed in before we went home, like that spectacular last-minute Michael Jordan half-court shot in a tie game, at the buzzer. Setting a date was nearly impossible, not knowing when the baby might get out. (Jackson couldn't attend the shower, because you know how germy grown-ups can be). Doris was dancing on hot coals for a few days, as we tried to narrow it down with everyone's schedule. At the last minute, we gambled and changed the date to a week earlier, because in the last two weeks before Richie flew out, Jackson improved, gaining momentum, gathering no moss. I could barely believe my eyes as his face became more and more the face of a man ready to face the world.

**B.D. WONG**

The weekend Richie arrived was an appropriate climax to this entire chapter.

| | | |
|---|---|---|
| *Saturday:* | **10:00** A.M.: | Richie arrives at the airport. |
| | **11:00** A.M.: | The dreaded circumcision. |
| | **12:00** P.M.: | Baby shower at Barry and Doris's. |
| | **4:00** P.M.: | Back to the hospital with Shauna for a "final for now" visit. |
| | **6:00** P.M.: | Our last nap as free men. |
| | **8:00** P.M.: | Our last dinner as free men and our first dinner together in a month. |
| | **10:00** P.M.: | Slumber party: "Rooming in." |

About that day:

I tried to schedule Jackson's circumcision so that Jewish Dad could be there. I thought this was important, even though I knew Richie would, pardon the expression, get the willies. Richie was disappointed that the *mohel* UCSF provided was named Dr. Takeyama, but felt better when he heard good reviews of his work. It's hard to entrust your son's penis to the scalpel of a person you don't know; it's hard enough to entrust your OWN penis to the scalpel of a person you don't know (or even worse yet, to entrust your OWN penis to the scalpel of a person you DO know), but when we watched Dr. Takeyama militarily present the stainless-steel swab bowl to the assisting nurse as if it was a Japanese tea ceremony, Richie and I both felt inexplicably better.

The Circ du Soleil went very well. The nurses were all impressed with Dr. Takeyama's, er, handiwork. Someday, on Venice Beach, Jackson may carry a picket sign protesting the barbarism and abuse of circumcision and hand out leaflets and curse us through a bullhorn in his Birkenstocks and unkempt dreadlocks, but until then, at least we look like we all play on the same team.

You're familiar with the teams, aren't you? "Shirts and—" —uh, never mind.

After the circ, we rushed to Uncle Barry and Auntie Doris's, which was in full party mode. I hadn't been paying attention to all the planning, but the shower hardly resembled a thrown-together-at-the-last-minute affair. As you can imagine, the spread was splendid, and there were many more people there than I expected, considering we had changed the date. Doris had been secretive about the "theme," and when we saw the cake, her undercover efforts proved worthwhile:

### *A STAR IS BORN*
### *WELCOME BABY*
### *JACKSON*

It was really neat. Earlier this year, five different friends and family members had all offered to throw us five different showers (to my mother's delight), but of course, we didn't ever get to have a one of them, so this was a special kind of consolation prize for us. Our loved ones were extremely generous, and Gramma Wong volunteered to help us pack it all up and ship it home to New York. Doris even had a "dress the baby doll" relay race with prizes and everything, but of course Richie's team cheated by not doing up all the snaps and was disqualified, which worried me regarding Richie's diapering skills and commitment to infant human waste management.

**B.D. WONG**

Some time during the festivities, I looked around the house, and there, present and accounted for, were so many of my aunts and uncles. All second-generation Chinese-Americans, who I often looked upon at the countless Leong Family gatherings over the years as stern, intimidating, disapproving figures. They are, in fact, pretty normal American relatives, who I had always imbued with a slightly exaggerated sense of foreboding tradition in my highly imaginative childhood. Perplexed by my artistic temperament and unconventional career. Quietly accepting of Richie as a member of the family, but *very* quietly. But there they were, comfortably sitting right beside the effervescent Shauna, offering Richie, Jackson, and me the very same hand-knit layettes, comforting blankets, and festively wrapped, noisy playthings that they have so warmly presented every single baby born into the huge Leong Family since I can remember. With the very same love, and the very same solidly solemn support. I could feel these (Alternative) Family Values passing down to me with each gift, and suddenly, I felt all growed up.

**357**

That night brought the ultimate challenge. Get out of here with your "Tribal Council," the true test of a man's mettle is his ability to spend an entire night in a hospital room, with his preemie son, freshly taken off monitors, alone, with no assistance, except in the event of an emergency. The hospital gave the three of us an impossibly small room for the night, with two miniature pull-out chairs and some sheets to put on them, and then wheeled Jackson's crib in and said, "Have fun." We could go back into the nursery to get the necessary items to prepare his feedings, but other than that we were on our own. The night is designed to help ease your fear of flying solo (or duet) with the baby, and yet if you fail miserably, if something undesirable happens, or if you completely wig out and need to go "No! No! I can't!

I can't! Take him back!" help is only that plaintive shriek away.

How did it go? I did the expected, by simply sitting next to the crib and watching the Chestnut Man breathe (with only the tank) for very long periods of time. Part of this is fear. But most of it is pure intoxication. It's so easy to be hypnotized by miracle in motion, by the gentle rising and falling of his tiny mound of a chest, by the independent flaring of those perfect nostrils, by the perfection of his triangular mouth. I just watched. When it was time to feed him, I fed him, and when it was time to give him his medicine, I gave him his medicine. It really was a breeze. Sue DeHaan and her merry band of Flo Nightingales trained me well.

Richie, on the other hand, slept through the whole night, snoring insufferably. The heaving of Richie's chest and the flaring of his nostrils were not quite as hypnotizing as his son's.

Then Rich van Winkle awoke, fresh as a daisy in a douche commercial, and I needed to be airlifted out of the hospital to the car.

Did it go well? You tell me.

The night we spent at the hospital was a Saturday, and our flight was on Monday morning. We didn't room in at the hospital on the very last night so that we could get some real rest on the night right before the flight.

As our last days in San Francisco drew closer and Richie and I began to feel more and more giddy and trusting that Discharge Day was finally approaching, so was a silent sadness steadily swelling.

**B.D. WONG**

In the last couple of weeks, one by one, the nurses on Jackson's Primary Care Team quietly, protectively, maternally began expressing their affection, bringing tokens of the unique bond that all of them shared with him. A bond which is completely unique to the patient-nurse relationship in the Intensive Care Nursery. Certainly no greater or less than the role that Shauna and Sue played, but powerful nonetheless. These women each played an integral role in Jackson's recovery . . .

What a curious word to use. "Recovery." Yet I can think of no other. You can't really *recover* from something if you were never well to begin with, can you? Your average nurse's usual pride must surely stem from aiding in the "recovery" of a patient, anyone from a few weeks old to a hundred, right? But when you're negative two and a half months old, and you've never known a moment of self-sufficience or independence, or a day without needing someone to be by your side for twenty-four hours just so you can live, but then indeed someone guides you through that process until the day when you actually can . . . what do you call *that*? The word "recovery" packs no wallop for me.

Jackson's discharge date is just a few days past his actual due date of birth. Just before Richie arrived that Saturday, Jackson reached that coveted weight of two kilos, not an unacceptable weight for a newborn, tiny but full-term baby. In some ways, his due date is his proper birthday, and his tireless nurses have guided him through his gestation with as much care as Shauna, who carried him so lovingly within her for most of it.

The pride and care that the nurses and Shauna have shown for Jackson is unquestionably maternal. Never possessive. But without that maternal drive, their unique relationship to him and their powerful contribution would not have been so great.

So one by one, at different times in different ways, the nurses stepped forward, like the magi, solemnly bearing gifts to a swaddled baby who, like the little Jesu, was kind of lost in the desert for a while. No, none of us ever said that final "G word" because it was just too painful. They just brought forth their frankincense and myrrh; I'm sure these objects will remain among Jackson's prized possessions.

My conversations with each of them were awkward, melancholy, and purposely un-final. I couldn't find the words to thank them for the gift they have given the Jackson Wongs. Maybe that's why I'm doing so here. The closest I came was a week before discharge, when the peppy Jennipher Goodner announced she wouldn't be on duty again before we left. After I packed up my computer and stuff to go back to my parents' at the end of that late night in the nursery, I hugged her and feebly mumbled "You're the best," but as lumps rose simultaneously in our throats, I cut the parting remarks off abruptly, and left.

Nurses who were not on duty on the final weekend suddenly showed up in their street clothes with gifts in hand. The star physicians, Dr. Francis Poulain, Dr. Stacey Levitt, and Dr. Roberta Keller, assembled by Jackson's cribside one last time Saturday morning, of course, for not only a final confab on his condition, but a brief exploration of when we might see one another again.

Then there's my parents. As you know, Jackson has taken center stage in his grandparents' household since the end of May, without ever having set foot in the place. This was at times very stressful on my folks, no doubt, and they always put their love and fear for Jackson before everything. But right when things got the most hectic and the most difficult to manage was when I also began noticing my parents' "empty nest blues" setting in.

When my father blurted out to some random stranger at the hospital, "I'm getting so sad," the last week before Richie joined us, I felt my heart sink like a solitary stone in a lonely summer swimming hole. My dad's desire to visit Jackson at the hospital gradually became more and more desperate, until the first thing he would immediately say to me in the early morning as soon as I came out of my bedroom eventually became a definitive "When are we going to the hospital?" as opposed to the usual, grammatically incorrect "What's our plans for today?" I began to hear the welling emotions I have uncannily inherited from him rising to the surface every time my parents left the hospital, when Dad always repeated this quirky phrase to his grandson, often five times in a row whenever he said good-bye:

"I'll see you SUBSEQUENTLY!" he would say as he was shuffling out the door, his voice getting tighter and tighter.

"I'll see you *SUBSEQUENTLY,* Jackson, *I'll see you SUBSEQUENTLY!*"

You see, it's much easier to say than the "G word."

Dad's just too superstitious to say the "G word."

New York is so far away, and I hardly see my parents enough. Time is marching on, and none of us are getting younger. The hidden blessing I have received throughout this entire saga was this time that I have spent at home, actually living with my parents again, just like I did when I was . . .

. . . first born.

See, the Circle never ends.

The activity in the circular driveway in front of the hospital at 505 Parnassus Street in San Francisco never ends either. For months, I have had a love-hate relationship with it. After weeks of parking in the UCSF garage ($$), or even attempting that impossible SF street parking, my parents and I just started parking in the fifteen-minute "white zone" in the Circle, knowing full well each time that we would be staying much longer. It was as if we felt we had earned the right to do so, having been there five times a day for three months. We would drive up the street toward the hospital, and my dad, always in fear of getting some family agenda wrong, always formally states his impression of the game plan aloud, to give my mom the opportunity to derisively say he remembered wrong, or wasn't listening.

"Park in the Circle, right?" he asks the inhabitants of the car.

"Park in the Circle," my mom confirms, like NASA.

You can't help but notice, whenever you are there, people driving up into the Circle and either letting someone sick off, or picking someone well up. Old ladies in wheelchairs. Teenage boys with bandaged heads, holding skateboards. Apparent drug users determined to stay clean. Going in with looks of dread. Coming out carrying half-deflated "get well soon" balloons and wilted flower arrangements. Not to mention the babies. All in a variety of optimistically plaid, handle-carried baby carriers. All freshly starting their lives with a gust of San Francisco wind in their squinting faces, all being secured into double-parked, idling minivans, rear-facing as per the law, siblings finally getting in their first territorial paw when the folks aren't looking.

On Monday, August 21, 2000,

five days after Jackson Foo Wong had "gestated" for forty full weeks,

at 6:00 A.M. Pacific Standard Time,

it was finally time for Richie, my parents, and me

to use
### THE CIRCLE
for its intended purpose.

We were very nervous about good ol' United Airlines, so Richie had suggested we take the first flight out on this Monday morning. I wasn't crazy about this, but of course, there was unintentional magic to Richie's method. When the weather blesses you on an important day of your life, it's easy to say that it seems as if you have God's blessing. A perfect day it was. But what impressed me more was the timing: how the sun rose over the hills at the very moment we drove up Judah Street toward the hospital, revealing a San Francisco morning so perfectly yellow and blue and brilliant and clear, I could no longer look upon this drive as my final approach to the hospital. The golden light of the sunrise made it so much more clearly *the beginning*.

We rushed inside, fashionably late.

Jackson got passed for a round of kisses like a sandbag in a flash flood volunteer's line. Abbie Hofstede, his original SF protector, his Rock of Gibraltar, was on duty, I suspect by her own contrivance. We woke up Francis Poulain, who was also on duty, and who rose to whisper *"au revoir."* Nurse Doris, who always seemed more like a funny old friend than a nurse, packed him snugly in his brand-new fancy French car seat for its maiden voyage. It was way too enormous for him, so Doris surrounded him with about ten rolled-up cloth diapers. He then vaguely resembled a small gopher burrowing up from a large snowbank. Nurse Karen Grass, another member of the JFW Primary Care Team, was also there for *her* closure. We transferred his good old nasal cannula to the portable oxygen tank and raided the baby supplies, throwing diapers, formula, nipples, pacifiers, and other free goodies, with J. Foo's medicines, into our brand-new Eddie Bauer diaper bag. I know, I know, French car seats and Eddie Bauer diaper bags . . . guilty as charged. We hastily took a few pictures. Then we just grabbed everything and rushed off, secretly grateful that our tardiness eliminated the possibility of lengthy farewells.

As we burst into the hall, we met Sue DeHaan head-on coming from the opposite wing. Her sunny face I will force myself to recall for the rest of my life when times get rough. By this time I was pretty emotionally tapped, and Richie had managed to keep it together. But when Richie saw Sue's beaming, gorgeous face, he finally lost it. For some reason Sue's particular countenance represents to us everything positive about our UCSF experience, and Richie's fondness for the only nurse who could dish out and take the sarcasm the way Richie can earned her a special seat at the captain's table. So his tears were proportionate to his affection and respect for her. We just couldn't properly express how we felt verbally, but Richie's screwed, weeping face was worth a thousand words.

We rode that once-infuriating whale of an elevator, one last time, which at six in the morning went straight from the fifteenth floor to the lobby like the #2 train going from Times Square to Seventy-second Street. We regathered everything, including ourselves, and got off in the lobby.

## AND *THEN,*

Nurse Doris, who was assigned to accompany us to the airport to hook up our oxygen on board the plane . . .

Gramma and Grampa Wong,

who, in their own special way, started this whole mess way back when . . .

Richie,

and me,

and the Chestnut Man . . .

stepped onto the rubber mat, and the electric doors obeyed . . .

and the Gods of Mount Parnassus blew Jackson's first breath of fresh air, full of the clean San Francisco Bay wind to meet us,

as we stepped out into . . .

## *The Circle.*

Are you proud of yourselves?

You did it.

You rooted him home.

What can I say? Like my dad, I'm way too superstitious . . .

We'll see you

**SUBSEQUENTLY,**

New York.

**WELCOME HOME**
**PRINCE OF HOPE**
**LITTLEST FOO**
**WONDERFUL WONG**
**TENACIOUS TOT**
**MAY GOD CONTINUE TO BLESS YOU!**

• **(EDDIE FORD)**

**Ken and I have been quietly, with bated breath, sending goodness your way since you first let us in on your little plan. I think of Jackson a hundred times a day as I tend to my little miracle (born 3/23). I imagine that his little**

*B.D. WONG*

tongue is tender and pink and sweet as he sucks the air in his sleep. I imagine that he looks so deeply into your eyes with such pure clarity that if you gave it the thought it deserves, you'd explode with wonder and joy. I imagine that he is like Rachel and all the countless babies I've had the joy of experiencing, and I am in love. We are sooooo glad you are finally home.

> · **MICHELLE POSNER** *is a Broadway production stage manager.*
> **KENNETH POSNER** *is a Broadway lighting designer.*

**Dear BD,**

I always end up reading these things late at night, thinking I'll just skim them quickly, get the highlights, and then go over them in detail later. And every time I get sucked into your writing and the beautiful wonderful world of your experiences and find myself crying over my computer at 3am.

But I consider my sleepiness the next day as a small tribute to you and your struggles, in the same way fasting for a day can be a tribute to something much larger.

I always want to use religious expressions or something sacred sounding in my wishes to you because ordinary words seem so banal. But "God Bless You" doesn't feel right coming from me so I just want to say, I feel for you and your family very very deeply.

Please more, more updates . . . . . from Home!!!!

**Love steven**

> · **(STEVEN PETRARCA)**

I'm proud, proud, proud. Of all of you. I think back on that predawn morning when I came to B.D.'s trailer to make sure everything was OK with his wardrobe and I innocently asked: "Did you have a nice weekend?" never dreaming that I was going to be able to share such an adventure.

Did I mention how proud I am?

Jackson's home . . .

- (KARYN WAGNER)


A final Caregiver's Corner:

Hi BD, believe it or not, it is a warm night in SF, and after watching an incredible moonrise, I have been sitting out on my deck reading your 3-part serial. I remember one night glimpsing you bent over your laptop as I buzzed past to find something or other on the North side; now I see what kept you so busy between feedings.

We live in a very insulated world up there in UC's penthouse, no matter how diverse our lives may be on the "outside." Your observations and musings (ok, and occasional rant-ing) reminded me how often I forget to look at things from a parent's perspective. It's all "been there, done that" for me. But for every parent, it's the first time in outer space, surrounded by aliens, and we all should know better. Thanks for your insights.

I'm glad you all survived your trip to Mars and are now hap-pily settling in at home in NY. You were a breath of fresh air in our cramped little climate-controlled nursery, and there has been a big lull since your departure. (You may be a San Francisco native, but you were Mr. Hollywood to us!!) Your circle of friends in NY (and all over the world, I imagine) sounds like a fantastic support system, so I know Jackson will never lack for extended family on either coast.

I wonder if you guys watched this same moon rise on your side of the earth tonight. I hope every day holds a bit of moonglow and wonder for each of you.

love to you three, Joan

- (JOAN BENEDUSI)

Two final postings from the Jackson Foo Wong Web Site . . .

Throughout the last few months, I was never sure how this would all turn out, and it was a little scary! I now know, and have to say that I will never again feel the joy that I have felt knowing that you're now parents, and I had something to do with it! Jackson is very lucky to have you both as parents.

Love you, Shauna.

The day I've anxiously been waiting for is almost here. Jackson, this Saturday I will meet you for the first time and I'm having a hard time waiting 'til then. I know you're doing great and getting stronger and bigger every day. I also know that your dads are doing a pretty terrific job too and I'm anxious to see them in their new role as parents. Josh and Daniel wish they could come and see you too, but they'll have to wait until you're ready. Until then we all send our love

—Sue, Matt, Josh, and Daniel

Truly circular things end the way they began. Even books . . .

"If I had to choose one to represent the spirit of them all, it might be this one: . . ."

WELCOME HOME . . . I knew the city was feeling like a better place to be this past week!

I can't wait to meet him, I really can't.

BD, I can't tell you how much these letters have meant to me. I love you, and I am proud of you, and I love richie. Jackson and Boaz have changed me. I made a baby blanket for jackson last week (oh, sorry, no surprise) and I got very quiet and sad. i mourned that i wasn't making one that said boaz. I felt bitter that I couldn't wrap it up and run over and give it to him. Joby came by and asked what was wrong. I just said i felt sad. she said, "but terri, . . . you got to make him one. He's here." she was right, and i felt better. and i went home and reread some of your letters. and i thought about the first message you left me on my cell phone, minutes after i got engaged. you said, listen to my words, and hear my voice. I refuse to look at this as anything less than a miracle. He is here, and now he is home. and in whatever way you can explain it, his brother is here too.

you know, i've heard it takes a village to raise a child. (Just today, little molly mcintosh, whose babysitter backed out at the last minute on a holiday weekend, came in to work with her mother. and we all helped. and everyone sang happy birthday to her doll, patience. It was a village at work.) It also takes really strong parents. Congratulations guys . . . and i am happy and proud to be part of jackson's village.

Love love love love and rainbows, and fyi, i am pretty great at halloween costumes . . . hey, wanna borrow a pumpkin costume made out of the memorable "Shroeder Catcher Pad" costume, which i believe graced the stage in skokie, mmmm, one performance? back when jackson was a flicker in his daddies' eyes . . . . . . .

terri

- (TERRI PURCELL)

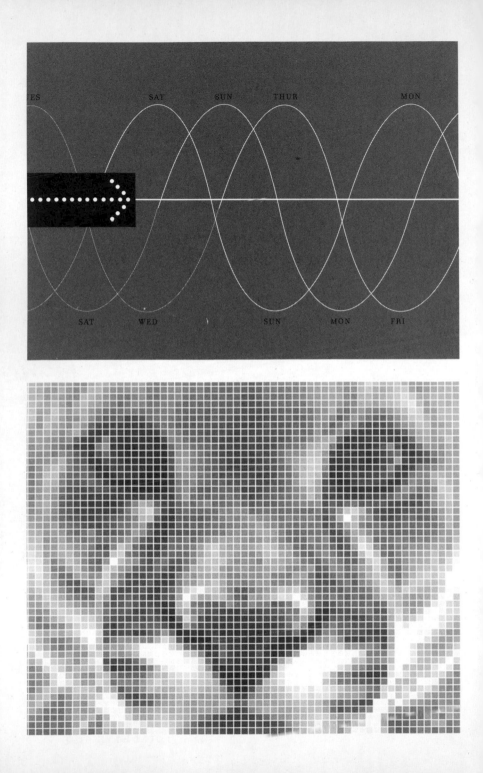

# "UP-ILOGUE"

**THE OKRA O'DONAHUE SHOW**
(last segment of episode)
or, plainly,
**A FINAL FUTURISTIC FANTASY**

**AIRDATE: SPRING 2025**
Somewhere, USA . . .

**THIS IS A TRANSCRIPT OF:**
**THE "25th Year of the 21st Century"**
**episode of**
*The Okra O'Donahue Show*

After commercial break #10 (Final Segment):

**374**

<u>Final Commercial Break</u>
1. Cell phone brain implant procedure ad:

tag: "You don't know 'Hands Free' till you
(sung) GET IT IN YOUR HEAD!"

2. Spot sponsored by the
Friends of Chastity Bono,
smearing opposing presidential candidate
Macaulay Culkin.

Back to show in 5, 4, 3 . . .

VOICEOVER:
And now, Okra remembers the first quarter of the century
in a final conversation with her very special guest . . .

(Closeup on OKRA. APPLAUSE.)

*B.D. WONG*

OKRA:
And we're back on *The Okra O'Donahue Show* with our amazing guest, Nobel Prize winner, poet, Olympic athlete,
and classical pianist Jackson Foo Wong.

(APPLAUSE.)

(Okra and her guest are revealed sitting in comfortable
armchairs. The latter wears a desert camouflage safari
ensemble. Under his open khaki shirt we see a T-shirt
which screams "SHIRK THE CIRC.")

JFW:
Thanks, Okra.

OKRA:
You are incredible.

JFW:
Thanks, Okra.

(JFW takes off his pith helmet.)

OKRA:
And gorgeous. Isn't he gorgeous?

(APPLAUSE.)

JFW
(smiling and shifting shyly): Thanks, Okra.

OKRA:
Great body, too. Tell us about your Nobel Prize.

JFW:
Um, which one?

(APPLAUSE.)

OKRA:
Forgive me. You're just so amazing.

JFW:
Thanks. Well, awards and things are nice, but really, I'm just happy to be alive.

OKRA:
Me, too. (As if she has said it a million times) "Life is a present we must reopen and rediscover every morning before we do our hair and makeup."

JFW:
. . . Yeah.

OKRA:
How do you do it?

JFW:
Well, I don't really do hair and makeup.

OKRA:
. . . and he's funny, too.

(LAUGHTER AND APPLAUSE.)

OKRA:
No, but how do you do it? How do you stay "happy to be alive"?

JFW:
I guess I had help. I come from a loving family. My dads wanted to have a baby real bad. They were among the first ones on our block to be a two-dad family, whereas now, you know, it's pretty much everywhere.

OKRA:
(who has been nodding enthusiastically) Yes, yes. Everywhere.

**B.D. WONG**

JFW:
My dads have always made me feel like I came into the world for a purpose. We all come into the world for a purpose, Okra. We have to get right down to finding that purpose, or purposes, as soon as we can, though, because time goes by so fast. That's why I race cars, to try to keep up with time.

OKRA:
Man of danger!

JFW:
Danger is a part of life. Thrill-seeking is a way to confront the danger and the fleetingness that's built into life. If you are able to meet fear head-on, then you can handle it when the real thing comes. And it will. Real danger, real scariness.

My parents get a little nervous, but they understand. I'm not foolish about it. I just went on my first safari. Not hunting, just observing the animals, and wrestling with them a little. It was inspiring. Dad is still crying about it, and I've been back a whole week now. Airport security had to remove him and everything.

OKRA:
So sweet. And where do you think this came from? The danger thing? Was it from your parents?

JFW:
Hmm . . .
(He pauses thoughtfully. Then . . . )

When I was a freshman at Harvard I was in the frat house and this package came in the mail, with no return address. It was this old paperback book. And I turned it over, and whaddya know? There's this big ol' picture of my dad on the cover!

See, I always knew where I came from since I was little, and how I had a twin brother who died, and how I was in the hospital when I was first born. My dads told me the basics. And then years go by, and I get this book in the mail, and it has my name in the title. It's by my dad! And it *really* told the whole story. My whole life, I never knew about everything that happened. I never knew about this book. Which, I guess, was a real book in bookstores.

OKRA:
I never heard of it.

JFW:
Well, I never heard of it, either, 'cause it turns out my dad kept it out of the house. He wanted me to have a normal childhood. He wanted me to read the book on my own when I was grown up, and learn about our experience that way.

. . . at the very end of the book, there's this thing about a talk show, and how I'm on it.

OKRA:
Kind of like this.

JFW:
(he thinks) Yeah . . . and he explains that when he wrote this part, I had been out of the hospital for a while, when he finally looked back on the whole thing.

My dad is big on what he calls the "noncoincidence" of life. He's always looking to seemingly coincidental things to point the way.

So, two things happened. One was he had this audition for a really good part in a play—my dad was an actor

before he got his seat on the Supreme Court—and for him,
a really meaty role was hard to come by, at this point
in his career.

In this play, the character he was auditioning for in-
spires the other characters in the play by making them
read the play *Our Town*, by Thornton Wilder.

And at the same time as this, there's this theater in the
Hamptons which is presenting the actual play, *Our Town*,
by Thornton Wilder. The same play that the *other* play was
quoting. And they offer my dad a part in *Our Town*, and he
takes it, 'cause it's a cool summer job in a nifty place.
But *Our Town* are not two words you just hear every day.
Let alone twice.

So my dad asks himself, "What is it about *Our Town*?" And
at this time, he's trying to finish up this book he is
writing about me and my brother and what happened in the
hospital.

And *then* my dad gets offered the part he auditioned for
in the first play. And he starts performances for the
actual *Our Town* in the Hamptons the very same week. And
he sits down to write the epilogue of his book, all right
at this same exact time. The same week.

In *Our Town*, the young girl, Emily, has died in the
beginning of the third act, and through a theatrical con-
vention she's allowed to go back in time for one day, but
all of the other "dead people" warn her not to do it.

She freaks out while she's watching the "flashback" of her
life, because she realizes that live people just don't
get it. They get wrapped up in their everyday stuff. They
don't appreciate the gift of life. They miss all of the
things, big and small, which make life such a privilege.

My dad writes in the book that he was frustrated because he couldn't bring me with him for more than a week of *Our Town* in the Hamptons. At this time in his life he was feeling overwhelmed by a lot of everyday stuff. Health insurance for nannies. Flaky contractors and sneaky, smarmy, stupid building developers. Sublets, with the baby sleeping in the walk-in closet. Acting jobs, and directors who "don't get" him. Money, money, money. And tons of other heavy stuff he had been spilling out at therapy every Friday.

And every night on stage that week in the play, there's Emily referring to the living as "just blind people," and she doesn't fully appreciate what she's got until she is called away from it all, by God.

And *her* dad in the play is being played by *my* dad. Isn't that trippy?

Dad was happy that someone asked him to compile all of his E-mails and write a book. He was proud that his gifts as a writer were being fully tapped and shared, something he didn't often feel as an actor. But he was ashamed that in a pretty short time, his appreciation for the experience he had in the hospital with me almost waned. Wore off. How could that happen?

They brought me home from the hospital, took me to numerous doctors' appointments. They took me to the ophthalmologist, who said my eyes were okay. They took me to the neurologist, who said not to worry. Eventually they took me off the oxygen. Eventually they took me off all the meds. One day I finally rolled over. One day I turned one. One day I started walking.

(sings) ". . . but there were planes to catch, and bills to pay, he learned to walk while I was away . . ."

**B.D. WONG**

They sold our apartment so I could have my own room. They bought a new one and moved in with my grandparents on Long Island while the new apartment was being worked on. My first summer living with my dads came and went. Labor Day, 2001, came and went.

And then something that everyone thought was unbelievable happened to the world, in the second week of September, and it really upset my dad, and I was crawling all over the place at Grandma Carol and Grandpa Paul's, and Dad was glued to the TV for a week, unable to move. All of a sudden, we were just like any other family in suburban Long Island. My dads were picking up toys and trying to get the baby to eat, and chasing the baby, and wiping food off the baby's face, when, literally, the Center of the World came tumbling down.

My dad with hair on top was very sad when this happened, and not long after this he was totally overwhelmed by life, and by all of the everyday woes on top of it all. Consumed. Ruled by. Constantly confused. Furious. It was kinda rough.

So, yeah, it took away from his appreciation for me. Even after that intense period of time in the ICN, which he assumed had forever changed him for the better. What happened that September, and then writing the epilogue, and *Our Town*, got him to face it all again.

I dunno. Maybe forgetting is just a part of life, Okra. Without the *forgetting*, there would never be that miraculous joy of *remembering*.

I mean, just because our baby dies, and we spend three months in a hospital watching his brother fight for his life, does that guarantee that afterward we will automatically be one of the ones who "gets it"? Does that

earn us the right to say from that point on that we now
"understand"? Just because we had one critically intense
"life or death" experience?

Or just because we wrote it all down?

Or read the book, or saw the movie?

No, Okra, it doesn't.

There isn't just one dramatic thing that happens in your
life that makes you "get it" forever. There are lots.
There will always be giants at the tops of our bean-
stalks peering down in wait to steal back their precious
golden lyres and petrify us. There will always be Cruella
Devilles wanting to skin us alive so they can turn us
into their own despicable, decadent fashions. And they
are all waiting in caves to trick us, and corner us, and
rob us, and enrage us. They are always there. They are a
part of life. They are always just about to move in next
door. There goes the neighborhood, huh?

OKRA:
Amen. Why is that?

JFW:
Sorry, Okra. I'm not the MAGIC EIGHT BALL.

(He laughs, and then) I know you want the answer. (He
looks out over the studio audience.) I would like to
put the answer on a refrigerator magnet myself. But I
can't tell you why. Except that if they *weren't* there,
we might as well be robots. Like the *Stepford Wives*.
There would be nothing to remember. Nothing to recover
triumphantly from. Nothing to compare our joy to. And,
without that comparison, our joy would become
absolutely, utterly colorless and meaningless. I don't

wanna to be a robot, Okra. So I like doing things that
give me a rush. See, only *humans* can have a rush.

You know, O, I'm sure my great relationship with my dads
is totally informed by their grief for my brother.

OKRA:
I'm sure it is. I love it when you call me that.

JFW:
My dad used the play in the Hamptons as a mini-vacation.
And as he wrote about me in that idyllic writer's harbor
setting, he did reconnect with everything I cumulatively
represented to him over the span of my life. Which I still
represent to him, Okra, and no matter what, I always will.

OKRA:
How could you not? You are dreamy.

JFW:

**383**

Well, I don't know about that. I *do* know that dreams do
come true. *But* I also know: there's *always* a "but."

When my dad sat down and wrote the epilogue, life since
our adventure in the hospital had become so *normal*. I
was having "the runs" a lot, and my dads were debating
over the phone about whether or not it was because of
the apple juice that I was drinking.

You know what? They could barely recall that terrifying
time when I couldn't poop on my own at all, runs or no runs!

Hey, I was just two weeks old then, but *I still* remember.

You know how I remember?

(He stands up and unpretentiously pulls up his T-shirt

and pulls down the waistband of his safari fatigues. Stretched across his lower abs is a nasty scar, maybe 8 inches long.)

This scar was a little more than an inch long when I had surgery. See, it's always right here, in case I ever forget, or don't get it. Get it?

OKRA:
I get it. I really do. (Okra can't stop staring at the scar. She fans herself with her note cards.)

(APPLAUSE.)

JFW:
Actually, O, it's okay if you *don't* get it. As long as you *realize* that you've forgotten. Then, you just have to find your way back as quick as you can. I mean, how can you live a whole life trying to get it every minute? It's exhausting. Actually, I don't think it's natural. Parking tickets, and everyday rejection, and terrorism and loneliness, they're all a part of life, too. You can't just ignore *them*.

What gets you back? There's your child's laughter. And there's birthdays. There's your grandma's tacos. There's your grandma, period. And bubbles.

And that's what books are for. To reintroduce us to the lust for earning our spot on the earth that we are always trying to retain. The thing that we keep saying to each other we shouldn't postpone. While we do our other chores. Actually, nowadays, it's not just books anymore. Sometimes the communication is electronic, too, or even a combination of both.

In *Our Town*, the actors in the play put objects in the cornerstone of a new bank which is being built. They put the *New York Times*, and the town newspaper, and the Bible, and the Constitution, and the works of Shakespeare in a time capsule. Lastly, they include a copy of the actual play which they are performing, *Our Town*. Everything they put in the cornerstone is in the form of print. Words. That's because when crazy things happen in the world around you, like, say, the sky opens up or something, there will always be pages you can turn to, to act as a gentle reminder, to help you put your electric locomotive back on the rickety toy track. The occasional derailment is inevitable. But we can always get ourselves back on track with someone's words.

Speaking of tracks, my Dad is big on taking the New York subway. He doesn't care how gross it is down on the platform, and how long you sometimes have to wait. He says you often find yourself just looking down the track, staring into the dark tunnel, *waiting*, feeling sweaty and grimy or freezing your ass off. Dad says a funny thing always happens when you are waiting for the subway.

In some stations, about a minute before the train comes, before it actually turns into the station, there's often a kind of reflection of the headlights as it bounces off the curve of one of the rails of the track. You always see it *very gradually* way before you see the headlights, or the train, or hear it, or feel it rumbling. And that reflection looks like a fine golden thread glowing brighter and brighter in the tunnel, and no matter how long you've been waiting for the train, when you see that golden thread, you always know that the train is coming, and that everything's gonna be okay.

OKRA:
I've seen that thread!

JFW:
Right? And Dad says laughter and tacos and Grandma and

books and E-mails from people you consider family, see, are the golden thread. They aren't the train itself. They're just the reminder that the train will be there, if you don't give up.

So don't be so hard on yourself when you momentarily forget how swell life is. That's natural. There's a lotta distractions. But there's also a lotta stuff on any bookshelf, on any computer, within reach, to make the forgetting only temporary. There's always a golden thread.

OKRA:
Should I should start a book club?

JFW:
Great idea. (He smiles broadly and laughs heartily.)

OKRA:
Wow. You're incredible.

(Okra makes her "disappointed face.")

That's all the time we have. Remember folks, reopen that present every morning *before* hair and makeup. This is wise, especially if your hair and makeup takes as long as mine!

(She takes Jackson's hand warmly.)

Our guest today has been the incredible, living, breathing, life-chasing, laughing, animal-wrestling, fun-loving survivor himself, Jackson Foo Wong. I'd like to thank him for the lessons he has taught to those around him.

You are an inspiration.

JFW:
Aw, no, Okra, I'm just a regular dude.

OKRA:
I bet your father wouldn't say so.

JFW:
(He smiles shyly.) No. I guess he wouldn't. (Waves)
Hi, Dad. (Waves) Hi, Dad.

OKRA:
Is there anything else you'd like to say?

JFW:
I'm just happy to be alive, that's all. (He winks.)

OKRA:
We're happy you are too, Foo. (She winks back.) Cutie.
(She turns to the camera.) I'm Okra O'Donohue. Thanks
for being there. Look for the golden thread.

**387**

(APPLAUSE.)

(Cue theme music.)

(Roll credits.)

(Segue to commercial.)

Peace.

**http://www.geocities.com/jacksonfoowong/**

HARPER ENTERTAINMENT (AN IMPRINT OF HARPERCOLLINS)

MICHAEL MORRISON, PUBLISHER

PRESENTS

A MAUREEN O'BRIEN PRODUCTION

OF A B.D. WONG BOOK

# Following FOO

(the electronic adventures of the Chestnut Man)

• a book about Intensive Collaboration •

STARRING
(IN ALPHABETICAL ORDER) SUE BAREZ   SHAUNA BARRINGER   RICHIE JACKSON
BOAZ DOV WONG  &  JACKSON FOO WONG

ALSO STARRING

CAROL & PAUL JACKSON AND BILL D. & ROBERTA WONG AS "THE GRAND-PARENTS"
WITH MARK HOWARD JACKSON   BRIAN DENNIS WONG  &
BARRY DOUGLAS WONG AS "THE BROTHERS CARE-A-LOTS-OF"
CO-STARRING MARC AYRIS   ROSALIND CHAO   TERRI PURCELL   KARYN WAGNER
& BILL WALKER AS "THE BIG E-MAILERS"   BACK COVER QUOTES BY JILL CLAYBURGH
MICHELLE KWAN & JOHN LITHGOW
FEATURING JOAN BENEDUSI   SUSAN DEHAAN   JENNIPHER GOODNER
KAREN GRASS   BECKY HENKELS   ABBIE HOFSTEDE   WENDY A. HOLMES
& CHRISTINE WHITE AS THE UCSF PRIMARY CARE TEAM NURSES

ROBERTA KELLER  STACEY LEVITT  FRANCIS POULAIN  SUSAN SNIDERMAN AS THE DOCTORS  DIANA FARMER  MIKE HARRISON  JENNY OGILVY AS THE SURGEONS AND STEPHANIE BERMAN & TRACY KEMPF AS THE SOCIAL WORKERS SPECIAL APPEARANCES BY ROBERT PERILLO  STEPHEN SPADARO  GARY GERSH AS "THE GODFATHERS 1, 2 , & 3"

PLUS NEARLY ONE THOUSAND *Foo Followers* WHO SENT ME THEIR HEARTS, AND CHANGED MY LIFE

EDITED FEARLESSLY BY MAUREEN O'BRIEN WITH TRUE IRISH PASSION, PATIENCE, & COMRADESHIP LITERARY REPRESENTATION BY ALAN NEVINS WHO NEVER, EVER GAVE UP • PRODUCTION EDITING TAUTLY MANAGED BY ANDREA MOLITOR • DESIGN IMMACULATELY MANAGED BY BETTY LEW BOOK DESIGNED BY JUDITH ABBATE CON BRIO • COVER DESIGN BY SUSAN SANGUILY CON ESTILO JACKET PHOTOGRAPHY BY THE PHENOMENAL SARAH SILVER (AUTHOR PHOTO) & THE ALWAYS TRUSTY JUSTIN KLOSKY (FLAP PHOTO: THANKS, "J.KLO" FOR EVERYTHING ELSE, TOO.) • WEBSITE DESIGN BY MICHAEL PIANE AND BARRY D. WONG • MARKETING BY DAWN DICENSO • PUBLICITY BY DEEDEE DEBARTLO DEDICATED BUT HARRIED ASSISTANTS TO MS. O'BRIEN RAKIA CLARK & KATIE HELLMUTH • CHEERFUL BUT BELEAGUERED ASSISTANTS TO MR. NEVINS KARIMA RIDGELY & MINDY STONE • RESILIENTLY EFFICIENT BUT NEVERTHELESS CONSTANTLY REVOLVING ASSISTANTS TO THE FIRM BUT FAIR MR. JACKSON BRIAN DAVIDSON  SABEEN EDWIN  MICHAEL MELAMEDOFF  &  EDDIE MERCADO

B.D. WONG IS GRATEFUL FOR THE EVER-CRADLING EMOTIONAL SAFETY NET WOVEN FROM THE BOLSTERING HEARTSTRINGS OF
PETER ARIZU   WAYNE BARKER   MARK BENNETT
MICHAEL J. MEENAN
ROBERT MOREA   KAREN SCOTT   BENNETT YELLIN
HE RETURNS THEIR LOVE UNCONDITIONALLY

HE THANKS EVERYONE WHO IS MENTIONED IN "FOLLOWING FOO..."

(...YEAH, EVEN THE BADDIES)

HE COULD NOT HAVE WRITTEN THIS BOOK WITHOUT THE BRILLIANT CO-PARENTING, PATIENT FORTITUDE
AND AMARANTHINE LOYALTY OF

# RICHARD ALAN JACKSON

AND THE EXCEPTIONALLY CARING AND TIRELESS PERFORMANCE BY

# MARIA EUGENIA CORRO AS "THE NANNY"

THANK YOU TO YOU FOR INVITING MY BOOK INTO YOUR LIFE.

AND LAST BUT, WELL, YOU KNOW, SPECIAL THANKS TO

# HEY, YOU UP THERE

I KNOW HALF THE TIME YOU'RE PROBABLY LAFFIN' AT ME UP THERE.
I GUESS NOW I'M LAFFIN' TOO.

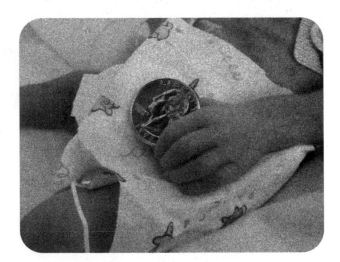